INDO–FRENCH PERSPECTIVES ON LOCAL GOVERNMENT AND DEMOCRACY

Centre de Sciences Humaines (Centre for Human Sciences): Created in 1990, the CSH is part of the network of 27 research centres of the French Ministry of Foreign Affairs. In 2007 it became UMIFRE 20 CNRS-MAEE, that is, a financially autonomous research institution under the dual tutelage of the French Ministry of Foreign and European Affairs (MAEE) and the French National Centre for Scientific Research (CNRS). The Centre's research work is primarily oriented towards the study of contemporary issues in the development of India and South Asia. The activities of the Centre are focused on four main areas, namely: Economic reforms and sustainable development; Politics and social change; Regional dynamics in South Asia and international relations; and Urban dynamics.

Centre de Sciences Humaines,
2 Aurangzeb Road,
New Delhi 110 011, India
Tel: (91 11) 3041 00 70
Fax: (91 11) 3041 00 79
Email: infos@csh-delhi.com
Website: http://www.csh-delhi.com

Institut Français de Pondichéry (French Institute of Pondicherry): Created in 1955 under the terms agreed to in the Treaty of Cession between the Indian and French governments, the IFP (UMIFRE 21 CNRS-MAEE) is a financially autonomous research institution under the dual tutelage of the French Ministry of Foreign and European Affairs (MAEE) and the French National Centre for Scientific Research (CNRS).

It fulfils its mission of research, expertise and training in human and social sciences, and ecology, in South and South-East Asia. Major research works focus on Indian cultural knowledge and heritage (Sanskrit language and literature, history of religions, Tamil studies, etc.), contemporary social dynamics (in the areas of health, economics and environment) and the natural ecosystems of south India (sustainable management of biodiversity).

Institut Français de Pondichéry
11 Saint Louis Street, PB 33,
Pondicherry 605 001, India
Tel: (91) 413 2334 168
Fax: (91) 413 2339 534
Website: http://www.ifpindia.org

Indo-French Perspectives on Local Government and Democracy

Edited by

LUCY BAUGNET
GIRISH KUMAR

MANOHAR

CSH
UMIFRE 20
CNRS-MAEE

CENTRE DE SCIENCES HUMAINES
2011

First published 2011

ISBN 978-81-7304-916-3

Published by
Ajay Kumar Jain *for*
Manohar Publishers & Distributors
4753/23 Ansari Road, Daryaganj
New Delhi 110 002

Typeset by
Kohli Print
Delhi 110 051

Printed at
Salasar Imaging Systems
Delhi 110 035

Contents

Preface and Acknowledgements

The idea of this book germinated around seven years ago when one of the editors (Lucy Baugnet, a Professor of Social Psychology at the Université de Picardie, Amiens) visited the Delhi-based French institute, Centre de Sciences Humaines (CSH). She was exploring the possibilities of an Indo–French joint venture in the realm of social sciences. Among others at CSH, she exchanged views particularly with Joël Ruet, the then (acting) Director, Stéphanie Tawa Lama-Rewal and Girish Kumar, fellows in political science division, CSH. As a follow-up, Kumar went to Amiens as a visiting Professor towards the end of 2003 and held a series of discussions with some of the faculty and doctoral students working in the areas of democratic decentralization, law and psychology. During his stay, Kumar also visited a local *Mairie* (municipal body) and gained first-hand experience of the structure and functioning of a French municipal body. As a result of these beief exchanges in Delhi and Amiens, the proposed Indo–French collaboration for an edited volume began unfolding in right earnest.

Tentatively, it was decided to contrast and question the process of decentralization in India and France. For, both the countires are mature democracies. Most importantly, the span of democratic experiences under the Fifth Republic in France and under the Republican Constitution of Independent India has almost been the same. The similarity ends there as there is a clear contrast in the decentralization processes and outcomes in both the countries. If India is ahead of France in respect of the extent of administrative and political decentralization, France has an ege over India in terms of resource mobilization for institutions of the local government. Besides, the importance attached to democratic expressions and exercises in both the countries are common, but again threat perceptions of respective local democracies are different.

The next step was identification of a team of experts, in both the countries, willing to share their interest in analysing the chosen themes from their perspectives and enlisting required institutional support from the Indian Council of Social Science Research (ICSSR), Fondation Maison des sciences de l'homme (FMSH) and CSH. It took, however, two more years to give concrete shape to the idea of working out a joint venture by cross-fertilization of social science disciplines with the idea of local democracy. On the whole, it was envisaged that the proposed volume would throw light on how local government institutions operate and their impact on management of resources within the broad frame of decentralization process at work in two entirely different socio-cultural and economic settings.

The pace was halting because of circumstances beyond our control. After a time-consuming process of translation of the chapters by the French contributors and incorporation of modifications suggested at various stages, the volume was finally ready for publication. We received support from many quarters in clearing the road blocks and surmounting all the hurdles, though it would not be feasible to name every person who gave us helping hands to this end. First of all, we are grateful to the contributors to this volume who waited patiently to see their work in print. This book would not have seen the light of the day without the support of Gilles Tarabout (Director, FMSH), Véronique Dupont (the then Director, CSH) and her successor Basudeb Chaudhuri. We owe a word of special appreciation to Arpita Mitra, the publications in-charge of CSH and her predecessor Rupa Sengupta for their persistent follow-up with the editors, contributors, translators and the publisher. We are thankful to Mr. Siddharth Chowdhury, Chief Editor at Manohar for his editorial suggestions and interventions, making the volume reader friendly. We also wish to thank the anonymous reviewer, courtesy Manohar, who went through the draft and offered valuable suggestions. Finally, we also wish to express our gratitude to the Director, Indian Institute of Public Administration (IIPA, which Kumar joined when the volume was halfway through) for his support to this joint venture. We believe this inter-disciplinary approach will be heuristic for future Indo–French research projects.

LUCY BAUGNET
GIRISH KUMAR

Introduction

LUCY BAUGNET
GIRISH KUMAR

To gather research and analytic contributions in order to cross-fertilize the perspectives on decentralization and local government in India and France can be considered at first sight as a risky venture in publishing. Without any doubt this function has a first obvious interest: informing a large audience about the ongoing processes which still remain largely unknown and making information about these accessible to English readers. As the title suggests, the idea behind this volume is to familiarize readers with the various strands of local democracy within the administrative and political frame of local governments in both the countries. But the interest goes further when we are dealing with two different cases in respect of many aspects: historical background, size and demographic characteristics, social practices and cultural values and types of economy. We would certainly require a theoretical and methodological framework to analyse in comparative terms (see Olivier Giraud's contribution to this collection).

These two systems, and this is the argument of this book—are democratic political systems and have introduced decentralization procedures regarding local democracy and governance.[1] In both cases, the system of government, i.e. democracy, is as well a fact as an ongoing project in the way it is designed and practised. As a matter of fact, the access to democracy in both cases has been achieved by adopting a Republican Constitution: ancient subjects were becoming citizens with a set of political and social rights. For India, this happened in 1947, after the end of the British rule; for France, it was following the Declaration of Human Rights of Citizens at the end of the monarchy in 1789. The Declaration has been a landmark for democracy in France, ketp up through the successive versions of the Republic. Both India and France began their post World War II journey as highly centralized states. This despite India having a constitutionally recognized federal structure, France and as a centralized state being member of the European Union[2] followed the French experiences, under its Fifth Republic (see I. Muller-Quoy's contribution).

The two countries' democratic experiences, mostly in respect of their local governments, have been at variance. India as a union of states has three different levels: the federal state, the states and the sub-state level that mainly refers to the local level panchayats (first raj institution—PRIs, taken for granted under colonization, re-actualized by the Central Act in 1973 and 1992–3 Amendments) and to urban local bodies (see Kumar). France, as a state, has an intermediate level (the regions) and the local-level communes, to which powers have been given by decentralization laws since 1982. Recently the creation of transversal groupings of Communes into 'communities' or into 'countries' has been undertaken. But these are not elected by universal direct suffrage and do not have responsibility as legal personality is a status of local government that makes them responsible in front of the law and can be charged in court (see Baugnet, Rangeon and Sanson).[3]

Therefore, the issues pertaining to local government and democracy have been examined in respect of their engagements in post-amendment phase for India and post-decentralizations laws for France. The lack of continuity of local government institutions, not rural but also urban, in India was also one of the reasons that we desisted from attempting a strictly comparative study.

Unlike France, it should be noted, India has two parallel sets of local governments: one for rural areas that is called 'panchayats' and a second called 'municipalities' for urban areas. The evolution of the local government has been traced back to the British period. The paper by Kumar dwells upon the genesis of modern three-tier panchayats ushered into India in late-1950s, and almost a decade after India became independent. It also needs mentioning that despite having introduced such innovative institutional arrangement keeping in mind its rural/urban divide, local governments have not been an enduring presence, until recently. In fact, the continuity of the both municipalities and panchayats could be ensured only in the early 1990s, thanks to the two major 73rd and 74th Constitutional Amendments.

The Amendments aim at invigorating local government institutions through the following mechanisms:

- Widening the base of representation, making it inclusive by ensuring representation of weaker sections including women;
- Providing institutional base for accountability of representatives to their constituents;
- Incorporating instruments of transparency and participation in the decision-making process;
- Expressing concern and care for poor;
- Demarcating functional domains of local governments by inserting 11th and 12th Schedules in the Constitution;
- Creating State Finance Commissions to restructure sharing of financial resources between provinces and local governments.

In France, since the Middle Ages, local bodies as communes had liberties attested by charters and representative councils for some Notables and Corporations. Since 1848 the principle of universal suffrage has been applied but restricted to men[4] until 1944 (see Sanson). But in this highly centralized state, local bodies, even elected, had administrative functions (see Muller-Quoy and Baugnet). Baugnet's chapter describes the decentralization process, which started in 1982 with the explicit and pragmatic objective of promoting the acceptance of responses better adapted to the diversity of specific local conditions, and designed a new democratic landscape:

- Empowering local territories by transferring powers, associated means, and budget control to locally elected representatives in order to lead to more concrete responses, closer to the citizens, their expectations and needs.
- Availing of a certain autonomy in decision-making related to their abilities, conferring legality that enables them to appear in judicial proceedings, accountability for their own budget. These are meant to give local bodies scope for governance.
- Defining principles of regulation between the different levels of

local bodies, vertical (principle of subsidiarity) and horizontal distribution, of responsibilites, development of cooperation between municipalities through the law on 'intercommunality'.
- Promoting flexible reorganization of territories (countries) and allowing local bodies the right to experiment with new practices, coordinate projects for the development of the territory and promoting sustainable development (Art. 72).
- Strengthening direct cooperation between municipalities and advisory boards (associations, elected representatives and minorities) at the intercommunal level.
- Invigorating a democracy of proximity, strengthening citizens' participation through the 27 February 2002 Act and instituting possible local decision-making by referendums and petitions for voters (Art. 72–1).

For sure the implementation of these constitutional and legal principles does take root from specific grounds. It is more pronounced, to begin with, in terms of its population size and rural/urban divide. In this sense, it will be easy to understand that while the Indian contributors have mainly focused on local democracy in the rural areas (see the papers authored by Ghosh, Inbanathan and Mahi Pal in this collection), the French ones focused mainly on urban ones (see the contributions of Rangeon and Sanson).

This is referring first to the characteristics of each territory as an objective phenomenom.

As François Rangeon observes in this volume:

> While a century ago only 10 per cent of the population used to live in cities, today 80 per cent of France's population (75 per cent of the European population and 50 per cent of the world population) is concentrated in urban and peri-urban areas. Yet, France is the European country wtih the highest number of municipalities.

More, the communes can vary in size, depending on the population. The decentralization process had a role in restructuring them, proposing different forms of associations which are not without importance in the political life (see Rangeon and Sanson).

In India, at the turn of the last century, i.e. in 1901, the urban population was just 10.84 per cent. It grew to only 17.29 per cent by 1951 when the first decennial census was conducted in independent India. Half a century later, India's urban population was mere 27.8 per cent, less than one-third of its total population. Here we can see a start contrast between India and France in terms of the growth of their respective urban populations and the rate of urbanization. In percentile terms both these countries had almost equal urban population nearly hundred years ago, but according to the latest count they stand far apart.

The institutional frame provided for local governments with emphasis on panchayats, their functional domain and the structural innovations inbuilt to ensure people's participation as well as accountability of the elected leaders to their voters are the main concerns of the Indian contributors. Yet, in view of the uniqueness of a representative local government for rural areas, the papers in the volume are based on the functional experiences of panchayats. Consider the following facts: seven out of ten people in India live in villages and more than half of the total Indian population happens to be illiterate (in rural areas the proportion is much higher and likewise as compared to men, women are more unlettered); the villages usually face with social and economic divides; and there's a huge population of agricultural labourers/daily-wage earners. Yet in order to make the panchayats all inclusive, a quota system was introduced to ensure representation of Scheduled Castes[5] (SC, erstwhile untouchables), Scheduled Tribes (ST, people who were earlier dependent upon the forests for their livelihood, people closest to forested land), as well as women. Amongst the people belonging to SC and ST categories, an overwhelming per cent happen to be illiterate, asset-less, poor, who have never held any official position for generations together. This is equally true of women belonging to these two categories and to some extent in case of women coming from upper caste families as well. This is not to deny, however, that women, irrespective of their socio-economic position, in the first place happen to be victims of patriarchy.

In France, the situation, at first sight, according to objective indicators, is very different. Education is compulsory until the age of 16 and the overall percentage of illiterates is around 5 per cent, mainly stemming from the immigrant population (where rate of female illiteracy is higher). Nevertheless, the general rule in schooling (notably in primary and secondary schools), in terms of differences of gender is, better success for girls than for boys. The situation of women in the society has improved in terms of autonomy and public life. But how come there are so few women in politics?

Despite of the rights and constitutional acts, as discussed by Sanson in this volume, 'At the end of the twentieth century, French politics remained a male bastion. . . . While they accounted for 53 per cent of the French electorate, the feminization of politics was extremely limited and experienced very slow progress.' The proportion of women mayors remains at a very low level (10.9 per cent in 2001) and most of the time it is in small communes. At the level of regions, the proportion of women as president is also quite rare, if not exceptional. As Sanson points out, despite

> the 8 July 1999 Constitutional Act amended Article 3 of the Vth Republic's Constitution, according to which, henceforth: 'the law promotes equal access to women and men in electoral mandates and elective posts' . . . but there is still a wide gap between laws and existing practices. The 6 June 2000 Act 'is aimed at promoting equal access to women and men in electoral mandates and elective posts'—the so-called Gender Parity Act—imposed what years of politics had failed to establish. . . . It did not have a spill-over effect in terms of equal access to the head of the municipal executive. Women have been imposed in politics and men will have to make place for them in a sphere that they had appropriated for centuries as if it were their exclusive prerogative.

Therefore, as illustrated, the topics which have been covered by the contributors in this collection shows some prior problematics: some topics remain a major concern for the implementation of decentralization and therefore important objects for analysis.

The decentralization process in France had restructuring effects on urban areas and rural space by introducing specific bodies for local democracy, and the issues and debates related to them are not yet solved. In the same way, the focalization of Indian contributors on the village decentralization of panchayats is due to actual concern related to their recent reforms, and also due to the questions arising from the various success of the implementation of local democracy in the different states federated by Indian Union. Yet, while French contributors have treated environment (see Jamay's paper), educational training (Agulhon) and reorganization at the local level due to the recent decentralization laws (Muller-Quoy), it is striking that the fiscal aspect is an important issue in India (Oommen). But this remains implicit, indirectly expressed by the French contributors as an issue, mainly in terms of attributed resources from the state to the local bodies.What makes up a problematic issue, and what does not, thus clearly differ between the two countries.

No doubt that the priority given to some specific aspect comes from the reality of the process itself in France and India; hence it also comes from the way this process is thought, applied, practised.

Apart from tracing the evolution of local governments in India, particularly for its vast countryside, Kumar deals with the impact of 1992 constitutional amendments ensuring the continuity of local bodies once and for all. Kumar has also argued that the spirit of the amendments have not been carried forward to their logcial conclusion. As the local governments, panchayats particularly suffer from lack of functional domain and correspondingly, adequate funds and functionaries.

The quest of Ghosh's paper is to enrich our understanding of local democracy by reinterpreting its unresolved problems. He begins with questioning the very motive for the attempts made so far by the state for institutionalizing panchayats: 'Was it the urge for providing more democracy to the grassroots, or whether it was the anxiety to enhance legitimacy of the centralized state?' To him, the quest was to ensure the legitimacy of the centralized state, which explains why the problems of establishing local democracy are still persisting.

The theoretical foundation of Indian democracy rests on the notion that the sovereignty of the state resides in the people. This abstract notion can be concretized by the active participation of citizens in the affairs of the state. The project of panchayati raj is essentially meant to promote such participatory citizenship, enabling its millions of people living in nearly six hundred thousand villages to take decision on vital matters that affect their everyday lives. But the way the (Indian) state has pursued the panchayats has raised questions about its very motive itself. This suggests that contrary to its stated objective (i.e. to give concrete shape to the notion of 'popular sovereignty'), the state has engaged panchayats to serve its hidden motive, that is, to ensure 'the resilience and legitimacy of the centralized state'. But is it a peculiar Indian case? Not, perhaps. The fact of the matter is that the very idea of collective decision-making through citizen participation, has taken a back seat in most of the countries. Ghosh has taken a leaf from Partha Chatterjee (2004) who observes that the modern states strive to secure 'legitimacy not by participation of citizens in matters of state but by claiming to provide for the well-being of the population'. The functioning of panchayats can largely be measured on these lines. This also explains why these local democratic institutions have remained engaged as local agencies to implement a plethora of rural development schemes designed at the top.

In fact, here lies the catch. The state needs popular participation for ensuring legitimacy even for the sake of development and welfare of people. This necessitates grassroots outreach with its elaborate development agenda covering, practically, all aspects of individual and social lives of people. But it has already been proved beyond any doubt that through its bureaucratic arm alone the state cannot deliver the goods and services to the people for whom these are meant. The panchayat was designed to fill in the gap but despite three successive attempts, including the 73rd Constitutional Amendment, the Indian ruling class has in general been extremely wary of creating centres of political power in the countryside. Caught in this quagmire, some Indian provinces have even taken recourse to alternative methods which are 'not only unorthodox but borders on naivety'.

What then is the roadmap of local democracy in India? In the first place, Ghosh concludes by observing that democratizing the local government is still not on the agenda of the ruling class in general. For, their interest is best served in maintaining the *status quo*, as the 'politics of patronage and clientelism' they have pursued over the decades still 'draws considerable strength from the absence of popular control over local governmental administration'. Therefore, in all likelihood they would appreciate deferring the matter of 'conferring autonomy to the panchayats' to a distant future, unless they are forced by 'other factors' to change their stance. What are these other factors? Ghosh has identified two such factors: one, the protest movements of various hues in the countryside more particularly in tribal areas. In fact, it is the failure of the local administration to address the felt need of masses which has given a spurt to these movements. Such movements have to be viewed 'as a protest against an administrative framework in which the ordinary citizens at the grassroots have no opportunity to participate in the making of decisions on matters that affect their everyday lives'. If articulation of such demands ventilated through movements becomes 'sufficiently audible, the political decision makers will have to rethink seriously about the issue of local democracy'. Two, fed-up with largely ineffective 'paternalistic administration' on the one hand, and their inability to directly access the formal centres of power, people have started seeking mediation/intervention of political networks, associations formed and led largely by elites or seeking services of a growing number of trouble-shooters to realize their needs and aspirations. Quoting Partha Chatterjee again, Ghosh concludes that through all such activities the poor people are making statements about the manner in which they would prefer to be governed.

Democracy has been defined by M.A. Oommen as an 'instrument in enabling people to vote every five years and elect their representatives'. In this assertion we find some components mentioned by the French contributors taking up a large part of the discussion on the nature of democracy: does it have to be representative democracy only? An articulation between a representative conception of democracy to a participative conception? A democracy of proximity? Self-governance? (see the papers of Baugnet, Rangeon, Sanson, and Agulhon).

M.A. Ommen's paper questions the core of democracy's implementation. Democracy brings political functionaries benefits in terms of personal advantages, since their role is an instrumental one. These dimensions have also been treated by the French contributors who have pointed out the touchy question of elites and notabilities in the representative conception of democracy (see the developments in the above French contributors and in Inbanathan paper). Yet, with decentralization, as often pointed out, the reinforcement of the local elites, rather than the participation of the basic citizen in local democracy, is the risk (see Sanson).

Underlying the common denomination of the decentralization process are particular connotations. Decentralization is defined by M.A. Oommen as 'the empowerment of the local people through the empowerment of local goverments'. For French contributors it mainly refers to the different steps of the implementation and transfer of powers in various domains to the territorial bodies elected by universal direct suffrage (see Nathalie Muller-Quoy's paper on the division of powers, Florence Jamay's paper for the questions it raises in the environmental domain).

As mentioned, one main line that shapes the French contributions is on which model can local democracy be improved. Is the shift from representative democracy (relying 'on the hypothesis according to which elected officials with the help of experts and technicians were the best to know what is good for citizens . . . and to decide for them': François Rangeon) to participative democracy, just a way of legitimation of politics, or may it become a successful practice?

In India, it is not difficult to guess that the motley groups of persons who have suffered discriminations of different hues for centuries would find it difficult to exercise power at the local level. But political empowerment of such categories of people is one of the main objectives of the 73rd Amendment. What has then happened during the last fifteen years? This issue has been examined at two levels in this volume. One, interpreting the not so encouraging result but more importantly, offering explanations as to why the results are contrary to the expected outcomes by juxtaposing them to ground realities. Two, in appreciation of the shortcomings of legislative intervention what corrective measures (read capacity building) were taken to overcome apparent inabilities of the representatives to reap the benefits.

The first point raised above has been treated in Inbanathan's paper with the right mix of macro and micro mapping of the ground realities. Panchayats, it needs mentioning, have been structured to meet people's demands and aspirations in a responsive way at the local level. Meeting the felt needs of constituents is just one form of 'accountability', Inbanathan argues but he adds that there is another dimension of 'accountability' which assumes that elected leaders be answerable to their voters. This can be realized in two ways: one, representatives should periodically inform of their actions; and two, they also be held responsible for whatever they have done or not done. The people should be able to hold their representatives 'accountable' for whatever actions they take in their capacity as their (people's) representatives. In other words, not only elected representatives need to affirm their commitment to their voters but they have to be equally responsive to the manner in which they are elected. If representatives are elected not by virtue of their own work or political attributes but because of their powerful patrons, they (representatives) tend to feel more answerable to their patrons and persons (who in the first place were instrumental in getting them elected) than the ordinary masses. This in a way distorts the perception of the elected representatives on the accountability issue and in turn weakens the process of democratic decentralization. Based on the study of a fairly large sample size of leaders taken from the two southern states of Karnataka and Kerala, Inbanathan has provided deep insight into the working of quota system in a highly iniquitous society. This paper also highlights the fact that how the notions of participation, transparency and accountability vary from one location to another notwithstanding the similar measures introduced through the same institution. This in a way affirms the significance of local factors at work and also the great diversities that exist even within the boundaries of a district, not to mention in its huge territorial spread.

The second point, the capacity building of elected representatives, has been taken up by Mahi Pal. The 73rd Amendment, the fact must be noted, led to the emergence of over three million elected representatives at all the three levels of panchayats across the country. Included among them were over one million women and about eight lakh (0.8 million) from the reserved categories of SCs and STs. A great majority of these representatives were illiterates/semiliterates and had entered an elected office for the first time, and hence they were completely unaware of the rules regulations, their rights and responsibilities, even what was expected from them.

Paradoxically, as per the requirements of their official position, they were expected to work out plans for economic development and social justice and implement them at their respective levels. This brought forth the issue of the capacity building of these representatives. And this happens to be the theme of Mahi Pal's paper. In view of the gigantic proportion of the task, the state had to seek partnership with the NGOs and other civil society groups. Mapping of the training needs of elected leaders, including women, methods adopted, strategies worked out, budgetary allocations for training needs under ensuing five-year plans have all been documented in the paper. The paper also draws from the evaluation studies of some of the training programmes conducted by the governmental training institutions as well as the impact of capacity building exercises conducted by a couple of NGOs in certain pockets. That apart, it also highlights the role of media and NGOs in awareness building of people at large without whose participation the project of democratic decentralization will remain incomplete.

Further on, some trends and questions are underlying the forms that decentralization take. Governance is one of them. Local governance is underscored as being an important matter. Largely presented, the local level by allowing a democracy of proximity, is said to provide a more responsive manner of matching the interests of people. It is concerned with the core of local democracy in its participative and representative dimensions; the locus of decision and control at this level is accurately perceived as a social and psychological parameter in its hierarchic dimension. It is in this matter that empowerment processes are politicaly clearly sensitive. The laws for parity in France and the amendments acts for SCs and STs in India have given concrete visible practices, more spread out maybe at this local level than at the other levels (see Nathalie Sanson's contribution for France). Have the citizens to be the actors of political and economic decisions? How are private and public interests concerned by governance? Has local government to gain from a supremacy of the public over the private interest? (see Florence Jamay and Catherine Agulhon's analyses). Public actions in France are modelled on the state model, i.e. centralized, strictly framed by legal rules, founded on the mechanism of representation and the principle of the supremacy of public over private interest' (François Rangeon). This is dealing with what the conceptions of local government is.

Closely connected, the idea of territorial governance is the third common preoccupation. Territorial governance refers to a flexible and negotiated form of public action, practised in an enlarged territorial frame, based on a vast redistribution of powers and on public-private partnership. Taking the form of a managerial process based on project orientation, programme-wise funding and a continuous evaluation of actions, territorial governance claims to break away from traditional methods of administrative functioning (see Catherine Agulhon's contribution for the complexity of the dynamic applied to vocational education).

If a theoretical and methodological frame has to be designed for factual comparaison (see Olivier Giraud's contribution), the different texts presented in this work broach various dimensions of the decentralization process and their implications for local democracy. As any one this one is dated: the state of the art and of the process itself are scanned.

The relationship between India and France as democratic republics is for sure coming from the past and nowadays they are not isolated or apart, but involved in larger macrocosmic tendencies. If they have been growing and are developing in original ways according to various variables, they both actually have to cope with the context of globalization and other macrophenomena such as emancipation by education and information. They are also aware of the necessary decentralization and empowerment that has to happen in order to strengthen the democratic process.

NOTES

1. In fact, putting a comparative account of the subject in general would have been either too simplistic or too ambitious to accomplish in the given time frame and limited available resources. For, given the diversities in their political backdrop, history, culture as well as the levels of economic developments, it would have been too difficult to measure the two countries on a comparative

scale. This is not to deny, however, that there are still a few indicators on which a comparative evaluation of strength and weaknesses of democratic decentralization could have been possible. This in fact has been taken as a suitable rationale, a backdrop, to this study.

2. It must be mentioned that France, by referendum, has recently rejected the adoption of the European Constitution. Even if the analysis about this vote tends to explain it more by the circumstances of the French political life than related to European matters, it remains that France, at the state level as an entity, is perceived itself as an independent state. At the European level, the local bodies express themselves through associations mainly at regional level: the Assembly of European Regions (1985), the Council of European Communes and Regions (1984), The Régional Committee (2004).
3. According to Rangeon, 'This new redistribution of powers is taking place not just to the benefit of traditional, local territorial bodies (communes, departments and regions), but also to the benefit of new territories, in particular urban agglomerations, rural areas and "communities of communes". "Intercommunality"—understood in France to mean voluntary cooperation among communes and not their authoritarian mergers—has seen considerable expansion, with practically the whole of the French territory being covered by "public establishments for inter-commune cooperation" (EPCI, or etablissements publics de coopération inter-communale).'
4. And for men in military forces in 1945, at the end of the Second World War.
5. According to the 2001 census, SCs and STs account for 15 and 8 per cent of the total Indian population.

CHAPTER 1

Local Government and Democracy in India: An Overview

GIRISH KUMAR

Unlike in France or for that matter any other European country, India has two different sets of local government institutions: one is the panchayat and the other is the municipality. The former offers an institutional frame to the concept of democratic decentralization in rural India, providing civic services as municipal bodies do in urban areas. It also operates as an agency responsible for implementing development as well as welfare schemes in the hundreds of thousands of villages dotting the country's vast rural expanse. The municipality, as known elsewhere, is an embodiment of urban local government, entrusted by and large with the same sets of functions and tasks, of course with necessary modifications. The most notable difference one can locate between municipal bodies in India and France is that besides discharging civic and urban development functions, Indian urban bodies are also engaged in ensuring representation of weaker sections in its folds as well as taking care of poverty alleviation programmes. Although this paper focuses on the evolution, structure, specific functions and a brief assessment of the functioning of panchayats, largely because of its unique characteristics, it also dwells upon the structure and functioning of urban local bodies.

It is widely believed that the panchayats, as village self-governing institutions, have existed in India from time immemorial. There is a mention of them in the scriptures dating back even to 1200 BC, though devoid of any hard historical facts. The urban local bodies, like railways, postal services or modern administration, including administration of justice, were established during the long spell of British colonial rule. Notwithstanding the similarity in the civic and certain other functions discharged by both these rural and urban local bodies, the pronounced differences in their nomenclature have remained in vogue for the very simple reason that even today nearly three-fourths of the Indians live in nearly 6 lakh (0.6 million) villages (total urban population in India is 27.78 per cent[1] as per 2001 census). For this reason, and because there are certain unique features of village life, rural regulation demands a different set of rules of conduct than the regulation of urban affairs, hence the dichotomy continues to exist.

The term 'panchayat' is derived from *panchas*, a council of five village elders vested with the authority to arbitrate disputes in the traditional village system. In addition, there were also 'caste panchayats'[2] to regulate the affairs of particular castes, which still continue to exist in many parts of the country. Far away and rather cut-off from the central authority, these village-level local institutions continued to conduct the social life of agrarian communities through the medieval period. That the affairs of these caste-ridden villages were regulated on the pattern of an egalitarian community under the feudal agrarian system is hard to believe. Much later, however, it was Sir Charles Metcalfe, the provisional governor-general of British India (1835–6), who described these villages as 'the little republics'. This glorified notion of the ancient village life was later repudiated by many including B.R. Ambedkar, the man largely responsible for drafting the Indian Constitution. He held these village republics responsible for the ruination of India. Whether these old village communities, governed by rigid caste-based rules ever lived together, except for their physical existence, has been commented upon by many including Jayaprakash Narayan (fondly called as JP who in his last years led the country against the authoritarian rule of Indira Gandhi in the late 1970s).

LOCAL BODIES UNDER THE BRITISH

The organized effort towards decentralization started in the last quarter of the nineteenth century. The stated purpose was to create an institutional structure to raise taxes to meet the increasing local demands of the people as also to create a band of leaders at the local level loyal to the British Crown.[3] Hence the resolution of Lord Mayo, the then British Viceroy, to set-up local-level institutions came into effect. Although a municipal body was established in Madras as early as 1687 with exclusively nominated members, in the cities outside British Presidency the municipal institutions were set-up only after 1842. Likewise, it was also decided to revive the traditional village panchayat system. This was put into effect with the passage of the Village Chowkidari Act, 1870 in the rural areas of the Bengal Presidency, comprising the territories falling under present states of West Bengal, Bihar and Orissa. Under this Act, the district magistrates were empowered to form village panchayats exclusively with nominated members. The brief for the village panchayat was to raise taxes to pay for the maintenance of the village chowkidar (watchman), who operated as the eyes and ears of the British colonial administration. But panchayats were not devolved any power to function as local self-governing institutions.

Over the period of next seven decades or so, the status of rural local bodies remained so, notwithstanding other resolutions,[4] including the 1882 Rippon Resolution which is considered to be a landmark in the evolution of local democracy in India. In sum, the village panchayat system, though slightly modified, continued under the British colonial rule.

The idea was further articulated by Mahatma Gandhi, who blended it with his idea of *gram swarajya* (village self-government) during the long freedom movement. Since Gandhi's views on decentralized power structure for independent India did not find favour with the dominant opinion of the Congress party, they were rejected after India gained Independence in 1947. In fact, with great reluctance the panchayats were incorporated in Article 40 of the Constitution that reads, 'The state should take steps to organize village panchayats and endow them with such power and authority as may be necessary to enable them to function as units of self-government.' This Article was, however, placed under the Directive Principles of State Policy that are not enforceable. Since it was not mandatory, the provincial governments did not feel obliged to organize and strengthen village panchayats. Thus the village panchayats formed during the pre-Independence period continued to function for almost a decade after India's Independence.

MEHTA COMMITTEE RECOMMENDATIONS AND AFTER

The municipal bodies created earlier during the British rule continued to function with necessary changes after Independence. In fact, these bodies were seen as the 'cradle of democracy' for many important leaders of modern India including both the first prime minister and the first home minister, who had cut their teeth as people's elected representatives at the municipal level. Therefore, to reform or reorganize urban local bodies was not on the agenda of the government for quite long. Contrarily, the present three-tier[5] Panchayati Raj Institutions (PRI) owe their genesis to the recommendations of the Balwantrai Mehta-led committee, set-up for an appraisal of 'Community Development (CD)' programmes[6] in 1957. The committee had envisaged that elected PRIs would help enlist people's participation for the effective implementation of the then on-going CD programmes. This was the first major step in promoting democratic decentralization in the country. Thus the recommendations of the study team gave birth to the first generation of modern PRIs with the state of Rajasthan taking the lead. While inaugurating the newly-created PRIs in Rajasthan (and subsequently in Andhra Pradesh) in October 1959, Prime Minister Nehru praised the pioneering efforts of the two states in taking 'the most revolutionary and historic steps' and hoped the others would follow suit. In response to his call, by the early 1960s most of the states had passed their respective Panchayat Acts and several of them had conducted elections for the panchayati bodies. The enthusiasm, however, did not last long. In fact, barring two states in the western part of the country, Gujarat and Maharashtra, the PRIs had practically collapsed in the rest of India once the initial euphoria was over and resultant contradictions could not be resolved.

That was in the mid-1960s. More than a decade later[7] attempts to revive these rural local bodies began with the recommendation of the Asoka Mehta Committee. The process was started in West Bengal in 1978, with Karnataka, Andhra Pradesh and Kerala (all these three southern states were ruled by non-Congress parties) following suit in the mid-1980s. The decentralized institutions thus revived were termed as second-generation panchayats.[8] Once again, however, excepting West Bengal, these second-generation panchayats could not survive once the political parties (all non-Congress), which had given them a new lease of life lost in the ensuing Assembly elections in these states. Perhaps, the continuation of the same Left Front government in power ensured the survival of panchayats in West Bengal. It would be apt to say that over the years both the panchayats and Left Front have reinforced each other's uninterrupted stay in their respective domain in West Bengal (Ghosh and Kumar, 2003; Kumar, 2006).

CONSTITUTIONAL SUPPORT TO PANCHAYATS

Until then, elections to local government institutions were not mandatory. In fact, except in Maharashtra, Gujarat (since early 1960s) and later West Bengal (since 1978), panchayat elections were never held regularly in any other state in the country. The setback received by the second generation of panchayats confirmed that unless these local governments are backed by constitutional support, i.e. making panchayat elections mandatory on the lines of periodic elections to national and state assemblies, their survival cannot be ensured. It may be recalled that way back in 1978, Asoka Mehta had called for constitutional recognition to panchayats. A process to this effect started later in 1989 under Rajiv Gandhi. Although it turned out to be abortive, it eventually culminated in 1992 with the passage of the 73rd and 74th Constitutional Amendments,[9] ensuring *inter alia* the continuity of both the urban[10] and rural local government institutions for ever in the country. Both these amendments were held as landmarks in the evolution of local self-governments in the country, which had begun with Lord

Rippon's resolution in 1882. For, apart from making elections to these bodies mandatory, the amendments also called for reservation of 'not less than one-third of seats' for women and marginalized sections of the society [known as Scheduled Castes (SC) (read Dalits) and Scheduled Tribes (ST) as per their population] at all the three levels and in the municipal bodies. Besides, these amendments also provided for the setting up of State Election Commissions (SECs, to conduct periodic elections), State Finance Commissions (SFCs, to periodically decide the extent of financial devolution) as well as appended list of functions to be devolved to the local bodies.

Above all, the amendments ensured that the seats at each level will be filled by directly elected members. It also had organic linkages between all the tiers by creating space for chairpersons of the village panchayats at the intermediate-level body and likewise, for presidents of intermediate panchayats at the district panchayats. In order to better appreciate the figures given above, it needs to be mentioned that administratively India is composed of 28 provinces/states and 7 union territories (UT).[11]

The provinces are administratively divided into districts, below the districts are blocks (the panchayat body set-up at this level is popularly known as Panchayat Samiti but the nomenclature varies in many states as Taluka/Mandal/Kshetra/Janpad Panchayat). The lowest tier within the framework PRI is the village panchayat, whose composition also varies. In several states a village panchayat is coterminus with a revenue village (relatively bigger in size) but the opposite is also true; that is, a village panchayat could consist of several adjoining villages clubbed together. This can be seen in states like West Bengal and Kerala. This explains why the total number of panchayats at the village level is 231,630 whereas the total number of villages in India is around 6 lakh (0.6 million). Thus for the governance of a total 700 million rural population in India, there are altogether 3,132,673 directly elected local leaders (see Table 1.1). Of them a little over one million happen to be women members (one-third of the total seats at each level is reserved for women) and nearly 8 lakh (0.8 million) belong to the categories of Dalits and Scheduled Tribes.

TABLE 1.1: NUMBER OF ELECTED LEADERS AT THREE LEVELS OF PANCHAYATS

Levels of panchayats	No. of units	Total no. of elected leaders
District panchayats	594	15,815
Block panchayats	5,912	145,412
Village panchayats	231,630	2,971,446

Source: Data Archives, Institute of Social Sciences, Delhi, 2005.

URBAN LOCAL BODIES

Municipal bodies are set-up in designated areas as per the criteria[12] defined by the census. These are as follows: (i) minimum population size of 5,000, (ii) population density of 400 per sq. km., and (iii) 75 per cent adult male population be engaged in non-agrarian occupations. But there are exceptions such as 'temple towns, pilgrimage and tourist' centres, rapidly industrializing areas and military stations. The small towns are covered under 'the discretionary criteria of urban settlement until these reach the required population threshold of about 10,000 for municipalization with fully elected councils. Again when a municipal area reaches about 300,000 population it is generally considered fit for according a municipal corporation status. The distinction between municipal councils and municipal corporations mainly rests not only in their executive structure, but also in the extent of their functional areas, tax powers and nature of state control' (Datta, 1994: 620). The 74th Amendment has divided the urban local bodies (ULB) into three categories: (i) municipal corporations for larger urban areas,[13] (ii) municipal councils for small urban areas, and (iii) nagar panchayats (town councils) for upcoming towns, representing the transitional phase of a rural area getting transformed into an urban area. In addition there are notified area councils, and cantonment boards.

The recently introduced 12th Schedule of the Constitution provides a long list of functions, a total of 18 functions to be precise (see Annexure I). In practice, however, the following functions are handled by the municipal authorities: (i) public health and sanitation, (ii) water supply[14] and drainage, (iii) primary education, (iv) roads and public works, and (v) maternity homes and health clinics. Besides these major functions, the municipal bodies also shoulder many but largely minor responsibilities.

> The usual practice is to divide state functions into various sub-functions and delegate some of these to municipalities, sometimes retaining their development component and delegating only the operational and maintenance tasks. There is also a common practice to divide municipal functions into obligatory and optional functions. (Datta 1994: 629).

Apart from the functional divide, there has/had been a divide in the exercise of power between the elected and bureaucratic heads of the municipal bodies, more particularly at the level of municipal corporations. Notwithstanding the fact that local urban bodies have been treated as nurseries of democracy, the state had vested real power in the hands of the commissioner (head of the municipal administrative staff), whereas the mayor or the chairperson had remained largely a ceremonial figure. With the introduction of the 'Mayor-in-Council' system,[15] the first time in Howrah (West Bengal) in 1980, over a decade prior to the 74th Amendment, an attempt was made to undo this mismatch on the municipal front. This initiative had twofold objectives: first, to introduce 'cabinet' type structure at the level of urban local government; second, in consonance with the fundamental principle that in 'local self-government, elected office, executive power and accountability have to go together, and makes a welcome change from the ceremonial, single person focus, to an arrangement of collective power and responsibility' (Singh, 2001).

This was an exercise to attach importance to the office of people's elected representatives. Yet another attempt, this time to bring representatives closer to the people, was made following a provision of the 74th Amendment. This called for setting up of 'ward committees' consisting of one or more wards within the functional boundary of the municipal body with a population of not less than 3 lakh (0.3 million) or more. By providing a forum for people's participation, it was hoped that these committees 'could play an effective role at the *mohalla* (ward) level in the delivery of municipal services'. The composition and size of these committees are at variance from state to state. West Bengal and Kerala, for instance, provide for the setting up of these committees at the level of each ward, whereas there are several states where this provision is applicable 'only in corporation areas for groups of wards with members to be nominated by the ward councillor or by the corporation as a whole or by the state government or a combination of these' (Singh, 2001).

CONSTITUTIONAL DESIGNS AND OVERLAPPING FUNCTIONS

Both the 73rd and 74th Amendments aimed at empowering the rural and urban local bodies but together and also separately these failed to demarcate the functional domains of panchayats and municipalities. The problem lies in the fact that these functions mentioned in the 11th and 12th Schedules are also given under the State List (function of the state governments) and Concurrent List (functions on which both union and provinces can legislate), hence there is a great deal of overlapping. This is not to deny that through the 12th Schedule the union had sought to widen the sphere of urban local bodies into the following three new areas: (i) economic and social planning, (ii) representation of weaker sections, and (iii) poverty alleviation. 'On the other hand municipalities are not being encouraged', as a perceptive observer of urban administration noted,

> to widen their human development activities, especially primary health care, nutrition, elementary and primary education, and personal social services. The main thrust of the 12th Schedule seems to be to reorient the municipalities from their preoccupations with public health and sanitation to water supply, roads, physical planning and environmental control, and shelter related activities—a bias originating from the Central ministry responsible for drafting the functional list. (Datta, 1994: 629).

This bias can also be seen in the functional list of panchayats wherein the latter were entrusted with special responsibilities to prepare plans for 'economic development with social justice' in respect of the 29 functions listed under 11th Schedule (Annexure II). It needs mentioning here that for long panchayats had been involved in implementing programmes aimed at poverty alleviation in villages. Likewise, social and economic planning is an integral part of the decentralized planning which panchayats along with municipalities are expected to carry out. This is equally true of representation and care of weaker sections, including women.

WHERE DO THE LOCAL GOVERNMENT INSTITUTIONS STAND TODAY?

Taking stock of developments a decade and half after the passage of the landmark amendments, three things are distinctly noticeable. One, state conformity acts were passed; elections for both panchayats and municipal bodies are now held regularly even in erstwhile laggard states; statutory bodies like SECs and SFCs have been set-up and are functioning; representation of women along with SCs and STs has been ensured. In short, all necessary formalities have been observed. Two, a smooth transfer of the three Fs—functions, funds and functionaries—so vital for the functioning of any vibrant institution—in appreciation of the letter and spirit of Article 243(G) of the 73rd Amendment, has not largely taken place. This in effect makes a mockery of decentralized planning. To a large extent this is equally true in respect of municipalities. Besides, PRIs are still suffering from an identity[16] crisis. It is apparent that by denying wherewithal and confusing the functional domain of both panchayats and municipalities, political elites in league with the bureaucracy are stifling the growth of local bodies as vibrant local institutions. Three, the instrument of reservation has merely ensured the representation of weaker section but has not led to real 'empowerment' of these sections of the society, again with notable exceptions. The institution of 'Gram Sabha'[17] (Village Assembly) and 'ward committee' at the municipal level have not emerged as multipurpose forums facilitating collective decision-making, transparency in the functioning of village panchayats/municipal bodies and ensuring

accountability of the local leaders to their electorates, performing the role of social audit, etc. In short, the inference is that the provisions of the amendment have either been worked on perfunctorily or subverted in the course of their implementation. Undoubtedly, there have been shortcomings; even necessitating the demand for yet another amendment (as called for) to realize the goal of self-governance.

From the above it is apparent that certain steps have been taken in the realms of both legislations and subordinate legislations providing a supportive framework, devolving certain functions and certainly some amount of funds, if not adequate, and over the years there has been an increase in the number of functionaries at the local level. This is not to deny that there is much to be desired on all the three counts. The central problem, however, is the core functions of the panchayats, which, to a large extent, explains people's apathy, and largely dismal performance of panchayats. The panchayats, it should be noted, are involved mainly in three types of programmes: construction or earth work to provide ostensibly wage employment, distribution of some relief, read implementation of welfare measures, and financing entrepreneurship of the poor. Taking the last item first, the Integrated Rural Development Programme (IRDP) renamed later as Swarna Jayanti Swarojgar Yojna (SJSY) is conceived on the wrong premises. It presupposes that largely illiterate, asset-less poor families devoid of the sense of ownership for generations are endowed with entrepreneurial skill. The poor may be hardworking but it is too much to expect them,[18] notable exceptions apart, to be equally enterprising. Besides, the programme does not take the 'risk factors' into account. Rather it overlooks, if not negates, entirely unfavourably socio-economic conditions, which are not conducive to entrepreneurship. As a result, billions of rupees have sunk over the years on these initiatives. Still the proportion of families belonging to below the poverty line (BPL) category is substantial.[19]

In respect of delivery of municipal services, the scenario is equally discouraging. Let us take stock of three basic services, as given below, to substantiate the facts.

WATER SUPPLY[20]

- Little more than half (51 per cent) of the households lack piped water facilities.
- A large number of cities have 2-4 hours supply.
- High physical losses.
- Poor operation and maintenance of existing assets.

SANITATION

- 43 per cent urban households are not connected with septic tanks or sewer lines.
- Only 22 per cent are connected to sewerage systems.
- Nearly half (47 per cent) of the urban households remove their waste to community dumping spots and 30 per cent to individual dumping spots.

WATER QUALITY

- 75 per cent of surface water resources are polluted.
- Sewer is the main source of pollution.

The above figures are enough to confirm the ineffective delivery of municipal services, though in major cities there are specialized agencies to ensure supply of drinking water or garbage disposal. In fact, the urban decay and the pathetic condition of towns and cities—even upcoming small towns which are unable to bear the influx of migrants—due to lack of infrastructure, led the union government to launch a comprehensive urban renewal programme. Named after the first prime minister, the Jawaharlal Nehru National Urban Renewal Mission (JNNURM) aims at creating an 'integrated framework with focus on economic and social infrastructures, basic services to urban poor, urban sector reforms and the strengthening of municipal governments and their functioning.'[21] Apart from mobilizing huge additional resources for rejuvenating the basic services, the mission provides comprehensive guidelines for additional resource mapping (through floating municipal bonds, for instance), recognizing space for private sector to play a prominent role in creating urban infrastructure through innovative public-private partnership, a regulatory framework including a new municipal accounting system, and so on. The ambitious JNNURM was launched in December 2005 which entails the formation of multi-level bodies to coordinate activities in 60 key cities initially identified for the stated purpose. The activities are to be worked out at the level of states and also at the level of two union ministries. Obviously, plans and underlying schemes are still at the preparatory stage, therefore it is only hoped that in future cities will look different. But given the multiplicity of institutional networks responsible for the coordination of sub-plans, plans within the state and their appraisal, release of funds with the involvement of two central ministries as well as multi-level funding arrangements, one wonders whether the mission would ever be able to meet its stated objectives and that too in the given timeframe.

ISSUES AND TRENDS

The impact of local governments can be measured with reference to the following points: functional autonomy, decentralized planning, leadership, participatory democracy, delivery of services, accountability and transparency. Let us take these issues one by one. Above all, perhaps what is most significant is the confusion persisting over the decades regarding the very identity of local government institutions: are they extended arms of the government, i.e. agencies responsible for implementation of programmes and schemes designed at the higher levels of government, or are they institutions of self-government? The 73rd and 74th Amendments did envisage the local bodies as 'institutions of self-government' but did not define self-government. Logically, therefore, it was expected from the provincial governments but none of the provincial assemblies cared to do so while delegating some authority and power to these bodies. Underlining the meaning of self-government was all the more crucial in the case of panchayats, since there were to be applied at all the three levels. 'Self-government', in plain terms, means a 'government without outside interference'.[22] It does sound very simple, even innocuous, but its implications are far-reaching. For it would require divisions of functions and powers between the 'union' and 'states' as also between the latter and 'panchayats' as well as within all the three tiers of panchayats. In other words, this would entail a thorough restructuring of the politico-administrative system of India.

In hindsight one can now argue that this crucial matter could not have been explained, let alone decided, by the provincial assemblies. In fact, it was beyond the competence of the state assemblies to unilaterally define the meaning and scope of 'self-government'. But they could at least have initiated a debate[23] on this crucial issue. The fact remains however that whether the framers of the 73rd Amendment expected too much from the 'provinces' or the latter failed to clarify the meaning of self-government, the central objective of the historical amendment was lost sight of. Thus panchayats (and municipalities) remained largely as agencies to implement the centrally/provincially sponsored programmes of rural/urban development, including social welfare. In other words, it was left to the sweet will of the legislators to devolve functions, funds and functionaries to these institutions. Accordingly, the extent of all these three Fs transferred to the PRIs, varies[24] from one state to another. This is not to deny that centrally-sponsored rural development[25] programmes happen to be the mainstay of PRIs. Over the years certain programmes have continued yet it has never been certain that a particular programme will continue for some years to come without any alterations. Consequently, the first victim of such an ad hoc approach is decentralized planning.

Yet routine work goes on, whether it is related to minor irrigation, repair or construction of roads and, culverts, a room in the existing school building, a compound wall or social forestry. All these involve construction activities or earth work that is the mainstay of the panchayats. Naturally, leaders are involved in them. Yet another function of the leaders is to select beneficiaries under various welfare programmes. Though officially these beneficiaries should be selected in the open session of the gram sabha, it is hard to imagine that a large number of elected leaders are engaged round the year in such activities. But this has been confirmed in several studies (Mukarji and Bandyopadhyay, 1993; Kumar, 2002;

to name a few). What panchayat leaders do not mention is their role as intermediaries or brokers (Manor, 2000; Inbanathan and Gopalappa, 2002; Kumar, 2006) they play on behalf of the common man while dealing with their cases with other institutions of the state such as block offices, courts, rural banks, cooperatives and even hospitals. But to say that all the elected leaders are equally enterprising would amount to exaggerating the facts. In fact, such smart leaders are in thin minority. An overwhelming percentage of elected leaders happen to be first timers (thanks to the roster system of reservation of seats for weaker sections including women) who simply grumble over not being approached by anyone. They are also ignored by the elected chief of the village panchayats. With the introduction of the (subject) committee system, there were expectations that a fair amount of work would be distributed among all the elected leaders but in practice the cabinet system has not gained ground. This has caused a great amount of dissatisfaction among first-time representatives who happen to be asset-less, illiterate or semi-literate, daily wage earners belonging to the scheduled categories, most backward castes or women. Yet the fact remains that the

> [I]nstrument of reservation has helped marginalized sections to avail formal leadership position. They may not have exercised real authority but their becoming a part of the institutional set-up is itself a no mean achievement. They are no longer excluded from the institutional domain; rather village panchayats have offered them space and opportunity to become part of the system, thereby bestowing legitimacy on the open democratic system. (Kumar 2006: 142–3)

As far as the transparency and accountability questions are concerned, the progress is very slow. The reasons are manifold. Firstly, the appropriation of political and social space in the villages by the ruling cliques, more particularly where dominant castes are in majority. And secondly, the economic and social divides in the villages along with the absence of public-spirited citizens who could forge people's collectives to facilitate 'participation' of people in the open forum of Gram Sabha. Thirdly, the lack of functional autonomy which, to a large extent, makes open forums meaningless. And, finally, the devolution of limited functions and funds to panchayats that leads to a great amount of frustration among both the masses and leaders alike.

What people really look for is the creation of livelihood opportunities, social and economic engagement, enhanced irrigation facilities, roads, electricity, better health care, education and future for their children. All these require huge investments and naturally remain beyond the functional domain of both village panchayats and municipal bodies. Those apart, municipal corporations in big cities, Delhi for instance, have no role to play in supply of drinking water or electricity for that matter. Hence the people remain largely unconnected with the institutions closest to them. Even panchayats have minimal role in improving the local-level institutions of the social sector.

Take, for instance, the case of primary education. This is one of the subjects mentioned in the 11th and 12th Schedules. Under the panchayat system primary teachers have not been made accountable to local leaders. On the contrary, alternative schools have been set-up wherein panchayat leaders and the community are involved. Although this is largely meant for poor people, these schools have shown encouraging results, confirming the fact that community involvement makes a difference in the performance of local-level institutions (Rana et al., 2002; Vyasulu, 2003). Yet primary school teachers have been kept out of the purview of the panchayat system in West Bengal, whose track record in decentralization efforts are relatively better and sustained for a long time, in contrast to a large number of provinces.

CONCLUSION

From the discussions above, three points clearly emerge out. First of all, the significance of both the 73rd and 74th Amendments can be located in broadening the scope of multi-level federalism than merely strengthening the functioning of the local governments. In view of the diversity of this subcontinent-size country, this is no mean achievement. This becomes all the more important if it is recalled that many thorny issues related to initial two-tier federalism, more particularly regarding control and sharing of financial resources between the first two tiers, are yet to be resolved. This also explains continuation of a heavy top-down approach to poverty alleviation programmes with very little concern for the autonomy of local government institutions.

Secondly, notwithstanding six decades of Independence from the colonial past, traditional disbelief of the bureaucracy and political masters over the means and ends of decentralization has not changed much. The political compulsions force them to create a democratic space for wider representation with special considerations for weaker sections, including women but the traditional mindset of state-level political elites, irrespective of the political spectrum they represent, do not carry forward the process of transformation. Further, in the constitutional design of two-tier federalism the union/centre encroaches upon the autonomy of provinces/states which the latter resent, but when it comes down to sharing of functions, power and resources with the third tier, they (provincial political elites) treat the local government institutions the same way as they are treated by the union. While this reflects the limits of constitutional intervention, it is also an affirmation of the fact that the battle for the local democracy has to be fought in political arena. And this would be a protracted battle.

Thirdly, the post-Amendment outcomes, howsoever modest they are, can be measured only when these developments are interfaced with constraints encompassing societal moorings, preferences and mental make up of society at large. That a highly stratified society like village India (stratifications are no less pronounced in urban areas, though their forms are changed) does not provide a suitable environment for the smooth working of democratic decentralization is a well-known fact. It calls for facilitators and mediators to iron out the social divides and transform individuals into 'people's collectives' to stand up against the prevailing adversarial interests and work for the shared goals.

Finally, in view of the growing clout of globalization, the role of the state is changing from that of a provider to a regulator. Accordingly, in urban areas, there is a strong possibility of the coming of private players in the delivery of even basic services. As a matter of fact, this has already been recognized in the JNNURM policy document. Thus the contours of local governments are likely to change and so would be their intended impact on local democracy.

Notwithstanding such constraints, there has been progress though haltingly with every attempt to improve upon the functioning of local governments in India. The latest constitutional amendments have created space for other stakeholders—civil society organizations, including NGOs, retired government officials and so on—and through them dispersal of power at the local level. Such villages or wards/localities in towns and cities are still in minority where people/residents have formed associations to intervene in running the affairs of local governments.

NOTES

1. This is the national average but there are wide variations at the state level. With 43.9 per cent urban population, Tamil Nadu, for instance, is the most urbanized state in India, followed by Maharashtra (42.4 per cent) and Gujarat (37.4 per cent). The corresponding figures for two least urbanized states, Himachal Pradesh and Bihar, are 9.8 and 10.5 per cent respectively. Numerically, however, the figure is very high. Of the 1,027 million total population of India, the share of urban Indian population in 2001 was 285 million, still almost 5 times higher a figure, compared to the total population in metropolitan France in 2001, which was approximately 59½ million.
2. The social structure of India was composed of caste groups wherein each caste was organized with a given set of occupation. Traditionally, the system had been strictly rigid, not allowing people to cross the barrier imposed upon or even to question its place in the social hierarchy. Accordingly, practically all the castes had their own panchayats entrusted with the task of enforcing their unwritten code of conduct among members of their own castes.
3. It needs mentioning that the 1857 uprising had shaken the foundations of the British rule. Though they ruthlessly suppressed, the rebellion necessitated a need for levying taxes to overcome the serious strain on imperial finances, hence the need of institutional structure to realize local taxes. Close to it was the necessity to create space in the public domain for the loyalists of imperial rule. Thus, by 1870 nearly 200 municipalities had been set-up throughout British India (Tinker: 1954).

4. The need for functional local bodies was endorsed by the Finance Commission in 1880 which had underlined that it was largely because of the absence of local bodies that the government could not supply relief materials to the famine-stricken people. Against this backdrop the historic Rippon Resolution of 1882 (named after a liberal viceroy Lord Rippon) came which provided for the setting up of local boards comprising largely non-official elected members, including the chairperson. Although its implementation was slow and tardy, the term 'self-government' had started gaining currency. This was further stressed upon in the 1909 report of the Royal Commission on Decentralization, though its recommendations, like that of the Rippon Resolution, remained largely on paper. A decade later within the proposed frame of diarchy, under the aegis of the Montague–Chelmsford Reforms (1919), it was accepted to transfer 'fully representative and responsible' local self-government to the provinces. In the next two decades, starting from 1925, local self-government acts were passed in over two-dozen provinces and native states. In between the Government of India Act, 1935, had also come into effect, guaranteeing autonomy to provincial governments. The elected provincial governments of 1937 remained in office for two years only. Thus by the time India gained Independence in 1947, there was not much progress with regard to the local government institutions.

   For a detailed historical account of panchayats during the pre-colonial and British periods, see Malviya (1956) and Mathew (2000) and for municipal bodies, see Tinker (1954), Bhattacharya (1972) and Datta (1994).
5. Under the federal arrangement, India has a centre and below it states/provinces. The administrative unit below the state is called the 'district' A few towns and hundreds of villages are governed by the district administration. This administrative structure was set-up during the British rule. Following Independence, one more tier was introduced between villages and the district, called the Block, roughly at every 1 lakh (0.1 million) population. Mehta Committee had recommended formation of panchayat bodies at all the three levels of district, block and village.
6. Launched in early 1952, the CD programme, a comprehensive village development programme, was all encompassing, covering a range of development activities: agriculture, animal husbandry, minor irrigation, education, village industries and special programmes for children and women, touching practically all aspects of village life. Since the CD programmes had failed to evoke people's enthusiasm, the brief for the Mehta Committee was to examine the reasons for the lack of people's participation in the CD programmes. The committee had felt that in the absence of an agency at the

village level, which could mobilize the 'entire community, assume responsibility and provide the necessary leadership for implementing development programmes, real progress in rural development could not come about at all'. Thus in order to ensure people's participation, it had recommended setting up representative bodies at three different levels below the state level. See, Mathew, op. cit., p. 6.

7. Nehru died in 1964. His successor Shastri, who did not share his enthusiasm for village self-rule, also died within a couple of years in power. Thereafter, Indira Gandhi, Nehru's daughter, took over in 1966. A year later the Congress was defeated in the 1967 General Elections for the first time, in as many as nine states. It had to seek support of other parties to stay in power in the centre. Thereafter, the Congress suffered a vertical split in the party. Besides, the entire north India was reeling under drought due to the failure of monsoon for three consecutive years. Thus, the ruling party itself was in crisis. Several states were facing political instability. Above all, the government was busy chalking out plans and strategies to overcome the food shortage. As a cumulative effect of these factors, Indira Gandhi resorted to a highly centralized rule which subsequently took the form of authoritarianism, culminating into the promulgation of Emergency (June 1975–March 1977) and abrogation of Fundamental Rights in the country. Following her defeat in the 1977 General Elections, a new democratic awakening swept the country, providing a suitable backdrop to re-examine all the contentious issues, including panchayat-centric democratic decentralization in the country.

8. A vital difference between the first- and second-generation of panchayats is 'the shift in emphasis from development *per se* to local government in its full meaning. The Balwantrai Mehta Committee had looked upon development as being central to the panchayat system, while the attempts in West Bengal, Karnataka, Andhra Pradesh and later in Jammu & Kashmir, were to make panchayats into genuine political institutions and thus the focal point of self-government with all its ramifications, a microcosom of the state itself.' (Mathew, 2000: 17) It also needs mentioning that besides advocating the creation of panchayats as political institutions, the Asoka Mehta Committee had recommended the setting up of two-tier, instead of three-tier panchayats. West Bengal heralded the coming of second generation of panchayats but settled for three-tier panchayats. See Ghosh and Kumar (2003), especially chapter 4.

9. For details of the amendment process and sequel of events these amendments led to, see Mathew (1994), Sivaramakrishnan (2000) and Kumar (2001).

10. Like panchayats, election to municipal bodies was earlier not mandatory. Therefore prior to the 74th Amendment, urban local bodies had for long remained under administrators disconnected with their democratic representative character.
11. These UTs are governed directly by the union government; the only exceptions are Delhi and Pondicherry which have their own elected assemblies, and therefore they enjoy partial autonomy.
12. See Datta, 1994.
13. The bigger metro cities like Delhi, Mumbai, Kolkata are also referred to as mega cities having a population of more than 10 million. They essentially represent urban agglomerates. In fact, with 93 per cent of its population living in urban areas, Delhi is the most urbanized mega city (cum state) in India. There are three urban bodies to govern its sprawling urban areas, viz., the Municipal Corporation of Delhi (covering almost 90 per cent of its urban space), followed by the (non-elected) New Delhi Municipal Corporation (taking care of Lutyan's Delhi comprising its centrally located parts covering union ministries, parliament, presidential estates and residential bungalows of top bureaucrats and political leaders as well as the diplomatic enclave. And for military establishment there is a Delhi Cantonment Board, covering less than 2 per cent of Delhi's population.
14. This is again not universal in nature. In Delhi, for instance, there is a separate body called Delhi Jal Board that is responsible for the supply of drinking water. This has nothing to do with the existing municipal bodies of the capital city of India. Moreover, in the era of liberalization and privatization, functions like sweeping, garbage disposals, and so on have been privatized in many cities in India.
15. On similar lines West Bengal government also introduced a provision for Chairperson-in-Council municipalities. Similar attempts were also made in Maharashtra, particularly in Mumbai and Nagpur, though soon it reverted to the old system: retaining the supremacy of the administrative head over the elected head of the municipal body.
16. What do panchayats really stand for? Do they happen to be a development agency, an extended arm of the government meant for implementing programmes/schemes designed at the top? The development motif attached to the image of panchayats as conceived by Balwantrai Mehta study team has dogged it forever despite clarity sought in Asoka Mehta Committee and pronouncements of the 73rd Amendment, which recognizes PRIs as in 'institutions of self-governance'. For a nuanced discussion on this issue, see Bandyopadhyay, Ghosh et al., 2003).
17. In order to encourage people's participation in decision-making pertaining

to urban services and also to ensure transparency and accountability of elected local leaders, the 74th Amendment provided for setting up 'ward committees' in municipalities with more than 3 lakh population. So far, these committees have been formed in 11 states. This is not applicable in case of smaller states and union territories. In the remaining dozen states the matter is under consideration.

18. Unlike self-help groups or Bangladeshi Grameen Bank programmes under which loans are advanced to poor, illiterate groups of people rather than individuals.
19. According to the latest estimates of the Central Planning Commission, since 1993–4 there has been hardly any change in the poverty figures of states like Maharashtra, Bihar, Madhya Pradesh and West Bengal. In fact, with nearly half of its total population (46.4 per cent) falling under the BPL category, Orissa tops the list, followed by Bihar (41.4 per cent). See, *Hindustan Times* (New Delhi), 22 March 2007.
20. Mumbai and Kolkata are ranked lowest among 27 Asian cities with million-plus population in a recent World Bank study. The figures given above have been compiled from data provided on the website of the Union Ministry of Urban Development, New Delhi, as cited in Mehta, 2007: 27.
21. For details, see the website of the Union Ministry of Urban Development, http://jnnurm.nic.in/
22. Soon after the 73rd Amendment became an Act, Nirmal Mukarji, a former cabinet secretary and a former governor of Punjab, wrote a series of articles raising doubts and concerns over the implications of the two amendments. See, *Statesman* (Kolkata), 11–13 May 1993.
23. For details of the issues raised and debates that followed in four provincial assemblies, see Kumar (2002).
24. As mentioned earlier, following the 73rd Amendment, a list of functions to be devolved to panchayats was inserted in the 11th Schedule of the Constitution. Since the list was illustrative, the transfer of all these three Fs was left to the discretion of the state assemblies. To what extent these vary can be seen in a compendium recently published by the Union Ministry of Panchayats (2006).
25. There are as many as 29 items listed under the 11th Schedule and against each item there are some centrally sponsored schemes. One of the biggest paradoxes is the highly complex arrangements for the identification, approval, fund release, monitoring and coordination of such schemes. For funds are transferred from as many as 14 union ministries/departments. The Ministry of Agriculture, for instance, funds a large number of

programmes listed under as many as nine heads—item nos. 1–3, 5–7, 16, 24 and 29 (see Annexure II). All these schemes fall under the broad rubric of rural development. Interestingly, however, there is a separate Ministry of Rural Development which sponsors schemes listed under item nos. 2, 4, 8, 14, 18, 21, 24 and 29. Above all, since 2004 an independent Union Ministry of Panchayati Raj is also operating.

REFERENCES

Bhattacharya, Mohit, *Essays in Urban Government*, Calcutta: World Press, 1972.

Datta, Abhijit, 'Institutional Aspects of Urban Governance in India', *Indian Journal of Public Administration*, vol. XL, no. 4, 1994, pp. 616–32.

Ghosh, Buddhadeb and Girish Kumar, *State Politics and Panchayats in India*, New Delhi: Manohar, 2003.

Government of India, Ministry of Panchayati Raj, *The State of the Panchayats: A Mid-Term Review and Appraisal*, vol. I, 2006.

Inbanathan, Anand and D.V. Gopalappa, 'Fixers, Patronage, Fixing and Local Governance in Karnataka', Working Paper 112, Bangalore: Institute for Social and Economic Change, 2002.

Institute of Social Sciences, 'Elected Representatives in all the Three Tiers of Panchayats in India', Data Archives, New Delhi, 2001.

Kumar, Girish, 'Overcoming State's Resistance: Panchayat Elections in Bihar', *Economic and Political Weekly*, 36(20), 2001, pp. 1681–4.

———, 'Constitutionalising Panchayats: The Response of State Legislatures', Occasional Paper No. 4, New Delhi: Centre de Sciences Humaines, 2002.

———, *Local Democracy in India: Interpreting Decentralisation*, New Delhi: Sage, 2006.

Malviya, H.D., *Village Panchayats in India*, New Delhi: All India Congress Committee, 1956.

Mathew, George (ed.), *Status of Panchayati Raj in the States and Union Territories in India*, New Delhi: Concept, 2000.

Manor, James, 'Small-time Political Fixers in India's States: Towel Over Armpit', *Asian Survey*, 40(5), 2000, pp. 816–35.

Mehta, Arun K., 'Financing Service Delivery in Municipalities', unpublished M.Phil dissertation, Chandigarh: IIPA and Panjab University, 2007.

Mukarji, Nirmal, 'The Third Stratum', *Statesman*, 11–13 May 1993.

Mukarji, Nirmal and D. Bandyopadhayay, *New Horizons for West Bengal Panchayats*, Calcutta: Government of West Bengal, 1993.

Rana, K., Abdur Rafique and Amrita Sengupta, *The Pratichi Education Report,* No.1, Delhi: TLM Books, 2002.

Singh, Kulwant, 'Trends and Issues in Decentralisation and Urban Governance in India', 2001.

Sivaramakrishnan, K.C., *Power to the People: The Politics and Progress of Decentralisation,* New Delhi: Konark Publishers, 2000.

Tinker, Hugh, *The Foundations of Local Self-Government in India, Pakistan and Burma,* London: Athlone Press, 1954.

Vyasulu, Vinod, *Panchayats, Democracy and Development,* Jaipur: Rawat Publications, 2003.

ANNEXURE I

Municipal Functions as Listed under the 12th Schedule

1. Urban planning including town planning
2. Regulation of land use and construction of buildings
3. Planning for economic and social development
4. Roads and bridges
5. Water supply for domestic, industrial and commercial purposes
6. Public health, sanitation, conservancy and solid waste management
7. Fire services
8. Urban forestry, protection of the environment and promotion of ecological aspects
9. Safeguarding the interests of weaker sections of society including the handicapped and mentally retarded
10. Slum improvement and upgradation
11. Urban poverty alleviation
12. Provision of urban amenities and facilities, parks, gardens, and playgrounds
13. Promotion of cultural, educational, and aesthetic aspects
14. Burials and burial grounds, cremations, cremation grounds and electric crematoriums
15. Cattle pounds, prevention of cruelty to animals
16. Vital statistics including registration of births and deaths
17. Public amenities including street lighting, parking lots, bus stops and public conveniences
18. Regulation of slaughter houses and tanneries.

ANNEXURE II

Functional Domain of Panchayats as Listed under the 11th Schedule

1. Agriculture, including agriculture extension
2. Land improvement, implementation of land reforms, land consolidation and soil conservation
3. Minor irrigation, water management and watershed development
4. Animal husbandry, dairying and poultry
5. Fisheries
6. Social forestry and farm forestry
7. Minor forest produce
8. Small-scale industries, including food processing industries
9. Khadi, village and cottage industries
10. Rural housing
11. Drinking water
12. Fuel and fodder
13. Roads, culverts, bridges, ferries, waterways and other means of communication
14. Rural electrification, including distribution of electricity
15. Non-conventional energy sources
16. Poverty alleviation programmes
17. Education, including primary and secondary schools
18. Technical training and vocational education
19. Adult and non-formal education
20. Libraries
21. Cultural activities
22. Markets and fairs
23. Health and Sanitation, including hospitals, primary health centres and dispensaries
24. Family welfare
25. Women and child development
26. Social welfare, including welfare of the handicapped and mentally retarded
27. Welfare of weaker sections, and in particular of the Scheduled Castes and the Sheduled Tribes
28. Public Distribution System
29. Maintenance of community assets

CHAPTER 2

State and the Grassroots: Unresolved Problems of Local Democracy in India

BUDDHADEB GHOSH

THE COLONIAL LOCAL ADMINISTRATION

When India became free, her Constitution makers chose to retain the structure of local governance inherited from the colonial past of the country. The hallmark of this structure was that the entire domain of local administration remained at the hands of the bureaucracy of the provincial governments and they were accountable only to themselves. The centrepiece of this uniquely organized local administration was an official called the district magistrate or the collector or the deputy commissioner. As his designation implies, this particular official was primarily responsible for two very important functions of the government, namely, collection of revenue of which land revenue constituted the major source, and maintenance of law and order. For any colonial power, these are the major concerns of governance. More than the substantive functions of his office, what made the district magistrate/collector almost a mythical figure was that he was flaunted as the representative of the imperial government at the district. He was not a mere civil servant, but a ruler *par excellence* exercising not only statutory powers, but also substantial discretionary powers over people who were 'subjects', not 'citizens' endowed with a set of rights. Of course, there were, even during the colonial regime, some developmental and welfare functions, but they were of minor nature. Except when there was some emergency with the potential danger of the breakdown of law and order, such as, famine or flood or drought, the district administration had a low priority for the developmental or welfare functions. Even when it discharged such functions, they were regarded as acts of a benevolent ruler dispensing justice and goodwill. By any standard, it was a highly autocratic rule.[1]

It is within this framework of district administration that the Raj introduced the rural local-self-government institutions in this country. As expected, these institutions were not adequately representative, being constituted on the basis of a restricted electorate. They also lacked autonomy and were starved of financial and administrative resources, besides being compelled to work under the constant surveillance of the district bureaucracy led by the collector. These institutions were not designed to undertake major developmental functions. Their main role was to provide civic services of a minor nature. Whatever developmental or welfare functions the government was discharging remained at the hands of the district bureaucracy. Such was the state of rural local government institutions on the eve of Independence.

MISMATCH BETWEEN THE INHERITED STRUCTURE OF LOCAL ADMINISTRATION AND DEMOCRACY

The Constitution makers of the country did not think it necessary to expand the role of the institutions of local government. They preferred to retain the structure of local administration in its entirety, as a result of which the district bureaucracy had no obligation to be accountable to the local people through their representatives at the local level. This arrangement would not have created problems had the character of the newly-formed Indian state remained the same. But radical transformation did take place in the character of the state after Independence and it carried the seeds of fundamental changes in the form of the governance system and its content. First, India opted for democracy with a set of political and social rights guaranteed to her citizens. Second, the political leaders of the newly-independent country declared at the dawn of Independence that the most important tasks of the state would be to eliminate 'poverty and ignorance and disease and inequality of opportunity'.[2]

These two factors changed the character of the state overnight, necessitating consequent changes in the manner as to how the country should be governed. The changeover to democracy meant that the people of the country were no more 'subjects' of an alien sovereign power, but had become right bearing 'citizens' to whom the governors of the country had responsibility and accountability. The commitment made by the leaders of the newly-independent state to end poverty, illiteracy, ill-health and inequality of opportunity meant that the focus of the state had to shift toward development and welfare functions along with affirmative actions for the underprivileged.

That the structure of the local governance system inherited from the past would be incompatible with the above changes in the form and the content of the governance system was not quite apparent at the beginning. From the point of view of the government, the incompatibility came to be noticed shortly after the state embarked upon an ambitious rural development programme in 1952. Known as the community development and national extension service programme, this development initiative, which very soon covered the entire country, envisaged planning and execution of village-based multi-sectoral activities for economic and social development and was regarded 'as an integral part of the programme for improving all aspects of rural life'. One of the important aspects of the programme was to transfer updated knowledge and skill to the villagers through an array of technically qualified extension officials in several disciplines for improving rural economy and society. In that respect, it may also be seen as the first major intervention of the newly-independent state to modernize the countryside. The programme also aimed at promoting communitarian principles and self-help efforts among the villagers. It was also expected to bring 'within its scope all rural families, especially those who are underprivileged'.[3] Thus, the purpose of the programmme was not only to provide coordinated services for bringing about all-round development of the rural people, but more importantly to ensure their enthusiastic participation and cooperation in various activities for improving the quality of life.

TOWARDS LOCAL DEMOCRACY

A programme of this kind needed, for its success, generation of sufficient local interest and local initiative through people's participation in full measure. The officials of the community development programme were not competent enough for the task. A study team appointed by the Government of India under the chairmanship of Balawantrai Mehta candidly admitted this and observed that the development programme that seeks to respond to the local needs, take cognizance of local priorities, generate local initiatives and ensure people's participation could not be successful unless it remained in the hands of local representative institutions (GOI, 1957). This realization prompted the study team to recommend setting up of three-tier local government institutions in rural areas—panchayats at the village (either one village or a group of villages), block and district levels. With active support of Prime Minister Nehru, political support to set-up the three-tier panchayat system was available instantly. By early 1960s representative rural local government institutions were set-up in most of the states to give a taste of local democracy for the first time to the people of the country's five hundred thousand odd villages. Nehru showed great enthusiasm for these grassroots democratic institutions and christened the new system as panchayati raj—governance through panchayats.[4]

The enthusiasm over panchayati raj did not last long. Before the panchayats could take their roots as institutions of local government, they began to stagnate after Nehru's death in 1964 and started declining in all the states except those of Maharashtra and Gujarat. Even the minimum requirement of holding regular elections to these bodies was not fulfilled by the states. A second attempt at reviving these institutions was made by three states, namely West Bengal, Andhra Pradesh and Karnataka in the late-1970s and mid-1980s following the report of another committee headed by Asoka Mehta, a socialist leader, in 1978 (GOI, 1978). Among these three states, only the panchayats of West Bengal survived and were firmly institutionalized. The institutions of the other two states declined after their first term was over, as they were not given political support by the new regimes, which came to power in those states.

Even in the states of Maharashtra and Gujarat where the panchayats have survived after their first appearance in early 1960s and in the state of West Bengal where these institutions have enjoyed uninterrupted continuity since 1978, the fact requires to be noted that they did not alter the structure of local governance in any way. The institutions of panchayats were not given functional or financial autonomy. They did not substitute any organ of the state government to discharge functions exclusively earmarked for them. They functioned principally as agents of the respective state governments in executing certain centrally sponsored development programmes, mostly under surveillance of the district bureaucracy. As such, they had hardly any scope or political authority in influencing policies, direction or priorities of local development. This means that there was less democracy at the grassroots level, if the 'meaning of democracy [is]', as Nehru said, 'the chance being given to people to decide for themselves on all basic issues'.[5]

In 1987–8, when Rajiv Gandhi, then prime minister of India, began his quest for 'efficient' and 'responsive' administration, the basic structure of local governance obtaining at the dawn of Independence remained practically unaltered. The bureaucracy dominated the scene with no existence of panchayats in most states or weak panchayats in a few states. The only change that could be noticed was expansion of the size of the bureaucracy, increasing insularity of various line departments and non-existence of any institutional machinery for ensuring horizontal coordination between different line departments at the field level. As before, the local bureaucracy was not directly accountable to local people. Panchayats, wherever they were present, acted as agents of the state government and had little resources or power of their own to meet local needs or local grievances. After extensively touring rural India and holding several conferences with the district officers, Rajiv Gandhi realized that 'at the interface between people and administration, the administration is unresponsive, inefficient, unsympathetic, often callous, sometimes even cruel to those whom they are meant to serve'.[6] He concluded that 'our district administration is not sufficiently responsive . . . because, it is not sufficiently representative'.[7] This realization made him a strong advocate of panchayati raj. As he took up the task of democratizing local administration—a task that his grandfather wanted to accomplish three decades ago—Rajiv Gandhi had noticed that earlier attempts to institutionalize panchayats had failed, because local government was a state subject and the question of the institutionalization of a viable local government system depended on the political will of the regimes in charge of the state governments. Experience showed that the policies taken by the state governments from time to time in such matters as holding of panchayat elections on time, providing support to these institutions or devolving functions and resources to these bodies depended on the political compulsions of the ruling parties of the respective states.[8] In order to ensure continuity and empowerment of panchayats, Rajiv Gandhi decided to give constitutional status to these bodies. Accordingly, he brought the 64th Constitution Amendment Bill on Panchayati Raj in May 1989 to set-up the third tier of governance at the district and sub-district levels. Unfortunately he could not get the Bill passed by the parliament. But the efforts initiated by him did not go in vain. Three years after Rajiv Gandhi's tragic assassination, panchayats and municipalities did find place in the Constitution through the 73rd and the 74th Constitution Amendment Acts, respectively. These amendments gave constitutional recognition to the panchayats and the municipalities as institutions of representative government at the local level.

CONSTITUTIONAL STATUS OF LOCAL GOVERNMENT AND ITS IMPACT

The constitutional amendments generated great expectations, because it seemed that the long-standing gap in Indian democracy was ultimately going to be filled by removing the problem that stood in the way of institutionalization of representative governments at the grassroots level. The implications of establishing institutions of self-government at the local level were, indeed, far-reaching, since the idea of carrying out governmental functions at that level through representative institutions directly accountable to the local people were totally alien to this country. It marked a complete break from the traditional pattern of governing the local by bureaucracy responsible to people's representatives only in form, but not in substance. In the constitutional amendments, many observers had noticed the possibilities of the reversal of this pattern and the emergence of a decentralized polity.

More than a decade has passed since the 73rd Constitutional Amendment came into force. To what extent has it been successful in fulfilling such expectations? It is true that the constitutional amendments have brought about substantial changes on at least three fronts. First, certainty of panchayat institutions has been ensured. Every state has to establish panchayats. Their space in the institutional structure of the Indian state is now guaranteed and not dependent upon the political will of the individual state governments. Second, continuity of the institutions through elections every five years is also now guaranteed. Even the defaulting states, which do not take their constitutional duty seriously, have to explain to the public, to the media and also to the judiciary the reasons as to why they cannot hold the elections on time. Third, weaker sections of people including women have entered the power-structure of panchayats through the reservation provisions made by the constitutional amendment. Positioning of innumerable elected bodies below the state level and representation within them of the people belonging to the weaker sections constitute an event that cannot be dismissed easily.

Despite these achievements, the grand possibilities of the constitutional amendments in replacing substantially the bureaucratic district administration by the empowered, accountable and participative local government institutions as envisioned by some observers did not materialize. For, panchayats have, by and large, failed to emerge as governments at the local level, described by some as the third stratum of Indian polity.[9] Those who noticed radical elements in the constitutional amendment believed that as institutions of self-government nearest to the people, panchayats would assert their autonomy and prepare the ground for dispersal of political power at an unprecedented scale. But the old order has refused to yield for the new. The project of democratic decentralization still remains an unfinished task.

What are the problems that beset the implementation of the constitutional amendments on decentralization? There are certain mandatory provisions in the constitutional amendments for putting in place the structures of local government at the village, district and intermediate levels. These relate to the constitution of panchayats at different levels, regularity in holding elections to the local bodies, reservation provisions for women and the underprivileged sections, recognition of the gram sabha (the assembly of all voters), constitution of state election commissions to conduct and supervise elections to the local bodies, constitution of state finance commissions every five years to look into the finances of these bodies, and so on. Implementation of these provisions has not posed much problem. Today, with the exception of one state, all others where the constitutional amendments are applicable,[10] have implemented these mandatory provisions of the Constitution. As such, the structures of the institutions of local government are now in place and they are being renewed more or less regularly through fresh elections at the interval of five years.

The main problem of implementation of the constitutional provisions on democratic decentralization lies in the question of empowerment of the Panchayati Raj Institutions. On this, it requires to be noted, the Constitution has not made any definite provisions, but it has given some positive indications about the attributes of the panchayats and their role in the system of governance, leaving the responsibility of working out the details to the legislatures of the respective states.

PANCHAYATS: GAP BETWEEN CONCEPT AND PRACTICE

The Constitution defines 'panchayats' as institutions of self-government and they are to be constituted at the village (which includes a group of villages), district and intermediate levels.[11] Thus the main attribute of the panchayat is that it is an institution of government and its location is at the grassroots level of a village or a group of villages or very close to that level. This has, indeed, far-reaching implications. Although panchayats would derive their 'powers and authority' from the enactments of the respective state legislatures and from the state governments, they cannot be treated merely as agencies or subordinate units of the government at the state level, because as self-governing institutions they have to be endowed with an autonomous functional jurisdiction. In other words, at each level, panchayats will have a sphere of independent action, such that the state government will not exercise any control over this sphere except giving general guidance and support. There could be other spheres of action where the state government and the panchayats would work together as equal partners, as it happens in the case of union and the state governments. In certain cases, these institutions may also act as agencies of the state government, but this sphere of action cannot be allowed to overshadow or diminish the distinctive character of panchayat as an institution of government having full authority to take decisions in certain spheres of the state's activities. Granting autonomous jurisdiction to panchayats implies that the Constitution intends devolution type of decentralization as opposed to mere administrative deconcentration, necessitating withdrawal of certain activities or even functions from the state government and transferring them to the local bodies.

This is a sharp departure from the way the local government institutions used to be treated in the past, as bodies subservient to the provincial or state governments. I hold the promise of transforming the system of governance of the country. For, each state government would then be required to share its power and authority with the institutions of self-government at the local level and once this happens, 'each state would become a federation', turning India into a kind of a 'cascading federation' or a 'federation of federations' (Mukarji and Arora, 1992: 270).

The Constitution also indicates the kind of role of panchayats are expected to play in the governance of the country. Normally, in most parts of the world the role of the local government remains confined to the delivery of civic services. A much bigger role is assigned to India's local governments by the Constitution. It is quite significant that the constitutional amendments give the mandate to panchayats at all the levels to prepare development plans for their respective areas. Not only that. The goal of such plans is also defined. This is expressed in Article 243G within the phrase: 'economic development and social justice'. It is well known that over the last six decades, the Indian state has been continuously pursuing the goals of development with particular emphasis on those who are economically poor or victims of various kinds of social injustice. Planning at the national and state levels has been an important tool to pursue these goals. Mandating the local councils to prepare area plans in order to achieve the same goals is an admission of the fact that macro-level plans remain incomplete or non-responsive to the urgent needs of people unless they are informed by the insights derived from the grassroots. Thus through the constitutional provisions on decentralized planning and on the goal of such planning, the institutions of local government are being made partners of the higher level governments for achieving the national goals of development.

The 11th Schedule of the Constitution, which gives a list of activities intended to be transferred to the local bodies, covers a broad spectrum of development activities ranging from activities in the social and economic sectors (education, health, women and child development, social security, farm and non-farm economic activities, and so on) to the development of infrastructure and institutions necessary for social and economic development. The thrust is, obviously, on development. But this does not mean that the Constitution prohibits the state legislatures to endow the local councils with regulatory powers also. The state legislatures are free to 'endow the panchayats with such powers and authority as may be necessary to enable them to function as institutions of self-government' (Article 243G). Thus the scope of the provisions on the transfer of powers and responsibilities to these bodies is quite wide, leading some experts to comment that the 11th Schedule represents the 'floor, but not the ceiling' and 'it is certainly within the competence of the state legislature to decide what powers and authority the panchayats should have in order that they function as credible institutions of self-government' (Mukarji and Bandyopadhyay, 1993: 7).

The constitutional directions to introduce empowered institutions of self-government at the grassroots level has been, by and large, ignored by the states, taking advantage of the discretionary powers given to them in giving concrete shape to the scheme contained in the directions. Except the Act of Kerala, none of the panchayat Acts framed by the different state legislatures has tried to grapple with the concept of self-government at the local level. Panchayats are denied autonomous jurisdiction, as exclusive functions/activities or local institutions for service delivery together with the financial and human resources are not devolved to them. The Acts merely permit them to work within the functional domain of the state, subject to such conditions as it may deem fit to impose. Excepting some minor civic functions which are invariably given to the gram panchayats, for all other so-called developmental functions assigned to the different tiers of panchayat, there are specific line departments of state government or parastatal bodies. They handle these functions. They have access to necessary resources as also staff for the discharge of the functions. Mere statutory authority to undertake functions already being performed by the state government is no guarantee that those would, indeed, be taken up by the PRIs, unless they have adequate funds and personnel to discharge them. Since these resources are not made available to them, the list of various functions that every panchayat Act religiously provides remains sterile. What the 73rd Constitutional Amendment intended is 'exclusive' functional domain for the panchayats, backed by resources. That has not happened.

Thus, institutionally, the panchayats could not in any way substitute the bureaucratic district administration. Like before, they are still regarded as additional institutions supplementing the work of district administration in development. Thus the legacy of the past continues, creating a sort of a myth that the administrative framework for the districts developed by the British Raj is immutable and any structure of local democracy has to adjust itself within it. No wonder, even in the states, which have shown political will to decentralize, devolution has not gone beyond the implementation responsibility of the development or welfare schemes/projects sponsored by the state or central government. As a result, panchayats have not blossomed into institutions of self-government. Instead they have become at best one of the implementing arms of the state government. The constitutional intention of deepening democratic governance by creating structures of local democracy and empowering them remains unfulfilled. The structures are in place, but they are not empowered.

DEMOCRATIZING LOCAL ADMINISTRATION: EXPLORING THE FAILURE

India's experiment on institutionalizing panchayati raj now covers a period of 50 years, considering the fact that the Balawantrai Mehta study team report ushering in the first generation panchayats was published in 1957. The above chronological account will show that the journey is far from being complete and even after the constitutionalization of panchayats, democratization of local governance system still remains a distant dream. Various explanations have been offered for the failure of the Indian state in extending democracy to the grassroots level.[12] It is not our intention to revisit them. Instead, we shall try to raise some other issues, which, it is believed, may be of help in understanding the problem from a different angle.

We would like to start by asking a question: what was the major motivation behind all the attempts made so far by the state for institutionalizing panchayats? Was it the urge for providing more democracy to the grassroots, or was it the anxiety to enhance legitimacy of the centralized state? We shall argue that the main purpose of all the attempts made so far to institutionalize panchayats has been to enhance the resilience and legitimacy of the centralized state, while the task of democratizing the local governance system through the institutions of panchayats has continuously been kept on the back-burner. That explains why the problems of establishing local democracy on a sound footing still remain unresolved.

As mentioned before, the first serious attempt to establish panchayats, as per the recommendations of the study team headed by Balawantrai Mehta, was prompted basically by the need of enlisting people's participation in the community development programme. Thus the basic motive behind the first generation panchayats was to legitimize a development and welfare programme designed at the top and implemented by the bureaucracy. Although the study team's report recommended that all aspects of rural development work should be transferred to the panchayats and after this is done, 'the state government should cease to operate' in such matters, in reality panchayats were introduced only to ensure people's cooperation in implementing the projects of the higher-level governments.

The same trend continued when a fresh attempt was made to revive the moribund panchayat system in the late 1970s and 1980s, following the report of another committee headed by Asoka Mehta. It is true that this committee recognized for the first time the political dimension of the institution of panchayats. The political consciousness of people, the report noted, had enhanced and they were demanding opportunities for direct involvement in the 'management of local affairs'. The report even gave the vision of a polity in which extension of democracy to the grassroots would 'encourage a two-way system of political linkages from bottom upwards through the state to national levels and vice versa' (GOI, 1978: 35). Such an enlightened view on the role of local democracy, however, failed to inform the committee's recommendations. The approach of viewing panchayats as agencies of the state governments for pursuing their development programmes dominated the thinking of the committee and formulation of its recommendations. Among the three states where panchayats were revived in the wake of this report, only the state of Karnataka made genuine attempts to 'build autonomous local government institutions in the villages and in the districts. Thc state even came up with the idea of district government'. The experiment, however, could not last long. In the other two states, namely West Bengal and Andhra Pradesh, the basic purpose of reviving these institutions was to acquire legitimacy and to enhance political influence of the ruling parties in power, namely the Left Front and the Telugu Desam Party (TDP), respectively (Bandyopadhyay et al., 2003 and Ghosh and Kumar, 2003). No wonder, panchayats of these two states lacked functional and financial autonomy. Being subservient to the respective state governments, they failed to make a transition to the genuine institutions of government at the local level.

Long back, Jayaprakash Narayan had asserted that the panchayat at a particular level 'should have power to do all that it [might] be competent to do' (1970: 105), but in reality these institutions were treated as merely 'limbs and agencies of the state government and no more' (ibid.: 134). Similar point was also made by E.M.S Namboodiripad in his note to the report of Asoka Mehta Committee. He said, 'democracy at the central and state levels, but bureaucracy at all lower levels—this is the essence of Indian polity as spelt out in the Constitution' (GOI, 1978: 160). 'I cannot think of panchayati raj institutions', Namboodiripad added, 'as anything other than integral parts of the country's administration with no difference between what are called the "developmental" and "regulatory" functions. What is required is that, while certain definite fields of administration like defence, foreign affairs, currency, communication, etc., should rest with the centre, all the rest should be transferred to the states and from there to the district and lower levels of elected administrative bodies' (ibid.: 163). The vision shared by Namboodiripad and Jayaprakash Narayan failed to create any impact upon the ruling class of the country. As our account of the present status of panchayats shows, despite constitutional support no state government, except Kerala, has cared to democratize local administration by empowering the local councils as autonomous institutions.[13]

SUBSERVIENCE OF PANCHAYATS: A CALCULATED DESIGN?

Thus after a period of half a century, the country's panchayats are nothing more than 'limbs and agencies' of the state governments. They are far from being 'integral parts of the country's administration'. Moreover, they are considered to be appropriate for discharging only one type of function, namely, the so-called developmental functions of the state. Even in discharging such functions, they would have no autonomy and would act only as agents of the higher level governments. This is the *de facto* status of panchayats in contrast to their *de jure* status as institutions of self-government.

The theoretical foundation of Indian democracy rests on the notion that the sovereignty of the state resides in people.[14] This abstract notion can be concretized by the active participation of the citizens in the affairs of the state. The political justification of the project of panchayati raj is to promote such participatory citizenship, so that the common people of the country living in nearly 6 lakh villages can get opportunities to decide for themselves, as far as possible, on matters that affect their everyday lives. But the manner in which this project has been pursued in the last few decades unmistakably suggests that its objective was never to give concrete shape to the notion of 'popular sovereignty'.[15] We have tried to show that the motive behind the project has consistently been to secure the resilience and legitimacy of the centralized state. This may not be very unusual. For, the idea of collective decision-making through citizen participation, which lies at the core of a democratic polity, is retreating fast from governmental practice in most countries. Partha Chatterjee (2004: 34) observes that a major characteristic of the modern states is that they secure 'legitimacy not by participation of citizens in matters of state but by claiming to provide for the well-being of the population'. One can find confirmation of this in the account of panchayati raj given in the preceding pages. This also explains why the role of these democratic institutions at the grassroots has remained confined only within the agency functions in the field of rural development.

NEW TECHNIQUES OF DISEMPOWERING THE PANCHAYATS

The problem before the Indian state is that its principal technique to secure legitimacy—development and welfare of people—requires popular participation for its success. It has to reach the grassroots with its elaborate development agenda that covers all aspects of individual and social lives of people. Time and again it has been realized that bureaucracy alone is unable to deliver the services in a manner that can satisfy those for whom they are meant. It is not a matter of coincidence that all the three generations of panchayats—first in late 1950s and 1960s, the second in the late 1970s and 1980s and the last one after the 73rd Constitutional Amendment in the 1990s—have been given the task of addressing the most crucial development issues of the contemporary periods. Yet, there has been a great hesitation in creating institutional opportunities through empowered local councils that could lead to the emergence of authentic voices of people in the countryside. The Indian ruling class has in general been extremely wary of creating centres of political power at the grassroots. Caught in this dilemma, some Indian states are taking recourse to methods which are not only unorthodox but border on naivety.

The first of such experiment was done in the state of Madhya Pradesh. Termed as *gram swaraj* (literally self-rule for village), a programme was launched on 26 January 2001 to introduce direct democracy at the villages, so that the power remains with people and not with their representatives. The state's Panchayat Act was amended to transfer all the powers of gram panchayat to the gram sabha which is an assembly of all voters. Under the previous Act this body was a deliberative body to oversee the functioning of the gram panchayat, as is the system elsewhere. Under the new dispensation, it was transformed into an executive body taking decisions on all matters coming under the purview of the gram panchayat. For implementing its decisions, the sabha would constitute eight standing committees and additional ad-hoc committees as and when required for execution of any specific work. All these committees would be responsible to the sabha (Behar, 2001). It was hoped that once gram swaraj gets firmly rooted, representative government at the village level would not be necessary, leading to the convergence of the village community and the village government. This audacious experiment obviously failed to live up to its expectations. Reflecting on its performance eighteen months after the launching of the programme, an observer noted that the democratic space provided for participation had remained grossly underutilized and the system was languishing. Interestingly, a major reason advanced for the poor performance of the gram swaraj system was the one universally given for the tardy growth of the panchayati raj, namely inadequate devolution of functions and resources (Behar, 2003).

Another variant of gram swaraj was taken up by the state of West Bengal in 2003. In an amendment to the Panchayat Act of the state, the gram sansad, which is an assembly of all the voters of a ward of the gram panchayat, was given substantive powers to take final decisions on the development and welfare activities to be performed within the area of the sansad. Except on special circumstances, the gram panchayat is not to be allowed to alter these decisions. The sansad has also been given even the responsibility of implementing the action plans prepared by it for which a committee to be called gram unnayan samiti is to be constituted through informal elections in a special meeting of the sansad. Thus in turning a deliberative body into an executive body, West Bengal is practically following the path trodden by gram swaraj.[16] So far, the experience of this experiment also appears to be disappointing.

Outside the framework of gram swaraj, another channel has been opened in the form of user committees and self-help groups (SHG) to create new spaces for participation in the management of various developmental activities including micro credit. These community-based organizations (CBO) are sponsored by the state governments for managing in most cases the donor-funded development projects. Thus there are irrigation water users' committee, watershed development committee, joint forest management group, parent–teacher committee, health committee and the like, besides women's SHGs. They exist parallel to the existing structures of local government institutions. Usually they have more funds than do the local councils. The state of Andhra Pradesh had taken the lead in pursuing a policy under which such CBOs would receive various kinds of support, while the question of empowerment of panchayats would continue to get neglected (Powis, 2003). Such a policy often finds support on the ground that it has the virtue of insulating development from local politics. Sudden proliferation of community-based committees and groups principally for managing specific development projects sponsored by the higher-level governments and more often than not funded by the donors therefore raises serious questions. While nobody denies the role of the CBOs as alternative channels of participation and as institutions for facilitating self-help efforts of the poor, the idea of treating them as substitutes for the institutions of local government seems to be a clever ploy to centralize political power. What is required is to establish a linkage between the user committees/SHGs and the local councils, so that they can integrate their activities to pursue the goals of development. Unless such a policy of integration is adopted, serious damage will be done to the project of democratic decentralization (Manor, 2005).

One cannot overlook the commonality in all the three types of decentralization described above. All of them ignore the question of strengthening the institutions of local government, but seek, at the same time, to create the fiction of transferring power to people directly. If the strategy in one case is to empower the gram sabha/ward sabha and to convert them into executive bodies in the name of introducing direct democracy, in the other case the method employed is more naïve in the sense that it seeks to depoliticize development by promoting and supporting the CBOs, bypassing the local government in the name of making people empowered and self-reliant. The irony is that in both these two types of decentralization, people at the grassroots remain totally dependent upon a government located at a distant place and on which it has practically no control. This perhaps suits the design of the political elites who are content to see that the 'local domain' remains a dependant domain with their self-governing institutions being denied the power and authority and the resources to meet even some of the basic needs of people.

THE ROAD AHEAD

What then is the future of local democracy in India? Clearly this is not an issue that is contested by the political parties. There is no indication yet that the political elites are seriously concerned with the issue of democratization of the local administration. On the contrary, they seem to be more interested in maintaining the *status quo*, as the politics of clientelism they pursue draws considerable strength from the absence of popular control over local administration. Hence, like before, in future also they will be wary of conferring autonomy to the panchayats, unless other factors force them to change their stance. Are such factors visible now? It is difficult to give a definite answer. But one cannot overlook the important fact that the aspirations of the faceless people at the grassroots to be recognized as 'right-bearing citizens' are increasing and it is becoming difficult for a non-participative state to satisfy them with its centrally designed policies and programmes.

How do we know that the efforts of common people to assert their rights are increasing? Two types of evidence are available to indicate that they expect responsiveness and accountability of the government in far greater measure than before. One comes from the various forms of militant movements particularly of the tribal groups and landless peasants to realize various demands originating from the perception of economic or ethnic injustice. These movements, which are grouped under the rubric of 'Naxal movement', have their origin in the non-responsiveness of the local administration in diverse areas of governance—be it land administration or police or forest management or irrigation and the like. The fact that the Naxalite movement has spread over 11 states and continues to remain as 'an area of serious concern' for the rulers of the country does not speak well of the capacity of the local administration to respond effectively and instantaneously to the needs of the local people. If the disgruntled people turn to the militant leaders for even temporary solution of their burning problems, the most proximate reason for this is that they cannot access any democratic institution to ventilate and realize their demands. In a paper tabled in the parliament on 13 March 2006, the union home minister admitted that the leaders of the Naxal movement 'operate in vacuum created by [the] absence of administrative and political institutions, espouse the local demands and take advantage of the disenchantment prevalent among the exploited segments of the population'.[17] The fact that the 'exploited segments of population' have chosen a violent path to realize their demands does not necessarily mean that they have lost their faith in democracy and are alienated from the state. This has to be read as a protest against an administrative framework, which is not only insensitive to the urgent needs of the common people, but also denies any opportunity to them to enter into dialogues with those who take decisions on matters that affect their everyday lives.

The other form of expression of democratic aspirations of the marginalized people may be noticed within the domain of what Partha Chatterjee (2004) calls *political society*. This is the site of political activities of the numerous non-elites, as distinguished from the site of civil society from where only a small number of elites engage with the state through various channels made available by the democratic constitution of the country. Thanks to the proliferation of various development and welfare programmes of the state targeted at identifiable groups and popularization of the concept of 'political equality' as concretized through the system of one-person-one-vote, the poor people are increasingly becoming aware of their rights. They have also entered today into a relationship with the agencies of the state and also with the political system. Their direct access to the institutions of the state is still limited. They also lack the skill of getting together in associations for pursuing their collective interests. Consequently they can exert little pressure on the formal centres of state power. Yet, they seek to influence the decisions of the machineries of the state. They do so by adopting other means such as, obtaining the services of mediators on whom they have trust, building alliances with the political elites to receive patronage, etc. It is important to note that through all such activities the poor people are making statements about their urgent needs and also about their expectations from the state. In other words, they are making strong demands for more responsiveness of the agencies of the state to their essentially localized problems.

It is this growing demand of common people for responsiveness of the machineries of the state that is creating enormous problems for the centralized state. In this context, the system of local administration where real powers of the state are exercised by the stipendiary bureaucracy having no accountability to the local communities is increasingly becoming irrelevant. The Indian state is clearly in need of a system of local goverance that is more responsive. This need cannot be fulfilled without institutionalizing local governments, which are accountable to the local communities. This means having representative government, such as panchayat, at the local level, which has better information about the local needs and is directly accountable to the local people. But, mere institutionalization of the local government does not automatically make the goverance system responsive. Responsiveness of the local government results, not only from its intimate knowledge about the 'needs' of people and its accountability to them, but also from the 'capacity' to meet such needs. This brings the question of autonomous functional jurisdiction of and commensurate devolution of resources to the local government institutions. As noted, there is still much hesitation in transferring powers and resources to these bodies. It is believed that sooner, rather than later, the political elites will realize that to resist the project of democratization of local administration by transferring powers and resources to the local government institutions will be potentially explosive.

NOTES

1. This structure of district administration took concrete shape after the Mutiny of 1857. The apprehension of future mutinies loomed large in the minds of the imperial rulers while building a coercive administrative machinery for local governance.
2. Jawaharlal Nehru's speech at the Constituent Assembly, New Delhi, on 14 August 1947.
3. See Second Five Year Plan, chapter 11.
4. While inaugurating the first Panchayati Raj System in India at Nagaur in the state of Rajasthan on 2 October 1959, Jawaharlal Nehru hailed it as 'the most revolutionary and historical step in the context of new India' (cited in Mathew, 2000).
5. Cited in Kumar, 2006, p. 20.
6. Cited in Bandyopadhyay, 2005, p. 84.
7. Ibid., p. 86.
8. On this, see Ghosh and Kumar, 2003.
9. See Mukarjee (1993).
10. The constitutional provisions on panchayats do not apply to the north-eastern states of Nagaland, Meghalaya and Mizoram, unless the respective legislatures of those states adopt resolutions to that effect.
11. The smaller states may opt not to constitute the institution at the intermediate level, but the constitution of institutions of self-government at the other two levels is compulsory in these states also.

12. Asoka Mehta Committee laid the blame principally on the bureaucracy and the MLAs and the MPs (GOI, 1978). For an analysis of political variables that led to the rise and fall of panchayats in four states, see Ghosh and Kumar, 2003. In a recent work, Kumar (2006: 298–309) has analysed the role of different stakeholders in the project of introducing local democracy.
13. If Kerala is an exception, this is largely because of the influence that Namboodiripad had on the Left Democratic Front government, which launched the boldest programme of democratic decentralization in the mid-1990s.
14. The Constitution of India draws its legitimacy from people. 'We, the people of India', its preamble declares, 'having solemnly resolved to constitute India into a sovereign, socialist, secular, democratic republic . . . do hereby *adopt, enact and give to ourselves* this constitution' (emphasis added).
15. In fact, very few among the national leaders had any faith in the capacity of the masses to govern themselves. B.R. Ambedkar's indictment against village as 'a sink of localism, a den of ignorance, narrow-mindedness and communalism' is quite well known. What is less known is the fact that the leaders of Congress party did not share Jawaharlal Nehru's enthusiasm for panchayati raj. Lal Bahadur Shastri who succeeded Nehru as prime minister is reported to have said, 'Panditji had full confidence in the people and thought that the janata (masses) [could] rule over itself. . . . I do not share his optimism' (see Dey, 1986: 38).
16. For a critique of the West Bengal model of direct democracy, see Ghosh (2003) and Bandyopadhyay (2003).
17. http//www.satp.org/satporgtp/countries/India/document/papes/06Mar13_Naxal

REFERENCES

Bandyopadhyay, D., 'Rajiv Gandhi and the Third Tier of Governance', in L.C. Jain (ed.), *Decentralisation and Local Governance: Essays for George Mathew*, New Delhi: Orient Longman, 2005.

———, 'The Caucus and the Masses: West Bengal Panchayat (Amendment Act), 2003, in *Economic and Political Weekly*, 15 November 2003.

Bandyopadhyay, D., Saila Ghosh and Buddahadeb Ghosh, 'Dependency versus Autonomy: Identity Crisis of India's Panchayats', in *Economic and Political Weekly*, 20 September 2003.

Behar, Amitabh, 'Gram Swaraj: Experiment in Direct Democracy', in *Economic and Political Weekly*, 10 March 2001.

———, 'Experiment with Direct Democracy: Time for Reappraisal', in *Economic and Political Weekly*, 17 May 2003.

Chatterjee, Partha, *The Politics of the Governed: Reflections on Popular Politics in Most of the World*, New Delhi: Permanent Black, 2004.

Dey, S.K., 'Panchayati Raj in Independent India: Some Personal Reflections', in George Mathew (ed.), *Panchayati Raj in Karnataka Today*', New Delh: Institute of Social Sciences and Concept Publishing Company, 1986.

Government of India, *Report of the Team for the Study of Community Projects and National Extension Service*, New Delhi: National Development Council, Committee on Plan Projects, 1957.

———, *Report of the Committee on Panchayati Raj Institutions*, New Delhi: Ministry of Agriculture and Irrigation, Department of Rural Development, 1978.

Ghosh, Buddhadeb, 'Much Ado About Nothing: Panchayat Reform in West Bengal', in *Panchayati Raj Update*, New Delhi, August 2003.

Ghosh, Buddhadeb and Girish Kumar, *State Politics and Panchayats in India*, New Delhi: Manohar and CSH, 2003.

Kumar, Girish, *Local Democracy in India: Interpreting Decentralization*, New Delhi: Sage, 2006.

Manor, James, 'User Committees: A Potentially Damaging Second Wave of Decentralisation?' in Jesse C. Ribot and Anne M. Larson (eds.), *Democratic Decentralisation Through a Natural Resource Lens*, London and New York: Routledge, 2005.

Mathew, George, 'Panchayati Raj in India: An Overview', in George Mathew (ed.), *Status of Panchayati Raj in the States and Union Territories of India 2000*, New Delhi: Institute of Social Sciences and Concept Publishing House, 2000.

Mukarji, Nirmal, 'Third Stratum', in *The Statesman*, Calcutta, 11–13 May 1993.

Mukarji, Nirmal and Balveer Arora (eds.), *Federalism in India: Origins and Development*, New Delhi: Vikas Publising House, 1992.

Mukarji, Nirmal and D. Bandyopadhyay, *New Horizons for West Bengal's Panchayats*, Calcutta: Government of West Bengal, 1993.

Narayan, Jayaprakash, *Communitarian Society and Panchayati Raj*, ed. Brahmanand, Varanasi: Navchetana Prakashan, 1970.

Powis, Benjamin, 'Grass Roots Politics and Second Wave of Decentralisation in Andhra Pradesh', in *Economic and Political Weekly*, 28 June 2003.

CHAPTER 3

Representation, Accountability and Patronage in the Institutions of Local Government in Karnataka and Kerala

ANAND INBANATHAN

Democracy in India has been instrumental in enabling people to vote every few years, and elect their representatives. At various levels, this has brought in political functionaries who have been instrumental in, or have claimed to be instrumental in, providing benefits to their constituents. Representation has largely been related to the benefits that accrue to the constituents, and constituents often relate to their representatives as potential beneficiaries of some form of personal advantage.

Panchayats in the country have been designed to have development interests of the people in view, and provide a more responsive manner of meeting such interests. Being responsive is one form of accountability to the voters and constituents, i.e. by meeting what the constituents need and want. However, accountability has other aspects to it, such as being answerable to the voters, and both by informing them of their (representatives') actions, and also being held responsible for whatever they have done (or not done). The people should be able to hold their representatives 'accountable' for whatever actions that were taken by them in their capacity as representatives.

While the institutions of local government have the provision of reserved seats for various groups of disadvantaged, the election to political office needs several attributes, both personal as well as the goodwill and support of various individuals in positions of political power. Representatives who are elected not only need to affirm their commitment to their constituents, but also have to be responsive to the manner in which they were elected, perhaps through patrons and patronage. Building up a political base of their own too is a matter which representatives need to provide for, through distributing benefits to their supporters, to ensure continued support (votes for example). In the context of accountability, political patronage tends to weaken the representatives' perception of their answerability to their constituents, and instead, brings to the fore the perception that patrons and persons who were instrumental in providing political support to get them elected were effectively more important than the ordinary people.

These issues will be discussed in the present paper, with empirical data from two south Indian states, Karnataka and Kerala.[1] These states have been perceived as being, in their own ways and at different times, at the forefront of introducing measures of decentralization. Three districts were selected in Karnataka—Mandya, Gulbarga and Dakshina Kannada—and also fifteen gram panchayats, four taluk panchayats, and three zilla panchayats (Table 3.1). In Kerala, three districts were selected, viz., Kollam, Kozhikode and Palakkad, and within these three districts, representatives from two district panchayats, six gram panchayats each in Kollam and Kozhikode, two gram panchayats from Palakkad (a total of fourteen gram

TABLE 3.1: DISTRIBUTION OF RESPONDENTS (KARNATAKA)

District	Gram Panchayat*	Taluk Panchayat**	Zilla Panchayat
Mandya	54	42	22
Gulbarga	55	37	42
Dakshina Kannada	55	29	29
Total	164	108	93

Notes: * Six gram panchayats in Mandya, five in Gulbarga, four in Dakshina Kannada.
** Two taluk panchayats in each district; and three zilla panchayats.

TABLE 3.2: DISTRIBUTION OF RESPONDENTS (KERALA)

District	Gram Panchayat	Block Panchayat	District Panchayat
Kollam	95	11	11
Kozhikode	95	18	24
Palakkad	18	8	0
Total	208	37	35

panchayats), and ten block panchayats, were interviewed in the study (Table 3.2).

PANCHAYATI RAJ IN KARNATAKA AND KERALA

The Karnataka Panchayati Raj Act 1993 followed the enactment of the 73rd Constitutional Amendment Act 1992. In keeping with the provisions and guidelines of the Constitutional Amendment, Karnataka had introduced the reservation of one-third of the seats for women, and reservations for Scheduled Castes (SC) and Scheduled Tribes (ST) in proportion to their population in the state, as well as one-third for Backward Classes. Reservations were provided for the posts of presidents and vice-presidents to the same extent as for the ordinary seats. The Constitutional Amendment had not made it mandatory for the reservation of seats for Backward Classes, and this issue was to be decided at the discretion of the states. However, even before the enactment of the 73rd Constitutional Amendment, Karnataka had in place the Karnataka Zilla Parishads, Taluk Panchayat Samitis, Mandal Panchayats and Nyaya Panchayats Act 1983, which had provided for the reservation of one-fourth of the seats for women, and reservations for SCs and STs. It had not reserved seats among the chairmen and vice-chairmen of mandal panchayats or for presidents/vice-presidents of the zilla parishads, which were the two democratic institutions of the then existing panchayati raj. Notwithstanding the earlier start that Karnataka had in devolving some powers to the panchayats, successive governments have not seen fit to empower panchayats to the extent that they can function in a relatively autonomous manner. With limited financial powers, for instance, the panchayats still function under some constraints (see for example, Rao, 2002).

Kerala enacted the Kerala Panchayati Raj Act 1994, which incorporated the requirements of the 73rd Constitutional Amendment. However, it had not devolved much powers to the panchayats at this time (Sastry, 1995). Increased devolution of powers came into effect only after the return to power of the Left Democratic Front (LDF) to the state legislature, in 1996. The LDF not only effected several measures to devolve powers, but also launched the People's Campaign for Decentralized Planning in 1996 (Isaac and Harilal, 1997). This was to ensure greater participation in local governance and also better utilization of the funds that had been devolved. Kerala's devolution of powers to panchayats, however, was not something that had a history before the enactment of the 73rd Constitutional Amendment. As Kannan (2000: 93) noted, '. . . the agenda of decentralisation remained stalled because successive governments had better things to do than decentralise their power'. Once the Constitutional Amendment came into place, Kerala, and particularly the LDF government, carried out measures to bring about greater transparency in governance, introduced several mechanisms of accountability, as well as devolved powers in finance and administration to the panchayats (see Franke and Chasin, 1997; Isaac, 2000; Das, 2000).[2]

REPRESENTATION AND ACCOUNTABILITY IN THE PANCHAYATS

Panchayats have been so designed that there is an important role for the rural people to participate in their functioning. Gram sabhas are the institution where direct democracy is, in principle, possible, with local people being involved in suggesting development activities and their development needs. These are expected to be incorporated in gram panchayat plans and more in conformity with the 'felt needs' of the people. However, the direct role of the people has some limitation, and in general, the development activities and functioning of the panchayats depend to a greater extent on the bureaucracy and the elected representatives. In the Panchayati Raj legislations of both states (1993 in Karnataka, and 1994 in Kerala), whatever suggestions and recommendations that are made by the gram sabhas only need to be given 'due consi-deration' by the gram panchayats.

A view that appears to suit the manner in which panchayats are to function is that the representatives should represent the people, and in the words of Pitkin (1967: 209), 'Representing here means acting in the interests of the represented, in a manner responsive to them'. Two attributes are immediately noticeable in this view of representation; one is 'interests', and the second 'responsiveness'. The matter of 'interests' is not as straightforward as it may sound. There are no common interests among all people, and discerning which interests should take precedence, and the order in which they would be implemented is a potentially divisive factor. However, in the panchayats, a distinction is normally made between community interests and individual's interests. Community interests include providing drinking water (for instance through tanks), proper drainage, roads, streetlights, toilets, etc., while individual interests include housing loans, electricity for homes, etc. 'Responsiveness' suggests the manner in which the representatives function, which takes into account what their constituents want, and thereby meet their interests. There is also the characteristic of accountability that is included in responsiveness. A representative is accountable to his/her constituents at the same time that s/he is responsive to them (Phillips, 1998: 4; Rao, 1998). In this context, communication between representatives and their constituents becomes crucial in whether representatives get to know what their constituents want, and if the activities taken up by panchayats meet the needs of the people. This is where gram sabhas are of particular importance, if they are sufficiently well attended by the local people, and if they choose to actually participate in them. Gram sabhas do not have to be the only means of communication, though they may come closer to what Habermas considered as 'public sphere', where political deliberation can take place, which is '. . . public use of reason jointly exercised by autonomous citizens' (in Hindess, 2000: 42; also Habermas, 2000: 288-94). People may be able to communicate with their representatives also through everyday talk, and this could be considered part of the deliberative system as well (Mansbridge, 1999). This two-way communication between the representatives and their constituents comprises not only the deliberation that one expects in the context of political institutions in a democracy, but such interaction also ensures that representatives are aware of what the people want, and development, therefore, would be more focused on the interests of the constituencies.

In some aspects, the panchayats in Kerala function in a manner somewhat different to panchayats in Karnataka, though in some others there is considerable similarity. While the Kerala panchayati raj also conforms to the requirement of a three-tier structure, the relative sizes of the panchayats vary, and gram panchayats are larger than in Karnataka. There is no fixed size for gram panchayats, and they could vary between a population of 20,000 to 40,000, and each ward comprising 2,000 persons has one representative (in Karnataka, the size is fixed at a population of 5,000 in most parts of the state, or 4,000 in the hilly areas). The importance of gram panchayats has been pegged at a much higher point in Kerala, with the block and district panchayats being of relatively less importance compared to those in Karnataka. Thus, not only have more functions been devolved to the gram panchayats in Kerala, but substantial funds have also been devolved. Karnataka's gram panchayats have not been given such importance, and in successive Panchayati Raj Acts (1983 and 1993) gram panchayats have been reduced in size (the 1983 Act had mandal panchayats at the village level).

A second important difference is the role of political parties. There is evidence to indicate that parties in Karnataka are much less involved in the functioning of the panchayats. They do play a role at the time of elections, where selection of candidates is normally the function of the party, and party officials at the district. They do not ordinarily intervene in day-to-day activities of the panchayats. In Kerala, the activities of the panchayats are far more politicized, which includes not only the elections, but also more often in the ordinary functioning of the panchayats. This was particularly noticed in panchayats where the leftist parties were in a dominant position, and also had a party member as president of the panchayat (the CPI[M]) for instance, is generally thought of as a centralized system (see Rammohan, 1998).[3]

An analysis of the functioning of the representatives in the panchayats requires, first of all, that their motivation to be in politics is above question. This issue becomes crucial inasmuch as the expectation is that only those who were interested in being elected representatives were the ones who were actually elected to the panchayats. In such a case, they would be expected to take greater interest in carrying out their functions as representatives. However, from our studies in the two states, there is reason to state that such an expectation is often belied by the representatives' lack of interest in being elected representatives of the panchayats. In Karnataka, a substantial number of representatives in all three tiers of the panchayats indicated that they had not been interested in politics when they contested the elections. Compulsions of various kinds were involved to persuade these persons to contest. Women, for instance were more or less compelled to contest by male members of their families, or other men, who were prominent members of the village (elites). The highest number of those expressing a lack of interest in politics was of women representatives in Gulbarga district. In fact, there were a higher number of women who stated their lack of interest in politics than those who indicated an interest in politics. Between the districts that came within the study, the highest number of those expressing low interest in politics was in Gulbarga, and the lowest were in Dakshina Kannada, with Mandya falling in between. Even among the male representatives, the number of those indicating a lack of interest in politics was higher in the gram panchayats than in the higher tiers. This seems related also to the competition that is involved in elections in the three tiers. Elections to gram panchayats are meant to be held without political party involvement or party identities. In practise, there is a disguised involvement of parties, through party officials and members who support candidates in these elections, as well as through the identification of well-known political figures whose photographs are printed on the candidates' campaign pamphlets (for example, Indira Gandhi or Rajiv Gandhi who, as everyone knows, were in the Congress I). Despite the involvement of party officials in the electoral campaign, it appears that for most of the village people, the indication of support for specific candidates was a personal recognition of the persons concerned, usually of the village elites or 'big men' of the village, rather than their party identities. In these circumstances, there were many cases where voting was not even necessary, since there was only one candidate who contested in each constituency, and who was therefore declared elected unopposed.[4]

In the functioning as representatives, a large proportion of the women representatives in particular, were only nominally the representatives and the *de facto* representatives were their husbands or other men of the village (Inbanathan, 2001; Vijayalakshmi, 2001; Vijayalakshmi and Chandrashekar, 2003). There were a lower number of representatives of the taluk and zilla panchayats who indicated a lack of interest in politics. Even among this much smaller number (than in gram panchayats) there were more women than men who indicated a lack of interest. Elections to taluk and zilla panchayats involved far more commitment of funds, time and energy, and the likelihood was much less, that anyone without interest in politics would contest. There were also indications that getting party tickets to contest cost the potential candidates substantial amounts of money (Inbanathan and Gopalappa, 2003), and therefore, less likelihood that anyone willing to raise these funds would do so if there was a lack of interest in politics.

A predominant section of Kerala's panchayat representatives indicated that they were interested in politics when they had contested the panchayat elections, with 96 per cent of the men saying that they did. The women were less inclined to make such a statement, with 63 per cent indicating that they had been interested in politics, while a little over a third of the representatives (37 per cent) indicated that they had not been interested in politics when they had contested the elections. However, in terms of their political experience at the time of elections (in whatever capacity—party activities, holding elective positions, involved in campaigns), while 81 per cent of the men had some political experience, only 35 per cent of the women representatives claimed some political experience.

Though this still leaves a substantial number who were completely new to politics (particularly the women representatives), it was certainly lower than in Karnataka's panchayats, where most gram panchayat members (95 per cent females and 84.8 per cent males) were new to politics. The persons new to politics who were elected to taluk and zilla panchayats were of a lower number among men, but women who were elected were still mostly new to politics (91.8 per cent females and 62.1 per cent males in taluk panchayats 45.2 per cent males and 84.7 per cent females in zilla panchayats; Subha, 1997: 111). As seen, those without any political experience at the time of their elections to the panchayats, particularly in the case of women representatives, was very high, and across all the three tiers of panchayats. The significance of the response from the women representatives is also indicative that the quota for women has been filled through bringing in women who were not interested in the functioning as panchayat representatives, and they were essentially brought in to fill the quota.

Having been elected, what forms of representation were observed in the panchayats? At the outset it should be noted that the interaction between representatives and their constituents was usually minimal. This was more pronounced among women representatives, and the interaction was lowest in the gram panchayats, rising slightly in the higher tiers. This may sound surprising, considering that the number of representatives in the gram panchayats of Karnataka was one for every 400 population, and they were usually residents in the same locality where they contested. Hence, moving about and meeting their constituents should be physically a relatively simple activity. However, social restrictions were probably more significant in this context than the bare fact of being a representative in a geographically small area. In any event, from our study, only 19 per cent of the women in Gulbarga indicated that they interacted with their constituents, and 68 per cent in Dakshina Kannada said that they did so, with Mandya women representatives falling in between these extremes. Taluk and zilla panchayat representatives indicated a higher proportion claiming to interact with their constituents. Many of the women said that there was no need for them to directly interact with their constituents because their husbands, who were more experienced in political matters did so, and therefore it was even better for the constituents than if they (the women representatives) interacted with them. Male representatives claimed to have met their constituents more often than the women representatives, but for the most part it appeared that, as in the gram panchayats, even unplanned or spontaneous face-to-face interactions with many of the constituents was a definite possibility. It seemed far less likely (also confirmed by many village people who were asked) that they went around the constituency to meet constituents in the taluk and zilla panchayats. What happened was that constituents went to the taluk or zilla panchayat offices, and asked for help/favours from the representatives, and this was the manner of interaction between representatives and their electors.

It is evident that with a relatively low level of interaction between representatives and their constituents, there was also a lower possibility of the representatives being able to find out the needs and requirements of the constituencies. While gram sabhas were poorly attended in most places, except for Dakshina Kannada in our study of Karnataka (Mandya and Gulbarga had far lower attendance in gram sabhas), the constituents had virtually no possibility of discussing development needs and requirements. Taluk and zilla panchayat representatives rarely attended the gram sabhas, and their overall interaction with constituents was also very low. Gram panchayat representatives often claimed that since they were residents of the same local area of their constituencies, they were fully aware of the requirements even without anyone coming to them to tell them about these needs. This also seemed to indicate their lower grasp of the essentials of the democratic principles involved, that they were to interact with their constituents as a matter of seeking their participation, rather than a purely mechanical condition of information gathering.

A further indication of the functioning of the representatives in Karnataka was the relatively large number of them who were not aware of the standing committees. In gram panchayats, the standing committees had only a nominal presence in most places, though Dakshina Kannada had a better situation regarding their representatives being aware of the functioning of standing committees, and in fact, who also took an active part in their functioning. Taluk and zilla panchayats had properly constituted standing committees, they were well attended, and their role was properly recognized by the members. Participation in the standing committees of the higher tiers of panchayats was significant in the decision-making process of the panchayats.

In Kerala as well, gram sabhas functioned in a manner that was less than participatory, with most gram sabhas hardly meeting the quorum requirement of 10 per cent of the members. Standing committees in Kerala's panchayats, however, functioned in a far more effective manner, and in gram panchayats, they had an important function in the running of the panchayats. With the gram panchayats of Kerala being of substantially larger size as well as having larger budgets for their work, they had more effective functions than the gram panchayats of Karnataka.

ACCOUNTABILITY

Accountability in a democratic system implies that representatives need to be responsive to their electors, inform them of what they have done in their capacity as an elected representative and finally, to be answerable for their actions (Sen, 1992; Shivaiah, 1994; Helgason, 1997; Polidano and Hulme, 1997; Sawer, 2000). Moncrieffe's (2001: 27) description suggests two aspects of accountability, one which she refers to as 'ex-post facto' accountability, which is 'answering for the use of authority', and the other, is 'ex-ante' accountability. The latter is a more inclusive category, and takes in constituents' interests, interaction and consultation between representatives and their electors, so that the representatives can be more knowledgeable about and responsive to their interests, and in short, improve the quality of representation.

ACCOUNTABILITY AND PATRONAGE IN KARNATAKA

A democratic system needs to have representatives who are both responsive to their electors/constituencies' interests as well as be answerable for their actions as representatives. Representatives in Karnataka's panchayats were in a general manner in agreement with the principle that they were accountable to their electors. However, the implications of this principle do not appear to have been fully understood by these representatives. Thus, there were members of panchayats who stated that they were accountable to the bureaucracy (among these were more of women than men). A few stated that they were accountable to their patrons (local elites), and others to community elders, or panchayat presidents, or MLAs/ MPs or even their families. In terms of numbers, in order of preference as it were, the largest proportion suggested that they were accountable to their patrons, and then in lower numbers to MLAs/ MPs, family, community elders, presidents/vice-presidents of panchayats and then the bureaucracy. The importance of patrons to the political advancement of individuals, as well as even in their first steps in the panchayats, towards being elected, is something about which the representatives are clearly aware. At the lower rung of the panchayats (i.e. the gram panchayats), the patrons have been very influential in the elections, selection of candidates and then in the campaign (if there was any need for an election), and if necessary in financially supporting candidates. The support also extended after the initial elections to the panchayats, to the election of the presidents and vice-presidents. There were more men in the taluk and zilla panchayats who indicated a preference to continue in politics, as compared to the gram panchayats where the numbers were far less. Cultivating important political personalities was a means by which they could advance in the political sphere—both in the party hierarchy as well as in electoral politics. In the context in which the elections are held (party politics), it is almost impossible for an individual to contest and win on his own. Evidently, when the representatives consider themselves as being particularly beholden to their patrons, even to the extent of thinking that their political success was entirely due to the patrons, they were more prone to accept that they were accountable to the patrons rather than to the electors. Patrons were able to direct or give instructions to the representatives whom they were instrumental in getting elected, and representatives were responsive to them (see Inbanathan and Gopalappa, 2003).

A few members of all the three panchayats had mentioned that they were accountable to the bureaucracy. This seems to be related to their dependence on the bureaucracy to give them information about the panchayats and their functioning. With most representatives being new to elected positions and even to politics (other than perhaps as voters), their sense of inadequacy in terms of knowledge of panchayat programmes, administration, and their role and functions in the panchayats gave them a sense of awe of the bureaucracy. Officials appeared to be both knowledgeable and in greater control of the panchayat programmes and functions in the perception of these representatives.

Panchayat members have certain powers to carry out their responsibilities and functions as political representatives. This is related to their political positions, which they get into either because of their own inclinations, or persuasion or compulsion of some others. State or parliament legislators have far more power than the incumbents of panchayat seats, and their (panchayat member's) influence and power over developments activities are circumscribed not only by the scale of funds involved, but also by the outcomes which they can personally influence.

PATRONAGE IN KARNATAKA

The traditional form of patron–client relationship was more often found in the gram panchayats of Karnataka than in the higher tiers. Patrons were members of the local elite, and they were sometimes elected members of panchayats. Very often they were not elected representatives themselves. However, the significant factor was that they were usually in possession of several resources, including political contacts, which sometimes extended beyond the villages, as well as wealth, and prestige. Local elites were also usually from among the castes higher in the social hierarchy, and rarely did we find those from the SCs in this category of local elite (even though as community leaders or elders, some individuals were able to influence activities in their own community). Villagers often referred to these persons as 'big men of the village', which also demonstrates that women were not among the village elite. As a positive feature, patrons initiated candidates into politics and advised them whenever that was required. On occasion, elites functioned in a manner that had a more negative and undesirable outcome, as when the patrons dominated the functioning of the panchayats through those they had brought into the panchayats, and otherwise carried out an 'extra-constitutional' function as elected functionaries even though they had not been elected to the panchayats.

In the patron–client type, clear and wide status distinctions exist between the patrons and the clients, and also, the representatives are mostly the clients. Patrons of the local elite were sometimes representatives themselves, but often were not elected representatives. Such relationships were significant to the political advancement of new aspirants to politics, and even to being elected to the panchayats. A direct form of dominance is seen when local elites are also elected representatives themselves. However, the system of reservation and the rotation of reservations makes it less likely that they can get elected every time, even if they were so inclined. Further, the elites were able to increase their dominance by their control over several representatives and hence, being elected was not a prerequisite for their dominance. Patrons too derived some other benefits from their clients. While it was the male representatives who claimed that their political support to the patrons was of importance to the patrons, women representatives did not have this aspect in view about their links with the patrons. Also, women were usually linked to the patrons through their husbands rather than through directly interacting with them, a deviation from the usual view of patron–client relations as being dyadic relations (see, for example, Scott, 1977). Patrons sometimes persuaded representatives who were their clients to distribute benefits to their supporters (other supporters of the patrons) through the panchayats. A few panchayat representatives also stated that patrons were beneficiaries of panchayat projects, as contractors of local projects, which were also instrumental in building up their political support base.

Dependence on patrons was not only of ordinary representatives, but also presidents of panchayats. Women were more likely to be dependent on the patrons, and the pattern of reservations appeared to favour the weaker or less able representatives in the eyes of the patrons (see Inbanathan, 1999). Patrons, or the village elite preferred to function as representatives, and through the more pliant representatives, rather than build-up a cadre of able representatives in the panchayats. The limited tenure of the presidents and vice-presidents of Karnataka's panchayats also reduced the possibility of the office-bearers improving their skills and confidence during their very brief tenure. Three presidents and vice-presidents with each a term of twenty months in the taluk and zilla panchayats, did not give sufficient time for capacity building. In the gram panchayats, the tenure of presidents and vice-presidents was thirty months, and hence, there would be two presidents in each five-year term of the panchayats. The short tenures and the need for fresh elections of presidents and vice-presidents gave much more scope for manipulation and patronage in the panchayats. A further problem, particularly in the higher panchayats, was that the cost of being elected as president had to be borne by three individuals (for president) in a five-year term of a panchayat. This also resulted in increased rent-seeking by office-bearers on the grounds of having to recover their election expenses (see Vijayalakshmi, 2005).

In taluk and zilla panchayats, there were less of patron–client relations (though still in existence) and more of purely political relations (on this distinction see Powell, 1977; Weingrod, 1977; Theobald, 1983, 1992; Korovkin, 1988), based and built up through the distribution of resources of various kinds. They were more a relationship of equals, or at least the inequalities in status were far less than found in patron–client relations. Choices were made, to be associated with political leaders who would benefit their own career advancement, and if such an outcome did not come about, they could leave this person and join another political leader.[5] MLAs and MPs also needed these local leaders and supporters to build-up their own support base. They had to ensure that these supporters benefited in some manner, and thus, remained happy to be associated with them. MLAs and MPs could not afford to antagonize these local leaders, since it were they who had direct links with the voters, rather than the MPs and MLAs themselves, who, the villagers stated, visited their villages only at the time of elections, and sometimes not even then. Without the local leaders who garnered votes for them, the state political leaders would be hard pressed to be elected.[6] Local leaders were sometimes elected representatives of these panchayats, but at other times worked for political parties in various capacities. MPs, however, had an additional means of linking up with local representatives, through the Member of Parliament's Local Area Development Scheme (MPLADS). Panchayat representatives occasionally made representations to MPs to use the MPLADS funds in their area (constituency). Funds are normally used depending on the political base of the MP, who would prefer to spend this money on his supporters rather than on people who may be supporters of other parties or political leaders (see also Gopakumar et al., 1998).

ACCOUNTABILITY AND PATRONAGE IN KERALA

Kerala's situation appears to be somewhat different from that of Karnataka. An immediate difference in the functioning of the panchayats in Kerala is the role of political parties. With political parties being more active in the functioning of panchayats, and electoral situations being such that the margin of support between the LDF and the UDF is never too large (see Cairo, 2001), parties are usually inclined to intervene more often (particularly the LDF) in the functioning of the panchayats. Further, even in the selection of candidates, there was a greater likelihood (though, clearly the situation of women representatives is not far different from that of women representatives in Karnataka) that candidates had been party workers when they were selected to contest for the panchayat elections. However, one should not overstate the differences, and ignore the similarities, which were also often observed.

Accountability in Kerala's panchayats had more of similarities with what was found in Karnataka, in the sense of answerability to the constituents. In the panchayats of both the states, such accountability was minimal. Representatives were more often likely to give information to the constituents in Kerala's panchayats, because this was mandatory, and the panchayats had to publish various details of their work and financial dealings. These were to be distributed to the electors, and with the levels of education and literacy in

Kerala, were read by some of the electors. However, consulting the electors on a regular basis was not as common as would be expected, although in gram panchayats, representatives stated that they met constituents now and then, on the road for example, and exchanged information with the electors. Such interaction did not involve many of the electorate, and was limited to only a small fraction of the ward members. Members of district and block panchayats were even less likely to meet their constituents unless these people went to them, most often in the panchayat office, for some specific purpose of their own. Gram sabhas were rarely attended by the block and district panchayat members, and the gram panchayat representatives were not able to have much of a discussion or interaction with the electors because not many of the electorate chose to attend them either. Representatives often claimed that they had group meetings with their ward members (gram panchayats) and discussed issues pertaining to their wards. Such claims were not usually well supported with actual details of what transpired in these meetings, and hence, were not likely to have taken place with the regularity that the representatives claimed they were held (i.e. once a month).

Representatives often stated that while they were to be accountable to the people of the panchayats (i.e. the electorate), they were also answerable to party officials and the party. The importance of the party is obvious as they are selected and supported by parties to get elected to the panchayats. They also have the practice of reporting regularly to party officials, as well as consult them on what needed to be done in the panchayat. While representatives may consider it feasible to be accountable to so many entities, ordinary people stated that they were rarely contacted by the representatives or informed about panchayat matters. One should also recall the reaction that may accrue if they were to cease being 'accountable' to the party, as they are to the ordinary people. Punitive action may be feared, and therefore, they would heed to party officials. Further, where women representatives are concerned, as with Karnataka's panchayat members, it is the husbands who were party officials or members, who encouraged them to contest, and for the most part then counselled or controlled their functioning in the panchayats. We may add a note here that the people's statement that they were rarely contacted by representatives was made in a political environment where the competing parties (or coalitions) are very close in the quantum of support that they can depend on. What could be a reason is that most political functionaries probably think that they need not regularly interact with the ordinary people during the five years that come between elections, and the campaign and interaction with people is only when they are seen as potential voters, and nearer the time of elections. This is clearly so in Karnataka, and evidently in Kerala as well.

While answerability for their actions would be considered as one aspect of accountability, Kerala's panchayats, as with Karnataka's, did not show any signs of having taken action against those who may have been held responsible for wrong doing. There was a small number of representatives who stated that corruption was punished, but details were not forthcoming.

Karnataka had introduced only a few and limited measures specifically to enhance accountability (considerable significance was attached to the gram sabhas). Kerala, on the other hand, introduced several measures for this purpose. These had been introduced not only to increase the participation of the people in the functioning of the panchayats, including the planning process, but also to make the panchayats more responsive to the people. Further, measures were also suggested to reduce the scope of corruption in the carrying out of panchayat projects and programme, reduce if not eliminate the possibility of patronage in beneficiary selection,[7] as well as means of redressal, such as through the institution of ombudsman. Audits such as accounts audits and performance audits have also been included among the means to monitor the functioning of the panchayats.

The institution of ombudsman has an ambiguous position in the scheme of things in Kerala. Initially, much was expected from this institution, and seven ombudsmen, people of various backgrounds including the judiciary, and retired officials who had held high ranks while in government service, were appointed to this position. The advantage of having ombudsmen was that ordinary people could bring to the notice of this authority malfeasance and wrong doings in the panchayats. Ombudsmen were to investigate these panchayats, and suggest remedial measures. After the new ruling coalition (UDF) came to power in the state (2001),[8] the number of ombudsmen has been reduced to one. With just one ombudsman for the whole state, the time taken to investigate the cases that are brought before him and to make a ruling on every case is not possible for one person to accomplish. Thus, most cases are long delayed, and as representatives themselves were quick to point out, payments were already made before the ombudsman was able to reach a conclusion on most cases of panchayat expenditure. Further, with only one ombudsman, who could obviously hold hearings only in one place in the state at a time, for most people of the state, travelling to and from the place where the ombudsman was at a particular time, was both tedious and time consuming, resulting in a lack of interest to pursue any case. There was no case in our study area where it was reported that a case had been investigated and closed by the ombudsman. Representatives were neither supportive of the institutions of ombudsman nor did they condemn it, and this ambivalence is probably also in tune with the role that the ombudsman plays. Contractors who had been interviewed during this study were not even sure whether the institution of ombudsman was functional. Representatives, however, were of the view that the ombudsman was not in a position to do anything significant to control or reduce corruption, which they affirmed is widespread. A final observation about the actual functioning of the ombudsman is that the principle on which it had started, that people could represent themselves, and their own case, was vitiated when the ombudsman's hearings began to take on the hue of a regular court of law.

Gram sabhas have been designated as an important institution of accountability. In the Kerala panchayat system, gram sabhas have been given even more importance than in Karnataka's panchayats, insofar as the number of functions is concerned. In fact, there were even people who suggested that the gram sabhas were the institutions which carried out a 'social audit' in the panchayats, a misnomer in many ways, but indicative of the manner in which gram sabhas were viewed. Gram sabhas in most panchayats did not serve the function for which they were designed, of involving and encouraging the participation of villages in ward sabhas (in Kerala, where gram panchayats could be very large, each ward, of 2,000 adults, holds a gram sabha). The functions for which they were convened were also not carried out, and only minimal discussions were held on the panchayats' functions.

In most panchayats, the manner in which local people were informed about gram sabhas was through party workers, *anganwadi* workers, SHG members, or the gram panchayat representative of the particular ward. Not everyone in the ward heard about the gram sabha, and sometimes only a few heard about them. A few representatives claimed that this was deliberately done to avoid the possibility of members of opposition parties attending the gram sabhas, or prevent larger gatherings in the gram sabhas. Sometimes, even if the date was known to the people of the ward, if the gram sabha did not start on time, some of those who came to attend the gram sabha left before it even started. Those who attended the gram sabhas were prospective beneficiaries of panchayat/development schemes, or were women SHG members who were told to attend the sabhas by gram panchayat representatives. A minimum of 10 per cent of the ward population is required to be present at the gram sabhas, for them to be considered as gram sabhas. However, representatives and local people indicated that this was rarely achieved (i.e. 10 per cent attendance).

An issue which may have some bearing on the accountability of representatives is their inclination to contest elections again, after their present term. A related issue is also, whether they think of politics as a possible career regardless of their contesting the elections which follows their completion of the current term as representatives. We presume that they may have a bearing insofar as their need to not only impress the electors with their ability and capacity to meet their interests, and also to be more interactive with their constituents. There were indeed representatives who stated that such a thought (of contesting elections again) was a motivating factor in their increased interaction with electors, as well as trying to be responsive to them. More of men than women representatives showed such an inclination. However, members of Left parties suggested that while they were interested in politics, it was left to the party to finally decide whether they should contest. Women, on the other hand, suggested that whether they contested may depend on a seat reserved for women, and they may be less interested if they were to contest from an 'open' seat. The system of reservation of seats ensures that the same constituencies as those they presently occupied would not be reserved for women in the next elections (considering that most women representatives had contested for seats in constituencies reserved for women).

PATRONAGE IN KERALA

We had started with an assumption that politics is not generally a vocation that is embarked on by individuals only on the basis of their own inclination. Someone else is needed to encourage, or sponsor the candidate, so that his/her chances of succeeding in politics increase, and more importantly they are able to get a party ticket and are then elected. The panchayats are a lower level of political institution than the state legislature and the parliament, and those who contest panchayat elections are often people with very little political experience. Support for fresh candidates (or even those who had been in politics for some years), and the source of encouragement could vary, for men and women. With the men, the political party is the main entry point, and most representatives had indicated that their political work and the support of a party official were instrumental in their entry into electoral politics. With women, the number who had indicated an earlier involvement in party politics, and the support from party officials to contest the elections, was much lower than with men. More often, it was their husbands (most of whom had party links, as workers, and party officials), who persuaded or encouraged them to contest the elections. Such encouragement, for men and women, is necessary to organize campaigns for elections. Most representatives also accepted that without party support, being elected as independents is very difficult, and very few people can succeed.

Along with the political party (which is an organization of diffuse and large size), it is specific officials in the party who are crucial and instrumental in sponsoring and furthering the individual's career in the party as well as in politics, i.e. these officials function essentially as patrons. For most women, their husbands advised them on what they had to do as representatives. There were those who claimed that they did not have any patrons or even need them. This appears to be a matter of how they perceived 'patrons'. That they needed supporters and well-wishers to sponsor their candidature as well as support in their campaigns is not disputed, even if they did not agree that it was 'patrons' who encouraged and supported their entry into politics. Patrons can be helpful and supportive of their protégés. The functioning of such patrons and their protégés, however, is not uniformly that of a patron–client relationship. That such relationships exist is not to be denied, but variations in these relationships lead to some ambiguity, and the less than unanimous feeling (among representatives) that patron–client relationships or even relationships of a purely political kind also exist.

While such support from political officials in the party has been clearly observed, there is less involvement of those whom we could call the elite of villages. In fact, representatives were initially inclined to even suggest that local elite were not involved in politics,[9] to later agreeing that they were occasionally involved in political activities, but they were not influential or influenced panchayat activities because of being local village elites. They were likely to be party officials themselves, in addition to being locally important persons. This contrasts with the situation in Karnataka, where local elites (the 'big men' of the village), even when they were not elected panchayat representatives, were involved in and influenced the functioning of panchayats, through their intervention in selecting candidates for elections, mostly in gram panchayats, selection of beneficiaries, locating development schemes, and so on.

There is a general belief among representatives in Kerala that patrons chose persons as prospective political protégés on the expectation that they would be beneficial to the patrons in some manner or other. Their power and political status are expected to grow with the support of panchayat representatives. There was also the belief that patrons preferred men rather than women in their scheme of political patronage due to their presumption that men can better aid political activities than women can, a perception not different from that of patrons in Karnataka.

Karnataka has a more individual–predominant patronage, with patron–client relations more common in the gram panchayats, and more of the purely political relations at the higher levels. In Kerala, such individual–predominant relations appear to be less pronounced, and while patrons and mentors appear to be present in Kerala's political parties, what is more visible is that parties are involved in a more direct manner in the functioning of the panchayats. In an institution where representatives are not likely to be elected in successive elections from the same constituencies, due to the reservation of seats for different groups, electoral accountability (on electoral accountability, see Prewitt, 1970) is an attribute which is less likely to play a significant role in the functioning of representatives. Likewise, their patronage is not of a type which leads to the building up of political support for themselves. Accountability too in the sense of being responsive to their electors is of less importance when they do not find themselves answerable to a recalcitrant electorate that would not choose to vote for them in the next elections. However, political parties have a longer tenure in local government, even though specific individuals may come and go. In Kerala's party politics where the LDF and UDF have alternated in the state government, and rarely continued in office for successive terms, their sense of being accountable is far more evident than that of individual representatives. Party members who have now been elected to the panchayats may feel more responsive to their electorate because of the party being held accountable for what they (representatives) had or had not done while in office. It is in this context that we find representatives stating that they are accountable to the party, which in a real sense may make the difference as to whether they are tapped by the party for other posts, or they are dropped from holding any other office.

On a related aspect, being responsive to their electors is in a sense to distribute benefits (patronage) to their supporters, who otherwise may not choose to support them. Patronage in the present context is also manifested through the party, i.e. the party functions as the patron, rather than individual party officials or members (on a similar phenomenon see Caciagli and Belloni, 1981). Thus, when local people got whatever benefits that they had sought, the immediate thought is not only that local representatives had been instrumental in getting them these benefits, but the party identity is also immediately at the forefront and clearly known. Further, it should also be noted that representatives do not always consider themselves as the authority in making commitments on benefits, or deciding on what the panchayats should do. This is particularly so with the Leftist parties, that party officials are not only consulted, but they also tell representatives what they should do. Representatives claim that party officials, through their regular interaction with them (representatives) as well as with local people, are well aware of what is needed, and can advise the representatives to take up various issues in the panchayats. This will ultimately redound to the credit of the party, and help later on in the elections. Such party-oriented efforts are less visible in the functioning of the panchayats in Karnataka, though it is no one's case that party politics are not noticed. However, in the gram panchayats where elections are held without the official participation of parties, local leaders (as such, and not as party officials) to get more prominence than the parties of the state. Even in the higher panchayats where party identities are important in the elections, and parties are clearly involved, there seems to be less involvement of party officials on a regular basis in the functioning of the panchayats, and their involvement takes place more often at the time of elections than otherwise.

CONCLUSION

Karnataka, in the 1980s, following the enactment of the 1983 Panchayati Raj Act, and Kerala in the 1990s, following the 73rd Constitutional Amendment, had brought in several innovations in the panchayat raj systems of the two states. At the time when Karnataka's Act, 1983, came into existence, no state had given the kind of support for women's participation, through the reservation of one-fourth of panchayat seats for women. Much has taken place since then, and reservations of seats for women, as well as SCs and

STs have been incorporated in the 73rd Constitutional Amendment, and all states have had to follow this principle. While the reservation of seats has given an opportunity for the disadvantaged groups to find a place among elected representatives of the panchayats, power has not been devolved to them to the extent that one may want. Thus, Karnataka has manifested political decentralization, but much less of administrative and financial decentralization. Kerala has been able to provide for more of all three attributes of decentralization. Further, while Karnataka has not brought in sufficient measures to increase transparency and participation, as well as institutions of accountability, Kerala has done much more towards this end. Ultimately, regardless of the kind of institutions that are present, we can see, as in Karnataka, wide variations in the functioning of the panchayats in the three districts which were chosen for study, viz., Mandya, Gulbarga and Dakshina Kannada. Similar differences have been observed in Kerala, where despite the institutions and measures that were introduced, participation, transparency and accountability vary from panchayat to panchayat. Likewise, with the measures meant to keep under control and also reduce the levels of corruption, such measures have not had the desired effect. Kerala may have marginally lower levels of corruption due to the measures that were introduced, but they have by no means reduced corruption to any acceptable levels (i.e. low). Evidently, something more than just the introduction of political institutions and other measures is needed for the reduction of corruption, as well as to motivate the people to take greater interest in the functioning of the panchayats.

NOTES

1. Both studies were financially supported by the Ford Foundation. The study of Karnataka's panchayats was carried out between 1989 and 2001, and the study on Kerala's panchayats was carried out between 2001 and 2003.
2. In an overall sense, decentralization in most parts of India would conform to the statement that, 'At present, India's decentralization to rural and urban governments is a patchwork of deconcentration, delegation and devolution' (Sethi, 2004: 3).

3. However, one should not get the impression that Left parties are monolithic entities, with a clear hierarchy and very unified and disciplined functioning. Like other parties, they too have factions, in-fighting, and several individuals who have more or less the same levels of influence within the parties (see for example, Haridas, 2006).
4. In the grama panchayat elections of February 2000, 27.7 per cent had been elected unopposed (source: State Election Commission).
5. A taluk panchayat representative stated that his association with a political leader did not benefit him since this man lost elections more often than he won. Hence, he left him and joined another leader, one who apparently won elections, and at the time of this study was the MLA of his area.
6. The view of a local elite, and political functionary, was that when a MLA asked him to campaign and organize political support for him (MLA) at an earlier election, it was on the agreement that some money would be paid. Subsequently, the MLA did not pay this money. In the next elections, the local elite refused to gather support for the MLA's election. The MLA realized that he needed the help of the person from the local elite, and came to see him, with the pending funds, and asked him to help.
7. Elaborate guidelines were brought into effect for this purpose, in a government order:
   GO (P) No. 181/98/LAD, dated 2 September 1998.
   While it is presumed that political institutions have an impact on the levels of corruption, and therefore, we would expect Kerala's panchayats to have benefited from the specific measures to reduce corruption, that corruption still exists and even thrives is a measure of the relative ineffectiveness of these measures. See also, for example, a multi-national study on corruption, which draws a relationship between political institutions of accountability and corruption, Lederman et al., 2001; see also Vijayalakshmi, 2005.
8. The state government found that the number of cases decided even with seven members (ombudsmen) was not commensurate with the costs involved in maintaining them, their office staff, etc., and thus, reduced the number of ombudsmen to one.
9. An extreme view of a few representatives was that there were no elites in the village at all.

REFERENCES

Cairo, Gemma, 'State and Society Relationships in India: Explaining the Kerala Experience', *Asian Survey*, 41 (4) 2001, pp. 669–92.

Ciciagli, Mario and Frank P. Belloni, 'The "New" Clientelism in Southern Italy: The Christian Democratic Party in Catania', in S.N. Eisenstadt and Rene Lemarchand (eds.), *Political Clientelism, Patronage and Development*, London: Sage, 1981.

Das, M.K., 'Kerala's Decentralised Planning: Floundering Experiment', *Economic and Political Weekly*, 35 (49), 2000, pp. 4300–3.

Franke, Richard and Barbara H. Chasin, 'Power to the Malayalee People', *Economic and Political Weekly*, 32 (48), 1997, pp. 3061–8.

Gopakumar, K., S. Manjunath and M.M. Srinath, 'The Member of Parliament's Local Area Development Scheme: An Avoidable Discretion?', Bangalore: Public Affairs Centre, 1998.

Isaac, T.M. with Richard Franke, *Local Democracy and Development: People's Campaign for Decentralized Planning in Kerala*, New Delhi: Left Word Books, 2000.

Isaac, T.M. Thomas and K.N. Harilal, 'Planning for Empowerment: People's Campaign for Decentralised Planning in Kerala', *Economic and Political Weekly*, 32 (1 & 2), 1997, pp. 53–8.

Habermas, Jurgen, 'The Public Sphere', in Kate Nash (ed.), *Readings in Contemporary Political Sociology*, Oxford: Blackwell Publishers, 2000.

Helgason, Sigurdur, 'Towards Performance-based Accountability: Issues for Discussion', Paris: Public Management Service, OECD, 1997.

Hindess, Barry, 'Representive Government and Participatory Democracy', in Andrew Vanderberg (ed.), *Citizenship and Democracy in a Global Era*, London: Macmillan, 2000.

Inbanathan, Anand, 1999, 'Decentralization and Affirmative Action: The Case of Panchayats in Karnataka', *Journal of Social and Economic Development*, 2, 1999, pp. (2): 269–86.

———, 'Representation and Accountability in Local Government: The Panchayats of Karnataka', Working Paper 96, Bangalore: Institute for Social and Economic Change, 2001.

Inbanathan, Anand and D.V. Gopalappa, 'Fixers, Patronage, "Fixing", and Local Governance in Karnataka', *Sociological Bulletin*, 52 (2), 2003, pp. 164–85.

Kannan, K.P., 'People's Planning: Kerala's Dilemma', *Seminar*, 485, 2000, pp. 92–7.

Korovkin, Michael A., 'Exploitation, Cooperation, Collusion: An Enquiry into Patronage', *European Journal of Sociology*, 29 (1), 1998, pp. 105–26.

Lederman, Daniel, Norman Laoyza and Rodrigo Reis Soares, 'Accountability and Corruption: Political Institutions Matter', no. 2708, Washington D.C.: Policy Research Working Paper Series from the World Bank, 2001.

Mansbridge, Jane, 'Everyday Talk in the Deliberative System', in Stephen Macedo (ed.), *Deliberative Politics: Essays on Democracy and Disagreement*, New York: Oxford University Press, 1999.

Moncrieffe, Joy M., 'Accountability: Idea, Ideals, Constraints', *Democratization*, 8 (3): 2001, pp. 26–50.

Narayana, D., 'Local Governance Without Capacity Building: Ten Years of Panchayati Raj', *Economic and Political Weekly*, 40 (26), 2005, pp. 2822–32.

Phillips, Anne, *The Politics of Presence*, Oxford: Clarendon Press, 1998.

Pitkin, Hanna Fenichel, *The Concept of Representation*, Berkeley: University of California Press, 1967.

Polidano, Charles and David Hulme, 'No Magic Wands: Accountability and Governance in Developing Countries', *Regional Development Dialogue*, 18 (2), 1997, pp. 1–16.

Powell, John Duncan, 'Peasant Society and Clientelist Politics', in Steffen W. Schmidt, Laura Guasti, Carl H. Lande and James C. Scott (eds.), *Friends, Followers, and Factions: A Reader in Political Clientelism*, Berkeley: University of California Press, 1977.

Prewitt, Kenneth, 'Political Ambitions, Volunteerism, and Electoral Accountability', *American Political Science Review*, 64 (1), 1970, pp. 5–17.

Rao, M. Govinda, 'Poverty Alleviation under Fiscal Decentralization', in M. Govinda Rao (ed.), *Development, Poverty, and Fiscal Policy: Decentralization of Institutions*, New Delhi: Oxford University Press, 2002.

Rao, Nirmala, 'Representation in Local Politics: A Reconsideration and Some New Evidence', *Political Studies*, 46 (1), 1998, pp. 19–35.

Rammohan, K.T., 'Kerala CPI(M): All that is Solid Melts into Air', *Economic and Political Weekly*, 33 (40), 1988, pp. 2579–82.

Sastry, K.R., 'Panchayat Raj Without Substance', *Economic and Political Weekly*, 30, 1995, pp. 1909–10.

Sawer, Marian, 'Parliamentary Representation of Women: From Discourses of Justice to Strategies of Accountability', *International Political Science Review*, 21 (4), 2000, pp. 361–80.

Scott, James C., 'Patron-client Politics and Political Change in Southeast Asia', in Steffen W. Schmidt, Laura Guasti, Carl H. Lande and James C. Scott (eds.), *Friends, Followers, and Factions: A Reader in Political Clientelism*, Berkeley: University of California Press, 1977.

Sen, Gita, 'Social Needs and Public Accountability: The Case of Kerala', in M. Wuyts, M. Mackintosh and T. Hewitt, *Development Policy and Public Action*, Oxford: Oxford University Press, 1992.

Sethi, Geetha (ed.), *Fiscal Decentralization to Rural Governments in India*, New Delhi: Oxford University Press, and World Bank, 2004.

Shivaiah, M., 'A Perspective on System and Measures to Enhance Accountability in Panchayat Raj (consistent with its status as a vehicle of genuine local self-government', in Amitava Mukherjee (ed.), *Decentralisation: Panchayats in the Nineties*, New Delhi: Vikas Publishing House, 1994.

Subha, K., *Karnataka Panchayat Elections 1995: Process, Issues and Membership Profile*, New Delhi: Concept Publishing Company, 1997.

Theobald, Robin, 'The Decline of Patron-client Relations in Developed Societies', *European Journal of Sociology*, 24, 1983, pp. 136–47.

Theobald, Robin, 'On the Survival of Patronage in Developed Societies', *European Journal of Sociology*, 33(1), 1992, pp. 183–91.

Vijayalakshmi, V. and B.K. Chandrashekar, 'Authority, Powerlessness and Dependence: Women and Political Participation', Working Paper 106, Bangalore: Institute for Social and Economic Change, 2003.

Vijayalakshmi, V., 'Gender Accountability and Political Representation in Local Government', Working Paper 102, Bangalore: Institute for Social and Economic Change, 2001.

———, 'Rent-seeking and Gender in Local Governance', Working Paper 164, Bangalore: Institute for Social and Economic Change, 2005.

———, 'Transparency, Accountability and Governance: Local Government in Kerala and Karnataka', in Niraja Gopal Jayal, Amit Prakash, Pradeep K. Sharma (eds.), *Local Governance in India*, New Delhi: Oxford University Press, 2006.

Weingrod, Alex, 'Patrons, Patronage, and Political Parties', in Steffen W. Schmidt, Laura Guasti, Carl H. Lande and James C. Scott (eds.), *Friends, Followers, and Factions: A Reader in Political Clientelism*, Berkeley: University of California Press, 1977.

CHAPTER 4

*Fiscal Decentralization to the Sub-State Level Governments in India**

M.A. OOMMEN

Fiscal decentralization is a subset of decentralization. Given the manifold ways it is interpreted in and the vast diversity of country experiences, decentralization has to be contextually defined and understood (Bird and Vaillancourt, 1998). For the purpose of this paper, decentralization is defined as the empowerment of the local people through the empowerment of the local governments. Fiscal decentralization therefore is fiscal empowerment of lower tiers of government which involves the devolution of taxing and spending powers along with arrangements for rectifying mismatches in resources and responsibilities (see Fukasaku and De Mello, 1999; V. Tanzi, 1996; and Oommen, 2004). This definition is important as it is in broad agreement with the 73rd and 74th Constitutional Amendments which seek to establish a third stratum of government in India. The local government has relevance not only because of its instrumental significance in providing efficient delivery of public services and local goods, but also because of the failure of national and state governments in providing basic services of comparable quality to the citizens during the last half century. On the basis of a detailed analytical study, Rao and Singh (2005) conclude that the Union Finance Commission, Planning Commission and the various centrally sponsored schemes have not made a substantial

*I wish to acknowledge the helpful comments of Prof. D.K. Srivastava on the first draft of this paper.

correction in regional disparities. In contemporary world, only India constitutionally empowers the local governments to prepare 'plans for economic development and social justice' along with the mandate to establish panchayats or rural local governments as institutions of self-government [see Articles 243G, 243W and 243ZD of the Indian Constitution]. Fiscal decentralization is the key variable in this new dispensation of governance. This paper tries to analyse the trend in fiscal decentralization in India focusing on the fifteen major non-special category states based on the data set relating to Panchayati Raj Institutions (PRI) and urban local bodies (ULB) given as Annexure to chapter 8 of the Twelfth Finance Commission (TFC) report. We are aware of the serious limitations of such a set of aggregate data reported by the various state governments. However, it is a matter of comfort that these data are canvassed through a common format prepared and collated by the TFC. This analysis is supplemented by a study of the second State Finance Commission (SFC) reports of five states.[1] The SFC is a constitutional counterpart of the Union Finance Commission (UFC) at the state level to mediate between the state and the local governments (see Article 243I and 243Y).

TREND AND EXTENT OF FISCAL DECENTRALIZATION

The extent of fiscal decentralization depends on the expenditure responsibilities and revenue assignments devolved to the lower tiers. The total expenditure of local governments (PRIs and ULBs), as a proportion of the combined expenditure of union, state and local governments, works out to about 6.4 per cent in 1998–9 and 5.1 per cent in 2002–3.[2] The decline in the expenditure of PRIs (from 3.9 per cent in 1998–9 to 3.3 per cent in 2002–3), which cover nearly 73 per cent of the people, needs special mention because decentralized governance is envisaged primarily to improve the quality of life in the rural areas. The PRIs expenditure in 2002–3 as a proportion of GDP works out only to 1.07 per cent. The own source revenue (tax + non-tax revenue) of local bodies as a proportion of the combined tax and non-tax revenue of the union, states and local governments for 1998–9 was around 2.7 per cent. This declined to 1.9 per cent in 2002–3. Reckoned in terms of GDP, in 2002–3, the own source revenue of local governments was only 0.39 per cent, more than 82 per cent of which is accounted for by ULBs. The extent of fiscal decentralization—already very low—has shown a pronounced declining trend. When we know that in most advanced countries local governments normally account for about 20–35 per cent of total government expenditure (in some countries like Denmark it goes as high as 45 per cent), India with two major constitutional amendments ostensibly to transfer power, authority and resources to local governments has very little to write home about.

The trend in the overall scenario of decentralization in India raises several questions. We may address some of them for the purpose of this paper: What has been the state-wise scenario? What inter-state differences are in the structure and pattern of transfers by states to local governments? What role has the SFC constitutionally created to rationalize state/sub-state level fiscal relations and transfers played in the context of decentralization?

THE THIRD STRATA OF GOVERNMENT AND FISCAL DECENTRALIZATION

Table 4.1 shows the state-wise progress in expenditure and tax decentralization as well as changes in the relative magnitudes of these variables by comparing two years, 1998–9 and 2002–3. The proportion of local governments' expenditure of all states to the expenditure of all states and local governments combined declined from 11.24 per cent in 1998–9 to 9.47 per cent in 2002–3. Among the fifteen major states shown in Table 4.1, only Bihar, Haryana, Tamil Nadu and Uttar Pradesh seem to have made some progress. In all the other eleven states the percentage has declined. The progress in Bihar and the other three states are due to their very low base in 1998–9. In 1998–9 the percentage of local government expenditure to total expenditure comprising state and local governments ranged from 0.92 per cent in Bihar to 21.73 per cent in Karnataka, followed by 20.90 per cent in Kerala[3] (18.76 per cent if RBI figures are used) and 20.36 per cent in Gujarat. In 2002–3,

TABLE 4.1: EXPENDITURE AND TAX DECENTRALIZATION AT THE STATE/SUB-STATE LEVELS (MAJOR STATES) (1998–9 AND 2002–3)

States	Local Government Expenditure as per cent of State Expenditure + Local Government Expenditure		Local Government Own Tax as per cent of State Own Tax Revenue + Local Government Own Tax Revenue	
	1998–9	2002–3	1998–9	2002–3
Andhra Pradesh	18.12	18.05	3.07	3.90
Assam	1.08	0.93	2.07	1.45
Bihar	0.92	2.65	1.53	2.40
Gujarat	20.36	14.06	12.30	8.04
Haryana	3.63	4.64	2.95	0.73
Karnataka	21.73	18.22	6.14	3.68
Kerala*	18.76	13.32	3.87	3.99
Madhya Pradesh	9.90	9.30	8.20	8.98
Maharashtra	16.30	13.60	9.97	5.17
Orissa	3.33	3.13	3.54	0.55
Punjab	5.62	4.71	9.67	7.55
Rajasthan	12.34	11.47	2.71	0.48
Tamil Nadu	9.19	9.42	3.63	4.22
Uttar Pradesh	3.98	4.64	1.27	1.36
West Bengal	5.93	4.69	3.27	4.87
All States	11.24	9.47	5.71	3.97

Sources: *Twelfth Finance Commission* and RBI's *State Finances: A Study of Budgets* for the Relevant Years.

Note: *State Expenditure figures are obtained from RBI's *State Finances: A Study of Budgets*. From the state total expenditure figures given in the RBI document, item IV of Appendix II (Compensation and Assignments to Local Bodies and Panchayat Raj) is deducted. We have checked with RBI sources and learned that all the payments to local bodies (ULBs + PRIs) are not included under this item. The real figures have to be obtained from the Ministry of Finance as audited by the C&AG. For Kerala we have used the figures from C&AG reports. As per the Report of C&AG, the figures for 1998–9 and 2002–3 are Rs. 1,309.78 crore and Rs. 989.98 crore respectively for Kerala. Hence the percentage when reworked will be 20.9 for 1998–9 and 14.1 for 2002–3. Similar figures for other states are not readily available and the given figures are possibly underestimates.

the corresponding range was from 0.93 per cent in Assam to 18.22 per cent in Karnataka and 14 per cent in Kerala (13.32 per cent with RBI figures) and Gujarat.

Karnataka occupies the top position in expenditure decentralization in both the years. It could be firmly confirmed from the table in Appendix A which gives the rate of growth of total expenditure in each of the fifteen states and that for all states for the period 1998–2003 that the decline in the ratio is due to the lower growth rate of the expenditure of the local bodies. While the all-states average rate of growth of expenditure increased at the rate of 11.6 per cent during the period, the rate of growth in the total expenditure of PRIs was only 6.87 per cent and of ULBs 4.07 per cent. Actually the trends for PRIs in Gujarat, Kerala and Orissa and for ULBs in Gujarat, Haryana, Karnataka, Madhya Pradesh and Maharashtra are negative (see Appendix A).

Turning to tax decentralization, Table 4.1 shows that at the all-states level the percentage of own tax revenue of local government as a percentage of state's own tax revenue plus local tax revenue declined by 1.74 percentage points in 2002–3 compared with 1998–9. Only in seven states do we see marginal increase during this period. The decline ranges from 0.62 percentage points in Assam to 4.80 percentage points in Maharashtra with Gujarat closely following. The magnitude and the pathology of the own revenue situation may be captured better in the three tables given in Appendix B. Table I shows the per capita own tax (OT) and per capita own source revenue (OSR) of PRIs along with the average growth rate from 1998–9 through 2002–3. Table II shows the corresponding growth rate for ULBs. Table III shows the ratio of own source revenue to total expenditure for PRIs and ULBs in the states under study for 1998–9 and 2002–3.

The per capita tax and per capita OSR of ULBs are several times higher than that of the PRIs in all the states (see Table I and Table II of Appendix B). Appendix B Table I shows that in 2002–3, the per capita OT of PRIs is below Re. 1 (zero in Bihar) or around it in five states. The highest per capita OSR among PRIs in all the five years consistently is reported in Kerala (as high as Rs. 101.96 in 1999–2000). The per capita OSR of PRIs is below the all-state average in the nine states in 2002–3. The rate of growth for all-states with regard to PRIs during the quinquennium 1998–9 to 2002–3, is over 7.7 per cent for tax and 5.7 per cent for own source revenue. The rate of growth in tax revenue of PRIs, however, is negative in Gujarat, Orissa and Punjab. Although the level of OSR of ULBs is very high compared to PRIs and in 2002–3, the per capita OSR ranges from Rs. 75.34 in Orissa to Rs. 743 in Punjab, the overall rate of growth of OSR of ULBs for all states has been negative (–3.14 per annum) during the period from 1998–9 to 2002–3. The growth rate of per capita taxes of ULBs is negative in Gujarat, Haryana, Karnataka, Maharashtra, Orissa and Rajasthan. Indeed, the own source revenue situation at the third tier of government, especially that of PRIs, does not seem to support a healthy decentralization process in the country. The ratio of OSR to total expenditure, which could be considered as a measure of the fiscal autonomy of the states [Appendix B Table III], presents a somewhat misleading picture. The picture of ULBs is apparently encouraging and definitely better than that of the PRIs. If we assume that a local government raises 50 per cent of its expenditure through OSR, it could be considered as fairly autonomous. By this standard except in a few states the ULB scenario is in fairly good shape. The share of OSR to total expenditure for ULBs is over 52 per cent in 2002–3 as against 6.7 per cent for PRIs for the same year. In the case of Assam and Punjab the high OSR ratio of PRIs is presumably because of poor expenditure assignments.

TRENDS IN REVENUE TRANSFERS TO LOCAL GOVERNMENTS

The effectiveness of fiscal decentralization to the sub-state level governments depends on: (i) appropriate expenditure assignments (illustrative guidelines follow from Schedules XI and XII of the Constitution) broken up into activities and sub-activities accompanied by transfer of funds from the concerned state department head of accounts in the state budget to the local bodies; (ii) appropriate revenue/tax assignments; and (iii) efficient design of the transfer system and its proper implementation. The latter, of course, is the primary responsibility of the SFC and the concerned state governments.

Table 4.2 presents the state-wise trend in the ratios of transfers (tax devolution plus grants-in-aid)[4] to the net state domestic product (NSDP), to state's total revenue, as well as to state's total expenditure excluding loans and interest payments. Besides that, Table 4.2 contains a column (no. 3) which shows the ratio of tax devolution to local governments as a percentage of state's own tax revenue. All these are different ways to measure the magnitude of transfers.

Table 4.2 which focuses on the magnitude of transfers made by the major state governments to local governments has to be seen along with the poor revenue and expenditure decentralization noted in Table 4.1 and Appendix B. Transfers to local governments as a percentage of SDP has declined in the country as a whole. However, it improved in ten states in 2002–3, albeit marginally, compared to 1998–9. SDP is not a good fiscal variable to measure the magnitude of transfers. The best way is to reckon transfers with reference to the state's expenditure and the state's revenue. We have also examined the tax component of the transfers *vis-à-vis* the own tax revenue of the state. In nine states total transfers registered a decline as a proportion of the total state expenditure. This includes such prominent states upholding decentralization like Karnataka, Kerala, Madhya Pradesh, Rajasthan and West Bengal. An important measure of fiscal decentralization is the percentage of tax revenue devolved (e.g. tax assigned, plus state taxes shared) to total state tax revenue. In 1998–9 it ranged from zero in Bihar to 52.63 per cent in Karnataka and in 2002–3, the same pattern continued except that Karnataka's share fell to 42.62 per cent. Karnataka was followed by Tamil Nadu and Madhya Pradesh in 2002–3. Transfers as a percentage of state revenue declined in nine states as well as for all states. Table 4.2 clearly shows that only Karnataka had an above all-state average with regard to all the four measures in all the years. Maharashtra and Rajasthan fell in the second best category as they qualified for all measures except tax devolution as a percentage of state's own tax revenue. In brief, the record of fiscal decentralization, to the sub-state level governments through transfers has been very poor. As regards Karnataka it is important to note

TABLE 4.2: SELECT INDICATORS OF REVENUE TRANSFERS TO LGs BY MAJOR STATES
(1998–9 AND 2002–3)

States	Transfers as per cent of NSDP (1)		Transfers as per cent of State Revenue (2)		Tax Devolution as per cent of State's Own Tax Revenue (3)		Transfers as per cent of State Expenditure (4)	
	1998–9	2000–3	1998–9	2002–3	1998–9	2000–3	1998–9	2002–3
Andhra Pradesh	2.68	3.39	19.54	21.20	4.44	4.54	15.33	16.48
Assam	0.03	0.04	0.17	0.18	0.27	0.29	0.16	0.16
Bihar	0.03	0.54	0.13	2.39	0.00	0.00	0.10	1.77
Gujarat	3.49	2.61	24.57	16.72	2.08	1.24	17.54	12.62
Haryana	0.27	0.58	1.88	3.87	0.88	2.59	1.28	3.43
Karnataka	4.81	4.43	33.74	27.52	52.63	42.62	27.34	21.01
Kerala	1.67	1.17	11.88	7.82	3.86	2.71	8.70	5.40
Madhya Pradesh	1.31	1.19	7.07	6.35	15.54	10.44	5.41	5.12
Maharashtra	1.71	1.99	15.05	16.87	0.36	0.31	11.41	12.07
Orissa	0.59	0.80	4.03	3.69	5.09	6.51	2.38	2.84
Punjab	0.13	0.17	1.12	1.03	1.28	1.24	0.68	0.76
Rajasthan	1.73	1.76	13.21	10.13	1.95	1.97	8.49	6.96
Tamil Nadu	1.09	1.27	8.12	8.26	12.03	12.00	6.50	6.68
Uttar Pradesh	0.58	0.25	4.45	1.59	9.58	2.99	2.83	1.25
West Bengal	0.44	0.45	4.97	4.76	0.09	0.66	3.16	2.92
All States	1.19	1.12	10.76	8.96	8.35	6.25	7.92	6.86

Source: *Twelfth Finance Commission*; RBI, *State Finances: A Study of Budgets*; and Government of India, *Economic Survey 2004–5*.
Note: NSDP—Net Domestic Product.

that the transfers are linked to the schemes transferred by the state government. The system that prevailed in 1993 continues. The local governments do not have any autonomy to determine priorities, discontinue schemes or change the composition of expenditures. Moreover, the gram panchayats in the state account for only 5 per cent of the total allocation of state funds to PRIs in 2002–3 and in 2000–1 as low as 3.5 per cent [see Karnataka second SFC Report (2002), p. 27]. In all other states the share of village panchayats is high. Indeed, the efficiency of resources use and the quality and effectiveness of the delivery of basic services depend on the quantum of expenditure at the cutting edge level.

Before we conclude this discussion, we may try to discern the pattern in the structure of transfers to local governments. Table 4.3 juxtaposes the state-wise distribution of per capita state revenue and per capita transfers in 2002–3 to PRIs and ULBs for the fifteen states. One important aspect to be noted from the table is the higher per capita transfers to the rural areas (PRIs) than the urban areas for the country as a whole. By and large this is true in the case of most of the states. This is a healthy trend. But there are significant exceptions. Assam makes no transfers to PRIs.[5] It is very significant that in Madhya Pradesh and Orissa which are admittedly backward states with a very high tribal population, the per capita transfers to PRIs is way below that to ULBs. In West Bengal the per capita transfers to PRIs is only Rs. 24.12[6] as against Rs. 232.37 for ULBs. Although Tamil Nadu's case is not as glaring as West Bengal, Madhya Pradesh or Orissa, the hiatus is very conspicuous.

Figure 4.1 seeks to illustrate the association between per capita state revenue and the transfers made to the local bodies. The per capita state revenue is shown in the x-axis and per capita transfers in the y-axis with the median lines relevant to these two variables being drawn making the whole figure into a box with four quadrangles identified as A, B, C and D (see Fig. 4.1).

In Figure 4.1 Quadrangle A represents the case of states with low per capita revenue (less than the median level of per capita revenue, or states with per capita revenue less than the middle 50 per cent, when the states are arranged in order of increasing per capita revenue), and low per capita transfers to the LGs (less than

TABLE 4.3: PER CAPITA STATE REVENUE AND PER CAPITA TRANSFERS TO PRIs AND ULBs (2002–3)

(*in Rs.*)

States	Per Capita Revenue of State	Per Capita Transfer (Combined)	Per Capita Transfers to PRIs	Per Capita Transfers to ULBs
Andhra Pradesh	2941.78	623.78	775.43	219.87
Assam	2464.25	4.54	0.00	35.53
Bihar	1318.96	31.57	34.21	8.97
Gujarat	3382.16	565.45	835.44	112.60
Haryana	3882.39	150.18	188.00	57.18
Karnataka	2955.19	813.14	1175.61	110.33
Kerala	3274.34	256.02	293.29	149.16
Madhya Pradesh	2114.19	134.29	65.23	325.92
Maharashtra	3073.10	518.57	816.05	114.69
Orissa	2225.93	82.08	56.54	227.43
Punjab	4369.67	44.84	47.72	39.25
Rajasthan	2190.99	221.84	250.56	127.62
Tamil Nadu	3266.99	269.74	231.31	318.52
Uttar Pradesh	1593.29	25.39	32.04	0.00
West Bengal	1729.35	82.36	24.12	232.37
All States	2656.85	238.04	269.55	152.10

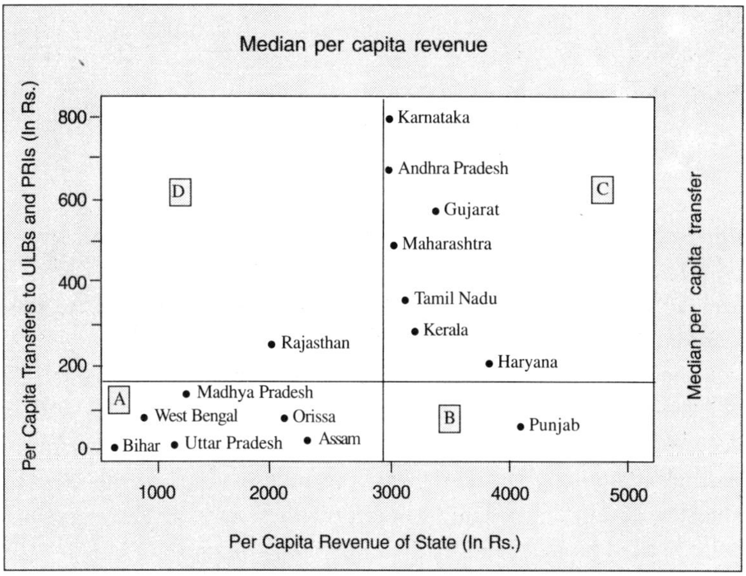

Figure 4.1: Per Capita Revenue of States and Per Capita Transfers Received by LGI's, 2002–3.

the median level of per capita transfers). Quadrangle B represents the case of states with high per capita revenue (greater than median level of per capita revenue) and low per capita transfers to LGs (less than median level of per capita transfer). Quadrangle C represents the case of states with high per capita revenue and high per capita transfers to LGs. Quadrangle D represents those cases with low per capita revenue but high per capita transfers.

What Fig. 4.1 shows is that though higher transfers are mostly seen to be made by the richer revenue states, it is not true in all cases. Punjab with the highest per capita revenue has the lowest per capita transfer. It is more or less the same story in the case of Haryana. The highest per capita transfer is made by Karnataka which is a state that falls in the middle when the states are ranked by their per capita revenue.

It may also be seen that most of the states with low per capita revenue devolve less or even nil to LGs, with Rajasthan standing out as an exception. Though a low per capita revenue state, Rajasthan devolves funds to LGs in much larger magnitude in per capita terms than Punjab, Haryana or West Bengal. This is shown by it being the sole state in Quadrangle D.

THE ROLE OF SFCs

Inter alia poor progress of fiscal decentralization may be considered as reflecting the ineffectiveness of the institution of SFC. It is as well be due to the failure of the states in implementing SFC recommendations. The primary task of the UFC is to mediate in the sharing of revenues between the centre and the states by rectifying the mismatches between responsibilities and resources as well as to reduce the horizontal fiscal imbalances between states in an equitable manner. The SFC, which is a counterpart of the UFC at the state level, is mandated to perform these tasks at the state/sub-state level. The task is probably more complex and onerous for the SFCs because of the lack of clarity with regard to expenditure responsibilities in many states. Except in a few states like Kerala where the responsibilities of the panchayats and urban local bodies are broken down into activities and sub-activities, every function of the LG is state-concurrent and therefore administratively complex. Because the local governments are constitutionally required to create institutions of local self-government and prepare plans for economic development and social justice under the new decentralization regime, the responsibilities of a SFC in ensuring vertical and horizontal equity and balance are very high. Economically poor gram panchayats and municipalities will have to be helped in providing comparable services through equalizing allocations (grants) which will compensate for genuine revenue raising problems and cost disadvantages such as distance, mountainous or marshy regions, and the like. In what follows we examine very briefly how five second-generation SFCs (Karnataka, Kerala, Punjab, Rajasthan and Tamil Nadu) have tried to improve vertical and horizontal imbalances in their respective states.

The size of vertical transfers logically depends on the goals to be achieved and the needs of local governments, which certainly will have to take into account the magnitude of the mismatches in resources available and the expenditure responsibilities. All the SFCs under study except Kerala have made estimates of vertical gaps. But none has made this exercise with reference to functional assignments and needs following from that. Actually a clear demarcation of the functional domain is not available in most cases. All the five SFCs agree on the need for providing basic public services of comparable quality at the level of rural and urban local bodies. Tamil Nadu, Punjab and Rajasthan SFCs estimate the fiscal gap, including capital requirements, by taking civic functions into account. Rajasthan Second State Finance Commission (SSFC) takes the view that investment requirements for providing civic services are 'large and ought to be met from plan funds including cess and externally funded projects' (Rajasthan SSFC Report: p. 82).

In Appendix C we present a broad outline of the scheme of vertical transfers of the five SSFCs which shows the magnitude of transfer, the instrument of transfers and the basis of vertical distribution between PRIs and ULBs. The size of transfers ranges from 2.25 per cent (this includes 0.05 per cent as incentive grant for raising additional revenue) of state's own net tax revenue in Rajasthan to 40 per cent of non-loan gross own revenue receipts (NLGORR) in Karnataka. All the SFCs except Karnataka consider net tax revenue as the instrument and source of transfer. Kerala SSFC which endorses the prevailing practice of giving one-third of plan outlay to the LGs as plan grants-in-aid, additionally recommends the devolution of a maintenance grant (5.5 per cent of net own tax revenue of state) based on a current cost of replacement and a general purpose grant to the tune of 3.5 per cent of the net own tax revenue.

We also see from Appendix C that the basis of vertical distribution between PRIs and ULBs is population in most cases. Besides population, Karnataka takes illiteracy rate and population per hospital bed into consideration and the ratio works out to 80 per cent for PRIs and 20 per cent for ULBs. Tamil Nadu takes population (50 per cent weight), needs (operation and maintenance, capital and debt), resource potential, and the rural-urban proportion with account and the ratio works out to 58 : 42. It is clear that the choice of criteria and the weightage given to them, which in turn depends on the objectives and priorities underlying the design of transfer of the concerned SFC, assume significance in determining the vertical share of PRIs and ULBs.

Turning to horizontal distribution, we may make some general observations based on the five SSFC reports. We have noted in Table 4.3 that in 2002–3 (see also Fig. 4.1) Karnataka had the highest per capita transfer. This was obviously due to the high vertical transfers through the transfer of schemes of the state government. The real question is whether it also results in higher horizontal equity or not. The answer is in the negative. For one, the allocation to gram panchayats[7] in Karnataka, as we have already noted, was only around 5 per cent of the total allocation to PRIs in 2002–3. The criteria for *inter se* distribution such as population, area, illiteracy rate, the ratio of population per bed and so on are applicable only in the case of zilla panchayats and taluka panchayats. Gram panchayats get only a fixed amount (Rs. 3.5 lakh per GP). In the case of the other states, the tax shares recommended to gram panchayats ranges from 60 per cent of the share of PRIs in Tamil Nadu to 100 per cent in Punjab. Kerala SSFC, besides giving nearly 70 per cent plan grant share to GPs, 78.5 per cent of general purpose grant is also earmarked for them.[8] While in Kerala the *inter se* distribution among the municipalities and corporations should be entirely on the basis of population, as regards GPs, a corpus of Rs. 100 million is recommended to be set apart as a horizontal gap filling to bridge the gap between obligatory expenses and own revenue plus general purpose grant of GPs. A 100 per cent gap filling in the case of second- and third-grade GPs, 50 per cent in the case of first-grade GPs and 25 per cent in the case of special-grade GPs are recommended. The balance is to be distributed on the basis of population.

The most rational horizontal distribution is to give adequate weightage to equity and efficiency. For *inter se* allocation among GPs, all SFCs other than Karnataka use population as the dominant criterion followed by area, tax efforts and some indicators of backwardness. The choice of a relevant backwardness criteria with appropriate weightage, incentivizing revenue efforts and ensuring delivery of quality of services assume significance. On this score most of the SSFCs require improvements and need to incorporate better efficiency and equity elements. Besides the horizontal gap filling recommendations of Kerala SSFC, two recommendations of the Tamil Nadu SSFC need special mention. One relates to the introduction of the report card system for the *inter se* distribution of Incentive Funds. Five per cent of the total devolution is set apart for providing incentives to local bodies for efficient resource mobilization as well as for delivery of quality public services. The report card system is a way of assessing the quality of public services from the perspective of citizens or users of civic services. Users can provide feedback on the quality, efficiency and adequacy of the services through the various entries in the card. The other is the equalization fund to compensate for fiscal disabilities. Any GP with less than Rs. 17 per capita tax (which is the state average for all GPs) is considered a weak village panchayat deserving this fund. The shortfall from Rs. 17 is made good from the equalization fund. It may be noted here that one may do well to compare fiscal capacity at a given average tax rate rather than the actual per capita tax, which may be low due to lower tax effort. Even so the promotion of equalization is a relevant effort towards horizontal equity. A great weakness of the Tamil Nadu SSFC is that it left 20 per cent of devolution to be discretionary and only 80 per cent as formula-based. A rational devolution mechanism should be fully formula-based which of course should be operationally simple.

By and large, the SSFC reports are better than their first-generation counterparts in terms of analytical content and quality of recommendations. Despite the innumerable shortcomings of the first series of SFC reports pointed out by the Eleventh Finance Commission (EFC) and those raised by the TFC about SFC reports they examined, that SSFCs raised the magnitude of vertical devolution compared to the previous regime cannot be gainsaid. However, the pertinent question is the cavalier fashion in which most state governments have treated the recommendations of the SFCs. All the five SSFCs under study have reviewed the progress the respective states have made in implementing the first SFC, devolution packages and recommendations. All of them report very serious lapses on the part of the state governments. The constitutional provisions contained in Article 243(4) that 'The Governor shall cause every recommendation made by the commission under this article together with an explanatory memorandum as to the action taken thereon to be laid before the Legislature of the State' have been violated by almost all the states. By dishonouring and soft-peddling on the recommendations of successive SFCs most state governments have put the fiscal decentralization process in reverse gear.

Presumably, the most striking mistake with regard to the transfer system emerging at the state/sub-state level following decentralization reforms is treating the transfers to LGs as an additional financial allocation. Yes, there is need for extra resources. But the basic principle that as part of decentralization of funds,[9] budgetary provision of an item of expenditure responsibility that has been transferred to the LGs should be followed with corresponding reduction in the concerned departmental budget of the state has not been followed in most states. So long as the necessary adjustments are not made the entire state transfers to the LGs become an additional burden on the state. It is a grave mistake on the part of the SFCs that they have not taken this into account in arriving at the vertical gaps. Economic efficiency and efficiency in governance are enhanced by the division of governmental functions among different levels depending on their comparative advantage or what is called the principle of subsidiarity. Although the Kerala State Assembly has made functional demarcations between the state and LGs, *inter se*, the Kerala government introduced a separate budget document for panchayats and ULBs as Appendix IV to the budget papers. There was no *pro tanto* reduction at the state departmental level except in the case of very few departments. So decentralization resulted in additional burden on the state exchequer even in Kerala. There is also need to insure local government from the impact of the fiscal imprudence of the state governments.

To conclude, even after more than a decade of decentralized governance under the new dispensation, the emerging fiscal decentralization scenario is disquieting. The percentage of local government expenditure in relation to total government expenditure has declined significantly during the period 1998–9 to 2002–3. The progress of expenditure decentralization in eleven out of the fifteen states appears to be on the decline. The revenue decentralization trend is also no better. That the average rate of growth in the tax revenue of PRIs and ULBs in most states has been negative or declining provides a wrong signal. It renders efforts towards building autonomous local governments impossible. As regards transfers to the local governments, reckoned in terms of SDP, state revenue and state expenditure, the overall trend has been very discouraging, although there are significant exceptions. Again while by and large per capita transfers to rural governments are higher than those to ULBs, the per capita transfers to ULBs is very high in states like Madhya Pradesh, Orissa, Tamil Nadu and West Bengal.

The performance of SFCs, which have the responsibility to mediate in the revenue sharing between the state and the LGs, leaves many things to be desired. Functional mapping with reference to state and LGs on the one hand and that among the three tiers of PRIs has not made much progress in most states. Sometimes functions are transferred without making any change in the budgetary head by way of devolution to local bodies. This makes transfers an additional burden on the state exchequer. Needless to say, economic efficiency and political efficiency are best ensured when the functions among the different levels are organized on the basis of comparative advantage followed by corresponding transfers. The design of the transfer system at the state/sub-state/level needs drastic reform. SFC recommendation is one thing, but implementation is the responsibility of the state. It is the state governments which should bear the major responsibility for the poor progress of fiscal decentralization in the country.

NOTES

1. They are Karnataka, Kerala, Punjab, Rajasthan and Tamil Nadu.
2. The expenditure data for local governments are from the TFC report and that for union and state governments are from *Economic Survey*, Government of India, for the relevant years.
3. For details, see note to Table 4.1.
4. Transfers consist of tax assignment plus tax devolved plus grant-in-aid transferred to local governments (PRIs and ULBs). The TFC data contain an item

'Others', other than own source revenue and tax devolution and grants-in-aid. As it is a mixed category we have not included it in the transfers.

5. This cannot be a case of non-reporting because it is zero in all the five years.
6. In West Bengal in the year 2001–2, the per capita transfers to PRIs was above Rs. 70.
7. Moving the 73rd Amendment on 1 December 1992 in the Lok Sabha the then minister for rural development said: 'The Constitution (73rd) Amendment Bill casts a duty on the centre as well as the states to establish and nourish the village panchayats so as to make them effective self-governing institutions.' This basic objective must be a governing consideration in the state/sub-state level transfer system.
8. The GPs' share is determined after allotting a one-time share for district and block panchayats in the general purpose grant based on their establishment cost and office expense requirements.
9. For the whole process to be complete, logically the functionaries also should be transferred to the lower tiers. This is a serious deficit in the democratic decentralization underway in the country.

REFERENCES

Bird, Richard M. and Francois Villancourt, *Fiscal Decentralisation in Developing Countries*, Cambridge: Cambridge University Press, 1998.

Fuka, Saku Kichiro and L.R. De Mello Jr., *Fiscal Decentralisation in Emerging Economies*, Paris: Development Centre OECD, 1999.

Oommen, M.A., 'Fiscal Decentralization in Kerala', in Geeta Sethi (ed.), *Fiscal Decentralisation to Rural Governments in India*, New Delhi: Oxford University Press, 2004.

Rao, M. Govinda and Nirvikar Singh, *Political Economy of Federalism in India*, New Delhi: Oxford University Press, 2005.

Report of the Second State Finance Commissions of Karnataka, Kerala, Punjab, Rajasthan and Tamil Nadu.

Reserve Bank of India, *State Finances: A Study of Budgets* for different years.

Tanzi, Vito, 'Fiscal Federalism and Decentralization: A Review of Some Efficiency and Macro-economic Aspects', in Michael Bruno and Boris Plesrovic (eds.), *Annual World Bank Conference on Development Economics 1995*, Washington: World Bank, 1996.

Twelfth Finance Commission Report, 2005.

APPENDIX A

AVERAGE RATE OF GROWTH IN THE TOTAL EXPENDITURE OF STATEs, PRIs AND ULBs (1998–9 TO 2002–3)

States	Growth Rate of State Expenditure	Growth Rate of Expenditure of PRIs	Growth Rate of Expenditure of ULBs
Andhra Pradesh	12.83	11.92	15.44
Assam	13.53	2.25	10.07
Bihar	4.93	96.20	12.57
Gujarat	8.95	-1.65	-5.68
Haryana	6.92	26.72	-9.41
Karnataka	12.41	5.86	-3.81
Kerala	10.04	-2.09	3.46
Madhya Pradesh	2.94	2.04	-1.50
Maharashtra	10.42	11.09	-0.25
Orissa	10.88	-3.37	19.45
Punjab	12.60	9.70	5.47
Rajasthan	10.22	5.67	9.48
Tamil Nadu	9.70	7.73	8.30
Uttar Pradesh	7.01	5.14	11.32
West Bengal	12.45	5.52	4.00
All States	11.59	6.87	4.07

APPENDIX B: TABLE I

STATE-WISE DISTRIBUTION OF PER CAPITA OWN TAX AND PER CAPITA OWN REVENUE WITH AVERAGE GROWTH RATE

State	Panchayati Raj Institutions											
	1998–9		1999–2000		2000–1		2001–2		2002–3		Growth Rate	
	Per Capita Own Tax	Per Capita Own Revenue	Per Capita Own Tax	Per Capita Own Revenue	Per Capita Own Tax	Per Capita Own Revenue	Per Capita Own Tax	Per Capita Own Revenue	Per Capita Own Tax	Per Capita Own Revenue	Own Tax	Own Revenue (OSR)
Andhra Pradesh	12.03	23.83	12.11	24.92	13.46	27.37	13.56	28.66	13.65	30.05	3.72	6.23
Assam	3.12	3.14	3.12	3.15	3.13	3.16	3.13	3.16	3.14	3.17	0.16	0.18
Bihar	0.00	0.84	0.00	0.42	0.00	1.04	0.00	0.47	0.00	0.85	0.00	1.33
Gujarat	22.52	25.48	22.34	25.80	20.99	23.95	19.50	22.14	18.48	21.10	-5.18	-5.17
Haryana	5.07	40.67	3.71	39.70	4.91	46.76	4.88	49.44	5.43	49.43	4.17	6.29
Karnataka	15.30	15.30	16.69	16.69	19.15	19.15	14.75	14.75	16.47	16.47	0.25	0.25
Kerala	38.08	72.68	42.84	101.96	49.16	93.08	48.08	81.36	51.27	94.07	7.36	2.94
Madhya Pradesh	28.24	29.26	28.01	29.61	28.38	32.00	27.46	31.33	33.34	37.55	3.17	5.71
Maharashtra	29.46	44.54	32.31	52.15	36.64	58.78	48.08	67.39	59.48	80.65	19.75	15.53
Orissa	0.16	2.05	0.15	2.81	0.15	2.89	0.15	2.77	0.07	1.71	-15.95	-3.70
Punjab	0.77	42.61	0.58	52.94	0.72	50.11	0.70	39.64	0.52	59.08	-5.64	3.71
Rajasthan	0.74	7.76	1.12	8.69	1.10	8.52	1.08	8.34	1.06	8.23	6.96	0.77
Tamil Nadu	10.09	15.26	11.26	17.24	13.10	16.39	14.51	17.68	13.64	18.34	8.95	4.01
Uttar Pradesh	0.75	3.70	0.90	4.15	0.89	4.47	0.81	4.39	0.80	4.57	0.07	4.89
West Bengal	1.24	5.28	1.22	5.26	1.56	5.64	1.62	5.69	1.63	5.17	8.71	0.37
All India	8.86	16.34	9.34	18.40	10.18	19.15	10.72	18.95	12.03	21.29	7.77	5.74

Note: OSR – Own Source Revenue (Own Revenue).

TABLE II

State	Urban Local Bodies											
	1998–9		1999–2000		2000–1		2001–2		2002–3		Growth Rate	
	Per Capita Own Tax	Per Capita Own Revenue	Per Capita Own Tax	Per Capita Own Revenue	Per Capita Own Tax	Per Capita Own Revenue	Per Capita Own Tax	Per Capita Own Revenue	Per Capita Own Tax	Per Capita Own Revenue	Own Tax	Own Revenue
Andhra Pradesh	92.32	238.22	105.20	249.17	125.53	302.48	153.36	340.70	203.78	401.53	21.66	14.53
Assam	42.18	95.92	45.06	89.55	52.15	104.85	54.81	105.34	59.49	122.41	9.23	6.72
Bihar	50.51	54.38	54.35	59.68	57.75	64.37	54.88	63.10	73.84	82.29	8.00	9.24
Gujarat	552.34	657.72	623.06	739.95	632.15	745.69	605.95	719.49	390.85	494.48	-6.94	-5.81
Haryana	151.92	237.66	116.82	255.57	95.20	205.84	104.31	207.39	50.37	144.50	-20.71	-11.34
Karnataka	231.29	304.34	223.15	263.54	215.85	241.43	225.49	254.80	182.57	188.49	-4.52	-9.44
Kerala	121.31	187.07	149.09	223.39	172.58	252.14	153.28	269.85	213.04	350.17	12.23	15.52
Madhya Pradesh	220.66	300.23	251.78	350.20	288.23	364.68	242.49	327.51	270.38	361.76	3.76	3.11
Maharashtra	359.65	475.89	346.02	470.11	391.62	542.61	412.15	577.41	209.14	247.00	-8.69	-10.47
Orissa	101.45	136.01	22.94	60.38	27.24	67.80	28.71	72.67	27.69	75.34	-21.12	-9.48
Punjab	435.54	584.61	556.58	732.49	590.99	818.83	559.81	807.82	540.27	743.80	4.46	5.97
Rajasthan	85.29	150.27	11.49	64.44	15.66	82.23	17.80	126.45	18.17	123.42	-23.32	2.84
Tamil Nadu	122.13	221.31	180.36	277.91	172.28	309.81	187.59	328.02	207.50	356.40	11.62	11.84
Uttar Pradesh	28.18	55.97	31.85	60.00	35.81	67.15	40.30	80.89	45.40	90.88	12.63	13.52
West Bengal	72.25	140.23	79.42	150.11	85.08	158.37	121.54	198.87	149.28	253.76	20.64	15.81
All States	182.59	263.91	193.71	277.53	206.91	304.25	212.33	207.80	174.59	260.06	0.02	-3.14

TABLE III

PERCENTAGE OF OSR TO TOTAL EXPENDITURE

States	Percentage of PRIs		Percentage of ULBs	
	1998–9	2002–3	1998–9	2002–3
Andhra Pradesh	3.93	3.34	64.09	60.81
Assam	99.86	98.83	69.55	67.67
Bihar	20.15	2.27	59.65	56.84
Gujarat	2.65	2.72	72.57	74.62
Haryana	45.35	20.82	77.94	94.00
Karnataka	1.67	1.45	70.00	56.48
Kerala	9.44	12.67	31.47	50.87
Madhya Pradesh	26.50	36.68	39.50	49.50
Maharashtra	7.88	9.98	73.01	49.68
Orissa	5.40	3.02	76.68	24.88
Punjab	66.33	55.32	100.78	113.85
Rajasthan	2.38	2.17	34.90	23.60
Tamil Nadu	14.68	12.39	41.11	46.61
Uttar Pradesh	11.60	10.62	25.11	28.96
West Bengal	16.89	17.64	39.53	60.21
All States	6.34	6.77	57.11	52.58

APPENDIX C

SCHEME OF VERTICAL TRANSFERS OF FIVE SSFCs

Name of State	Instrument of Transfer and percentage to be Transferred	Basis of Arriving of the Divisible Pool	Basis and Proportion of Vertical Distribution Between PRIs & ULBs	Remarks
Karnataka	40 % of Non-loan Gross Own Revenue Receipts (NLGORR)	Normative estimate to provide minimum public/civic sesrvices of comparable quality in rural and urban areas	Population, SC/ST, Illiteracy rate and population per hospital bed. PRIs: 80% ULBs: 20%	Raised NLGORR ratio from 36% recommended by first SFC to 40% by the SSFC.
Kerala	*Plan:* Grant-in aid—$33^1/_3$% of the state plan *Non-Plan:* (i) 5.5 % of Own Tax Revenue for maintenance of assets (ii) 3.5% of Own Tax Revenue as general purpose grant (unconditional) (iii) 10% of plan grants (excluding special component plan and tribal sub-plan) to be distributed as Incentive Fund (in proportion of additional revenue collected by GPs and ULBs).	Maintenance grant based on current cost of replacement. (Details spelt out). General purpose grant based on normative assessment of establishment cost and office expense requirements for District Panchayat and Block Panchayatt. The balance is distributed as Gram Panchayat—78.5% Municipalities—8.5% Corporations—13%	Population of Urban and Rural areas	It may be noted that the general purpose grant is in lieu of assigned taxes, shared taxes and various statutory and non-statutory grants-in-aid.

Contd.

APPENDIX C (*Contd.*)

Name of State	Instrument of Transfer and percentage to be Transferred	Basis of Arriving of the Divisible Pool	Basis and Proportion of Vertical Distribution Between PRIs & ULBs	Remarks
Punjab	4% of net collection of Own Taxes.	Normative projection of income and expenditure and estimating vertical gaps of PRIs and ULBs.	PRIs—67.5% ULBs—32.5% *Inter se* distribution among ULBs: Population (70%), SCs (15%) and shortfall of per capita tax as compared to average per capita tax of all ULBs. Enter share of taxes of GPs' *Inter se* distribution: Population (65%), shortfall of per capita own income as compared to per capita own income of GPs in the state (15%) Population of SCs (15%) population in mountainous areas (5%).	Income includes additional resource mobilization and expenditure includes capital needs and quality of services.
Rajasthan	2.20% of own tax revenue plus 0.05% as incentive for resource mobilization (Total 2.25%)	• Assessment of minimum requirements based on additional responsibilities • Gap to be filled by additional	Population the basis PRIs—76.6% ULBs—23.4%	Incentive scheme of a matching allotment by state for tapping taxes and non-tax sources.

	• 15% of net proceeds from entertainment tax • 1% of net receipts from royalty or mineral in gram panchayat of the districts where these activities are carried on.	revenue efforts • Sharing of royalty on the basis of collection.		District-wise distribution of PRIs: Population (80%), Area (10%), BPL families. (5%), Illiteracy (15%), ULBs: 85% population, 15% for less developed municipalities.
Tamil Nadu	Net own tax revenue. 8% in the first two years (2002–3 and 2003–4), 9% in the next two years (2004–6) and 10% in the last year (2006–7). 5% of central devolution for vertical and horizontal devolution. Horizontal distribution for village panchayats: Population (60%), SC/ST population (10%), agricultural labourers (10%), area (10%) and asset maintenance (10%). Out of 100% global sharing, 13% set apart for reserve, equalization and incentive funds.	Resource gap on the basis of normative assessment of needs for providing minimum basic services.	Population: 50% Needs: 25% (Operative & Maintenance, Capital Debt) Resource Potential: 25%	Quantitative and qualitative aspects of civic needs considered in resource gap estimates. Capital needs also considered. Zero base budgeting recommended. Several measures to ensure fiscal responsibility recommended. 80% Formula based 20% left to discretionary decisions.

CHAPTER 5

Strengthening Panchayati Raj Institutions: Role of Training, Civil Society and Media

MAHI PAL

INTRODUCTION

The 73rd Amendment Act, 1992 (hereafter referred to as the Central Act) was enacted in 1993. This amendment has been a watershed in the history of Indian federalism because it has not only given more powers and functions to the Panchayati Raj Institutions (PRI) but also created adequate space for women and marginalized groups in the federal set-up. The decentralized democracy has been extended to the fifth scheduled areas[1] of states through the provisions of the Panchayat (Extension to the Scheduled Areas) Act, 1996 (hereafter referred to as the Extension Act).

As a result of the implementation of the Central Act, more than 3 million people have been elected as members and chairpersons of different tiers of the PRIs across the country. Of them, more than 1 million are women and about 0.6 million are from the Scheduled Castes and Scheduled Tribes. It is important to mention here that most of the elected representatives are not only first timers but also illiterates who are expected to prepare plans for economic development and social justice and execute the same at their respective levels. Hence, there was a need to sensitize them about the meaning of the plan and its various components/dimensions in order to enable them to perform their assigned task effectively. Besides government institutions, various agencies are involved in the task of capacity building of these people. Exposition of the strengths and weaknesses of the PRIs is also needed to be documented/published for taking up remedial measures by policy makers. In the above context, the role of training, civil society organizations and media is very pertinent in strengthening PRS in the country.

We have by now a decade of experience of the functioning of the PRS in the country. Elections have been held in a number of states for the third time, in some states, the States Finance Commissions have submitted their second report on panchayat finances to their respective governments.

At this juncture, it appears appropriate to analyse the extent of role played by training, civil society organizations and media in strengthening the PRIs during the last decade and to suggest policy interventions for making their role more effective in decentralized governance, planning and development. This paper seeks to deal with these issues.

I. TRAINING

Imparting training means building the capacity of the panchayati raj representatives to perform their roles effectively. Bolger (2000) defines capacity as 'abilities, skills, understandings, attitudes, values, relationships, behaviours, motivations, resources and conditions that enable individuals, organizations, networks/sectors and broader social systems to carry out functions and achieve their development objectives over time'. Here the term 'building' denotes processes of the capacity.

According to CIDA (1996), 'Capacity building is a process by which individuals, groups, institutions, organisations and societies enhance their abilities to identify and meet development challenges in a sustainable manner.'

On the basis of above, it may be said that capacity building is a process of empowerment of people/communities/organizations. Meaningful intervention through capacity building requires interaction of experience-by-doing, access to resources, facilitation, mediation, and training.

As mentioned above, elections to the panchayats in all the states have recruited more than 3 million representatives at various levels of the PRs. Of them, an overwhelming majority are new entrants, particularly from the marginalized sections. Article 243G of the Constitution expects the panchayats to prepare and implement plans for economic development and social justice including the 29 subjects listed in the 11th Schedule of the Constitution. Hence, the role of training is very important. In this context, the then prime minister of India P.V. Narasimha Rao, while inaugurating the first National Conference of Ministers/Secretaries of Panchayats on 3 July 1993, after the enactment of the 73rd Constitutional Amendment Act 1992, said:

> Since a large number of members will be coming from the weaker sections of the society, it will be necessary to give them comprehensive training about their roles, responsibilities and overall philosophy behind these Panchayati Raj Institutions. They have to know the procedures, rules and working of the Government and these local institutions, to effectively discharge the role assigned to them. This training should not be a one time affair and should be conducted at regular intervals for continuous updating of knowledge and skills. States should take stock of the situation and make provisions for training of both officials and non-officials. Ministry of Rural Development has also been working on evolving a comprehensive training programme for the functionaries and will suitably assist the States in their efforts. (Conference of Ministers, 1993: 6)[2]

The subsequent conferences of the ministers, secretaries, consultative committees and *sammelans* have discussed the importance of training in empowering panchayats and their representatives and also worked out some modalities for the same. The then Ministry of Rural Areas and Employment had organized a programme for the training of trainers in three institutes of national eminence.[3] These institutions have trained 326 trainers. These trainers in turn have imparted training to panchayat functionaries at the state, district and sub-district levels.

Keeping in view the fact that institutional training cannot be given to all the PRI representatives and also realizing the potential of the distance education system, the Indira Gandhi National Open University, with the support of the Ministry of Rural Areas and Employment, launched a massive programme of education and training for the elected representatives of PRIs through the distance mode of learning. A multimedia approach comprising preparation of: (a) self-learning print material, (b) audio-visual programmes, and (c) counselling programmes was adopted. For information education and communication activities, the ministry provided funds for the publication of *Panchayat Unnati* to the National Institute of Rural Development.

If we compare pre-73rd Amendment regime with the post-73rd Amendment one, in terms of training and capacity building of Panchayat Raj Functionaries, we find a sea change in the allocation of funds under this head of the Ministry of Rural Development.

Table 5.1 depicts the situation during Seventh and Eighth Plan periods. There was merely Rs. 21.50 crore allocation during Seventh Plan which rose to Rs. 35 crore during Eighth Plan. Along with this, a new scheme named Panchayat Development and Training was also introduced during the Eighth Plan to give impetus to training activities. Further, if this is compared with the Tenth Plan, there is a lot of difference in this regard which is evident from the following figures. There is an allocation of Rs. 150 crore for training during the Tenth Plan which includes Rs. 20.90 crore for state institutes of rural development/extension training centres, Rs. 0.50 crore for other training courses, Rs. 20 crore for panchayat development and training, Rs. 10.60 crore for panchayat awards research, Rs. 2 crore for information technology and Rs. 1 crore for information and communication. Against an allocation of Rs. 19 crore, an amount of Rs. 17.73 crore was spent during 2002–3. The approved outlay under the scheme during 2003–4 onward has been given in Table 5.2.

It may be seen that the allocation under the scheme reduced from Rs. 39 crore during 2003–4 to Rs. 24 crore in the next two years, for reasons beyond comprehension. In fact, the allocation should have been more in view of the grassroots reality that both the institutions and the representatives will be ineffective if there is lack of awareness about PRS. It may be noted here that the data on actual expenditure against the allocation could give the correct picture of the use of allocated funds, but that is not available in

TABLE 5.1: SCHEMES FOR STRENGTHENING TRAINING INFRASTRUCTURE AND THEIR FINANCIAL ALLOCATION AND UTILIZATION DURING SEVENTH FIVE YEAR PLAN AND ALLOCATION DURING EIGHTH PLAN

(*Rs. in crore*)

Name of the Scheme	Seventh Plan Approved Outlay	Actual Expenditure	Percentage Utilized Actual to the total	Eighth Plan Approved Outlay	Percentage Change in the Eighth Plan over Seventh Plan
Establishment/ Strengthening of State/Regional Training Centres	10.00	11.98	119.80	15.00	50.00
Organization of Training Courses/ Seminars	1.50	0.59	39.33	5.00	233.33
Strengthening of Extension Training Centres	10.00	6.15	61.50	10.00	No Change
Panchayat Development and Training	Did not exist	—	—	10.00	N.A.

Sources: Computed from the Seventh Five Year Plan and Eighth Five Year Plan, 1992–7, Planning Commission, Govt. of India. Quoted from Mahi Pal, 'Gap between Availability and Requirement of Training Infrastructure Under Panchayati Raj', *Journal of Rural Development*, April–June 1994.

TABLE 5.2: APPROVED OUTLAY OF TRAINING AND RELATED AREAS FROM 2003–4 TO 2005–6

(*Rs. in crore*)

Year	Approved Outlay
2003–4	39.00
2004–5	24.40
2005–6	24.00

Source: Annual Report (2004–5), Ministry of Rural Development, Government of India.

the annual reports of the ministry. It is heartening, however, to note that the allocation for training has been enhanced manifold during Tenth Plan period.

Now let us see the impact of training on the elected representatives as brought out by the various evaluation studies.

A study of the impact of training on the performance of panchayat functionaries in Madhya Pradesh conducted by the Institute of Social Sciences in 1997 concludes:[4]

> Notwithstanding the deficiencies in content coverage, methodology, etc., the training programme has been widely welcomed by the elected representatives. They want more of it on a continuous basis . . . (it has) brought about a significant change in the style of living, and work among women. The veil[5] is practically off, 'sarpanch-pati'[6] syndrome continues but it will soon fade away. Women have started coming to meetings, though in small number. They do attend training courses, but are often accompanied by their male relatives. . . . Training is bringing women out of the their shell and giving them necessary exposure for meaningful participation in public affairs . . . imparting information and knowledge about development programmes and schemes and this has a highly educative value. Women's exposure to health and education needs will have an immediate as well as a long term effect on social development. Training has brought about general awareness and these are major gains for building a sound system of governance through panchayats. (ISS, Panchayati Raj Training, p. 5)

It is clear from above that there is positive impact of training but the report also pointed out certain deficiencies in terms of the duration of training, attendance, content and coverage of training programmes, methodology of training, availability of infrastructure at training institutes/centres and lack of motivation on the part of the trainers.

In order to make training effective, the report suggested, among others that both officials and non-officials should be trained; training should be a continuous process having both basic training and refresher courses; method of training should be interesting, participatory and it be imparted in decentralized manner; involvement of NGOs is imperative; having at least one institute for every two districts, creating and strengthening the existing infrastructure;

trainers may be selected keeping on the basis of their knowledge, experience, attitude, academic interest, commitment to the PRIs; and there must be proper follow-ups after the training.

Furthermore, during a workshop[7] (ISS and HIRD, 2002) on the subject, the general consensus was that the training imparted to elected representatives of panchayats was useful; after training they came to know more about the main provisions of the 73rd Amendment Act and the powers and responsibilities of the panchayat as given in the Panchayati Raj Act. However, the training did not give them any exposure to the concept and implementation procedures of the plan for economic development and social justice as well as preparation and maintenance of panchayat accounts. As a future line of action, it was suggested by the participants that: co-ordinated efforts are required to avoid overlapping and repetition; group of trainees may be range between 15–20; use of success stories; adoption of trainee-centred approach; evolving proper feed-back; creation of two more training centres, one in the western part and another in the southern part of the state because there are currently only two institutions for imparting training to elected representatives, both of which are situated at Nilokheri. This place is far from the western and the southern parts of the state (Mahi Pal, 2003: 507–9).

Besides, HIRD has organized training for panchayat functionaries on its campus and at the block headquarters. Of the total panchayat functionaries at the apex tier, merely 32 per cent participated. At the intermediate level, the participation rate was 34 per cent and, at the lowest level it was 67 per cent. Four reasons could be attributed for the rather dismal participation rate in the case of some districts in the training camps. One, only one and half years were left for the elections to the next panchayats. These elected representatives might have thought that they would not gain much from the training. Second, elected representatives have affiliations with different political parties and were, therefore, associated with Assembly elections in Rajasthan state. Third, often the members from different political backgrounds used the training course as a forum for highlighting the deficiencies of the chairperson of a particular district, chairpersons and his/her group members stayed away from the training course to avoid confrontation and/or the exposure of their deficiencies as chairpersons or members of the Zilla Parishad (ZP). Fourth, the administrative machinery of the ZP also discouraged the Zilla Parishad functionaries from attending these programmes thinking that awareness building may create problems for them (administration).

The experiences of the trainees have thrown up two more critical reasons: one that training should be a continuous process focusing mainly on conduct of business, powers and functions devolved on the PRIs, micro planning, financial management and social development and, two, initially conducting separate courses for women, which could later be followed by joint courses so as to facilitate the process of their overcoming gender taboos and working alongside their male counterparts.

The Task Force on PRIs constituted by the Planning Commission, Government of India, has evaluated the performance and outlined the perspective and modus of training of PRIs as follows:

> The training programmes conducted for elected representatives of the PRIs have been for a short duration and failed to sensitize them regarding their social responsibilities. They have tended to concentrate more on infrastructure creation and construction-oriented governmental schemes. However, the social concerns of an area such as health, education, sanitation and food security require greater attention. Training programmes, therefore, have to internalize social issues. The periodicity of the training also needs to be increased. Training of PRIs on such a vast scale cannot be handled only at the district level. Training at Panchayat Samities and even mobile training units to provide in-situ training, would have to be created in the Tenth Plan period to take up this enormous task. Similarly, the Government functionaries who have till now been the instruments for implementation of centrally sponsored schemes, have to be sensitized about the need to effectively transfer powers and functions to PRIs. This calls for extensive training programmes. Though a number of training institutions exit in the country for training PRI functionaries, these are clearly inadequate to address the problem. The Central/State Government may direct Ministries /Departments to earmark certain proportion of funds in each scheme for training PRI functionaries as well as the bureaucratic formations dealing with these programmes. (Task Force on PRIs, 2001: 84)

The findings of the study on the Accounting System and Training in Panchayats in Rural Sector conducted by the Institute of Public Auditors of India in the states of Kerala, Madhaya Pradesh, Tripura, Tamil Nadu and Uttar Pradesh are worth recalling in this context (Table 5.3).

This study gave a fairly balanced assessment of the impact of training imparted to the panchayat functionaries and what more is required in this context. In a nutshell, panchayat functionaries are required to be imparted training on formulation of plans, budgets,

TABLE 5.3: FINDINGS OF A STUDY ON THE ACCOUNTING SYSTEM AND TRAINING IN PANCHAYATS

Issues	Findings
Whether staff qualified to keep accounts?	Most of the staff members were not qualified.
Training imparting institutions.	State planning boards and state institutions have been set-up for imparting training in Kerala, Tamil Nadu, Tripura and Uttar Pradesh
Whether training programmes were adequate for maintenance of financial records?	Not adequate. Only 18 per cent of functionaries received some training in Madhya Pradesh. None except the panchayat secretary in Tripura.
Whether elected representatives were aware of their rights and duties?	No.
Whether the meetings of the gram sabha were held as they should be, as per the rules?	Either not held or if held infrequently with lack of people's participation in plan formulation.
Whether useful works were dentified and completed?	Unproductive works and non-durable assets selected by the handful of functionaries and hence the expenditure incurred was not optimized to the society.

finance, accounts and audits. In other words, they should be capacitated to utilize both tied and untied funds of the panchayats they belong to.

The Participatory Research in Asia (PRIA) a Delhi-based NGO, has mobilized villagers for the meetings of the gram sabha and ward sabha[8] in the states. The outcome of the efforts of this organization in the states of Himachal Pradesh and Haryana are worth reporting here. In Himachal Pradesh about 55 per cent women participated in the meetings of the ward sabha. As a consequence, the participation of women and weaker sections has increased in the meetings of the gram sabha.[9] The impact of a similar exercise in the state of Haryana was that: (i) people participated with enthusiasm in the meetings of the gram sabhas; (ii) marginalized sections of society not only participated in these meetings but also raised issues like health, water and sanitation; (iii) strong linkage was established with elected representatives and various subject committees such as Village Education Committee, Parent Teacher Association.[10]

After having worked in the central ministries including the Planning Commission, training and research institutions and panchayats, the author of the present paper holds the considered view that training/capacity building of various stakeholders has to be in the action mode. Merely imparting training in classrooms is not sufficient. In this connection, an external agency, may be an NGO, can initiate the process of training which can cover the holding of meetings of the gram sabha, constitution of various subject/standing committees, proper conduct of meetings and establishing organic link between and among different tiers. In other words, the Panchayat Act has to be implemented practically in the panchayats by activating and involving the various stakeholders.

II. NON-GOVERNMENTAL ORGANIZATIONS/ CIVIL SOCIETY

Panchayats are expected to prepare plans for economic development and social justice at their respective levels. The grassroots reality is that most of the elected representatives are not only illiterate but also hail from the marginalized sections of rural society. Not only this, most of the women elected representatives of the panchayats have been represented by their husbands and other relatives. The problem scaled up so much that in 1997, the Ministry of Rural Areas and Employment issued a letter to the state Secretaries of Panchayati Raj and Rural Development (dated 20 May 1997) stating that:

> . . . it has been brought to our notice by a number of organizations and individuals including Hon'ble Members of Parliament in various forums, that quite often women representatives are not able to carry out their functions effectively and independently, if they are sought to be influenced by members of their family such as their husbands/brothers, etc., who may be accompanying them to attend meetings of Panchayats.[11]

Indeed, excepting some aberrations, there is not much change in the participation of women in local governance. It also appeared from the conclusions drawn at a workshop[12] that due to the stranglehold of the caste structure in rural society there is neither respect for the office of elected representatives nor the simple social values of giving equal regard to fellow human beings. This has resulted in the paradoxical situation where, on the one hand, Panchayati Raj Act provides *de jure* powers to the office of the sarpanches and on the other, *de facto*, they remain bereft of these powers. The bureaucracy, which is expected to work under the guidance and supervision of the elected representatives of the PRIs, is either away from the scene or succumbs to the pressure of village politics and power games. The solution emerging from the workshop was that, in addition to raising the economic status of the Scheduled Castes women representatives, there is an urgent need to simultaneously to sensitize and re-orient the social and administrative systems and to provide intensive training to enable them to perform their role effectively.

The role of the civil society becomes critical in this scenario. During the early phase of the implementation of the 73rd Amendment to the Constitution, not much emphasis was laid on the involvement and participation of the civil society in strengthening the PRIs. It may be mentioned that the M.L. Singhavi Committee which had strongly recommended the implementation of the 73rd Amendment to the Constitution had this to say about the role of the civil society:

> The Committee is of the view that the proposed National Institute of Local self-Government should, in respect of its research and evaluation functions, utilize universities, research bodies and voluntary organizations, such as All India Panchayat Parishad, which should have a consultative nexus with it and which would be an invaluable resource for dissemination of information as well as for proper motivation. (Committee for the Concept Paper, p. 13)

But the All India Panchayat Parishad[13] has not done much constructive work in this regard because it has itself been unable to sort out its internal problems.

However, some civil society organizations have played an effective role in strengthening grassroots democracy. For instance, the Kerala Shastra Sahitya Parishad, which has played a crucial role in strengthening PRIs in Kerala, is a household name in this context. Besides organizing training camps on various issues of decentralized governance, planning and development, the Parishad has published a dozen of handbooks like *Guides to Panchayat Development*, collection of secondary data, local history. It has also developed an innovative approach to agricultural development, soil and water management, and environmental cleanliness. 'It was these activities, both human resources and the study materials, that acted as the spring board to the people's planning campaign' (Parameswaran, p. 13). Besides, state-wide Voluntary Technical Corps (VTC), comprising 8,000–10,000 technically experienced persons recruited to examine and vet the projects prepared by the panchayats, has been set up. These VTCs have examined between 1 and 1.5 lakh projects prepared by the panchayats for implementation during the Ninth Plan period (Varghese, 1997). Similarly, various registered organizations have played their role in capacity building of the panchayati raj functionaries.

It must, however, be mentioned in the context of the role of civil society in strengthening PRIs that community-based organizations, exceptions apart, have not played any remarkable role largely because of the lack of concensus amongst the functionaries of these organizations. This is also true of a large number of NGOs. The mid-term appraisal of the Ninth Plan referred to a case of Andhra Pradesh in this way:

> A respondent from RDT, an NGO in Andhra Pradesh, commented that there are a few villages in which the committees have the capacity to become partners of the government for development. But 60 per cent of the institutions are not democratically elected. (MTA, p. 186)

Another important issue pertains to the respectability of the PRIs themselves in the eyes of the villagers. In this connection, the mid-term appraisal of the Ninth Plan has this to say:

> . . . the Panchayat is not seen as a very valuable organisation by villagers; the main reason is perceived lack of individual benefits, also lack of transparency and lack of influence and a high presence of corruption. People place much higher value on other development activities which bring a larger number of individual benefits and are more transparent. . . . The savings group has a purpose. All women meet to deposit money and to decide on who can take loans. We will get benefits. There is no work for the individual in the Panchayat, and especially not for women. What will we gain from participating there? Whether we go or not does not make a difference. (MTA, p. 187)

In such a situation, there is a big challenge before the civil society to create an environment where everybody in the village sees a future in participating in the decentralized democratic channels opened by the 73rd Amendment Act through the PRIs. For this purpose, the following suggestions are relevant:

There are umpteen associations and organizations in the forms of mahila mandals, youth clubs, parent–teachers associations, self-help groups (SHG),[14] farmers' clubs, health committees, education committees, etc., which have been created by the state and constitute the components of civil society organizations. But these are mostly lying inactive. Activating these institutions for strengthening the PRIs is strategically most critical. In this connection, experiences of the Empowerment and Sustainable Development Initiative, an NGO facilitating the process of organization of meetings of gram sabhas, show that women who were members of the SHGs did participate in the meetings of gram sabha. In other words, CBOs that have been formed through a proper social mobilization process have the potential to make PRIs vibrant and pulsating institutions.

Table 5.4 shows the participation of women who were members of SHGs, mahila mandals and others in the meetings of the gram sabha.

It may be seen from Table 5.4 that in village Butana, almost 56 per cent of participators were women. It was more than 80 per cent in Bairsal village. These could be due to the initiative of the SHGs and, in turn the initiative that these SHGs members may takan along with them other women of the village, because women felt comfortable to attend meetings in groups.

Secondly, there is need to promote social capital[15] formation by forming and nurturing SHGs and networking these associations. Our experiences show that with some exception (for example, Kerala) the stock of social capital in India is very low and whatever is available is lying latent. In fact, social capital is an asset that remains dormant until agencies activate and use it to generate a flow of benefits to the people. Hence, the more capable NGOs should work towards activating various components of the social capital for not only strengthening PRIs but also for activating the

TABLE 5.4: EXTENT OF PARTICIPATION OF WOMEN IN THE MEETINGS OF THE GRAM SABHAS

Name of Gram Panchayat	Date of Meeting	Participation			
		Male	Female	Total	%age of women participation to total
Raipur Roran	2 May 2004	35	30	65	46
Poojam	2 May 2004	15	25	40	63
Butana	4 May 2004	20	25	45	56
Arjaheri	7 May 2004	15	25	40	63
Bairsal	14 June 2004	5	30	35	86
Sandhir	15 June 2004	30	35	65	54

Source: 'Gram Sabhas Put Social Development Agenda before Gram Panchayats', ESDI, 2004.

idle physical and financial capitals in rural areas. Seeing the significance of social capital, the Tenth Plan document in its chapter, 'Poverty Alleviation in Rural India—Strategy and Programmes', observed that: 'The promotion of a movement which enhances social capital and forges linkages with other formal and informal stakeholders engaged in developmental activities would be a major thrust during the Plan.'

It may further be mentioned that, after the implementation of the 73rd Amendment Act, there is at least one elected representative in every street of every village across the country. The NGO sector has a big challenge before it because if this sector does not have good rapport with the panchayats or if the latter do not appreciate the work of the voluntary sector, the elected head of the panchayat may take the view that another head of the panchayat is meddling with his/her work. As the work of the panchayats is expected to increase in the years to come and the role of the voluntary sector is also expected to increase keeping in view the circumstances which are already established or are emerging. In this situation, panchayats must be motivated to consider the voluntary sector as facilitators and not as interferers in their sphere. In fact, the sector should be both motivated and mature enough to harness full benefits of the environment which has been created by the government at the local level for the local people.

In view of this, a long-term strategy for investment in their capacity-building is needed. Indeed, expertise of a different kind is required, strategies of a different nature need to be designed, personnel with different attitudes and orientation need to be mobilized to tackle the problems of the panchayats. In the context of the role of voluntary sector in the future, what the then prime minister said about national development while addressing a conference on this sector in 2002 is worth recalling here:

> I would like to liken nation-building to a chariot that is driven by five horses. These are: the central Government; the State Governments; Panchayati Raj Institutions; the private sector; and, last but not the least, voluntary organisations and community-based groups. The chariot will run fast and in the right direction only when all the five horses run in tandem. (All India Conference on Voluntary Sector, p. 24)

What the Task Force on PRIs said while outlining the possible role of the NGOs and PRIs is worth quoting here:

> The NGO-PRI relationship should not be adversarial, but complementary. NGO-PRI relationship would have to be based upon one basic premise that neither NGOs nor the PRIs should consider the other as contenders to their respective position. Primacy of the panchayats, as a distinct tier in the representative system of governance has to be accepted by the NGOs. Similarly, the superiority of the NGOs in terms of access to knowledge, latest technological advancements as well as their capacity to deliver has to be appreciated by the PRIs (Task Force, 2001: 77)

In short, there is an imperative need for adopting collective and collaborative approach by the civil society organizations for strengthening PRIs.

III. MEDIA

Media, signifying information, education and communication (IEC), has a very crucial role to play in mobilizing people for the development process at the micro, meso and macro levels. This role assumes greater relevance when we note that huge amounts of funds are now routed to and through these institutions. For example, the approved outlay for the Ministry of Rural Development for the year 2005–6 was Rs. 24,480 crore, mostly to be spent through the PRIs.

Seeing the relevance of media in rural development and empowering PRIs, the Ministry of Rural Development has taken up various IEC activities through the print and electronic media and through outdoor publicity. The purpose of these activities is to create awareness amongst the target groups of the programmes of the ministry and mobilizing them towards participatory development, to sensitize opinion makers and urban elites about the issues relating to rural development and to create awareness amongst the general public. The allocation under the IEC was also doubled to Rs. 20 crore during 2004–5, from Rs. 10 crore during 2002–3.[16]

In spite of these developments, there is a lot more to be done by the media in the context of PRIs and other governmental schemes so as to bring about social change in the rural areas. The media covers the PRIs without any positive/analytical/inferential and indicative context. Generally, newspapers report that such and such thing happened in a particular gram panchayat or PR institution. This sort of reporting has no relevance unless the event is analysed in its retrospecting and prospecting dimensions. In fact, the realities of PRI happenings need to be reported in the following way:

1. The extent to which the provisions of the 73rd Amendment Act resemble with grassroot realities across the states.
2. Impact assessment of the PRIs in effective implementation of various programmes with villagers' participation, particularly the marginalized sections, in both the short-term and the long-terms perspectives.
3. Identification of the forces which are responsible for strengthening and weakening the PRIs in the country and specific states.

In the context of the role of the media in society, senior associate editor of the *Tribune* pointed out that 'the media (is) deviating from its role of social responsibility . . . publishing newspapers or periodicals was to highlight the real issues concerning the masses so as to exert pressure on the rulers or the policy framers to make policies to suit the needs of the people.'[17] In fact, it would not be an exaggeration to say that a large section of the media persons are virtually illiterate about the PRIs and their relevance and role in rural development and thereby in the nation's governance and ultimate well-being.

The solution to this problems lies in imparting proper training to the media persons about the various facets of decentralized governance, planning and development. In fact, the media needs to be sensitized and motivated to write on issues which concern panchayats, their self-governance status, election process, and so on, in a villager-friendly language. As a part of the training of the media persons, the model of China's Peasants' Dailies is worth emulating in the context of sensitizing media people in India. To quote a perceptive observer:

. . . as a rule, every reporter and editor must spend at least two months in the countryside every year, during which time they are expected to familiarize themselves with the local peasants, their aspirations and difficulties. The paper engages 300 peasants as regular stringers and about 700 as irregular correspondents. The paper chooses the most typical letters for publication while referring the rest to relevant organisations. Very often, investigation groups are sent to the countryside if the letters touch upon matters of significance. (Gupta, 1989: 22).

The civil society organizations can play an important role in making the media aware about the grassroots realities by organizing visits to rural areas, holding press conferences on issues of rural local governments and circulation of press notes and write-ups.[18]

There are more than three million elected representatives of panchayats across the country at the village, block and district levels. Some of them may be given an opportunity and trained as per the methodology of the Peasants' Dailies of China. Folk media may also be used to make villagers aware about PRIs and their role in rural development. The experience of using folk media for the stated purpose is worth quoting:

Most of them were very impressed. They told that using folk media would definitely help in bringing about a positive change in the attitude of the rural masses towards the role of Gram Sabha and inspire people to participate in its meetings. The women—most of whom were illiterate—enjoyed the show very much. They said that lectures and discussions became boring after some time, but programmes like this could be watched for hours. (Panwar, 2003: 5)

Evidently, and understandably, traditional media has an edge over modern media because of the former's localized nature, personal touch, familiarity of the audience, economy, and so on.

CONCLUSION

To conclude, training, civil society organizations and the media have very crucial roles to play in strengthening PRIs in India. But among the three, civil society organizations have relatively greater responsibility in terms of building capacity of elected representatives. Media personnel have roles to perform too, positively and constructively. As for training, it should not only be imparted to the elected representatives of the PRIs, but also to the members of the gram sabha, as well as members of various subject/standing committees constituted at different levels of the PRIs. The training should be in pre-, during and post-election modes of these bodies. Issues of gender equity and social justice, social audit, mobilization and management of financial resources should be focused on in these training courses. The courses should be designed and operationalized in the action mode. The training institutions should also be strengthened in terms of software (faculty position) and hardware (infrastructure). As indicated in the discussion, the capacity of the local-level NGOs and CBOs has also to be enhanced by those NGOs which have considerable on-ground experience about the functioning of the PRIs. Media personnel should also be trained in the various facets of PRS to enable them to analyse the functioning of the panchayats in the right perspective instead of merely reporting or exposing the good and bad happenings in the process of discharging their responsibilities as people's organizations. In short, an integrated approach combining the efforts of the civil society organizations and the media is required. In this process, the state has also a very critical, rather catalytic, role to play in activating and facilitating the process of strengthening panchayats with the help of these institutions.

NOTES

1. Those areas of states dominated by Scheduled Tribes.
2. This conference had come out with fifteen recommendations for promoting panchayati raj in the country and one of these was related to training, which read as: 'It is necessary to impart adequate training to all functionaries involved in the Panchayati Raj System at every level. In order to do this, the existing Panchayati Raj Training Centres at different levels require to be revitalized and strengthened in their capacities. A comprehensive calendar of training programmes to impart training to all important functionaries should be formulated from 1993–4 onwards' (Conference of Ministers, 1993: 51).
3. These institutions are: National Institute of Rural Development, Hyderabad, Lal Bahadur Shastri National Academy of Administration, Musoorie, and the Indian Institute of Public Administration, Delhi.

4. The Institute of Social Sciences, New Delhi, conducted an evaluation of the training programme for the panchayats functionaries in Madhya Pradesh in 1997 with the purpose of ascertaining the nature and quality of training being imparted, to locate gaps, if any, and to suggest measures to strengthen the programme and plan for the future. To meet the objectives of the evaluation, twelve training institutions and 306 functionaries (247 elected representatives and 59 others) were interviewed.
5. The women representatives of panchayats use the veil (*ghunghat*) because as per rural custom and traditions they are not allowed to interact with their husband's elder brothers, father-in-laws and villagers publically.
6. Husband of the village council president.
7. As a part of the process of evaluating the impact of training on capacity-building of panchayat leaders, a one-day workshop was organized by the Institute of Social Sciences in collaboration with the Haryana Institute of Rural Development (HIRD) at Nilokheri on 3 December 2002. The workshop was a platform to share experiences of elected representatives of all tiers of the panchayats as well as of those who acted as trainers for such trainings.
8. The gram sabha consists of all voters of the gram panchayat and it is held at gram panchayat level whereas ward sabha consists of voters of a constituency of the gram panchayat and is held at the constituency level.
9. PRIA District Resource Centre, Kangra, in collaboration with five voluntary organizations carried out this mobilization process from February to March 2003 with the help of a local resident of the panchayat who acted as a citizen leader and was designated as a panchayat mitra (village council friend). This campaign was carried out in 60 gram panchayats. As many as 3,855 women and 3,200 men participated in these meetings.
10. Between November 2005 and December 2005, PRIA carried out this mobilization campaign with the help of a network of local volunteers in 150 gram panchayats in 8 districts comprising Karnal, Jind, Kaithal, Ambala, Panchkula, Sonepat, Panipat, and Jhajjhar. Similar processes were also carried out by this organization in Mahendragarh and Fatehabad districts of Haryana.
11. A Member of Parliament has suggested during the meeting of the Consultative Committee on Parliament attached to the Ministry of Human Resource Development, that women representatives attending the meetings of the gram panchayats along with their husbands served to diminish their own role and status. The state governments were therefore requested to take necessary steps, including this one, and issue guidelines to the panchayats at all levels to ensure that the women members of PRIs were not reduced to figure heads or proxies.

12. Recently, HIRD organized a workshop of SC elected representatives of panchayats for understanding the problems being faced by them in carrying out their public/official duties and for eliciting suggestions from them as to what sort of support system is required for their effective functioning.
13. All India Panchayat Parisad is a national-level organization of the PRIs. Its main purpose is to further the interests of the panchayats.
14. Self-help group is a group of 10-20 members. Only one member from a family is eligible for membership of the group. The members of the group take decisions democratically for their various activities.
15. Contemporary literature discusses two related but different takes on social capital. The first one is related to sociologist Ronald Burt, Nan Lin, and Alejandro Portes and the second one is related to political scientist Robert Putnam. The sociologists refer to it as resources such as information, ideas, support that individuals can get by virtue of their relationships with other people, as social capital. These resources or capital are social and are only accessible through relations unlike physical capital in the form of tools and technology or human capital in the form of education and skill, which are essentially the property of individuals. The structure of the given network (who interacts with whom, how frequently, and on what terms) determines the flow of resources through that network. Those who occupy key strategic positions in the network are said to have access to more social capital than the others. The political scientist approach to social capital refers to the nature and extent of one's involvement in various informal networks and formal civic organizations. According to this approach, engagement and interaction of individuals determine the extent of social capital. A range of social and economic problems are linked to the endowment of social capital. Scholars have recognized that social capital is multi-dimensional in nature.
16. During 2003–4, the Ministry instituted thirteen Pandit Deen Dayal Upadhyaya Fellowships for Journalism in Rural Development with the view to building up a core group of journalists who will specialize in social sector issues, bring out the imbalances noticed in the media coverage of rural development issues, and encourage the media to bring about requisite social mobilization for rural development and facilitate people's participation in the development process through the PRIs.
17. Haryana Institute of Rural Development organized a workshop 'Role of Media in Rural Development' in which personnel from different streams of the media participated. Addressing this workshop, A.J. Philip, Senior Associate Editor of the *Tribune* exhorted the media to highlight the real issues concerning the vast population of a nation living mostly in rural areas instead of trivializing the news to entertain readers or viewers.

18. The Participatory Research in Asia (PRIA) has promoted partnerships with media at the state and national levels by organizing exposure visits for media persons to intensive areas of intervention with the purpose of providing the latter a first-hand experience of rural local self-governance institutions.

REFERENCES

Annual Report 2003–4, Ministry of Rural Development, Government of India, 'Panchayati Raj Training in Madhya Pradesh: An Evaluation', Institute of Social Sciences, 1998, p. 148.

Annual Report 2004–5, Ministry of Rural Development, Government of India.

Bolger, J., 'Capacity Development: Why, What and How', Canadian International Development Agency, Policy Branch, vol. 1, no. 1, May 2001.

CIDA: 'Capacity Development: The Concept and Its Implementation in the CIDA Context', Canadian International Development Agency, 1996.

Conference of Ministers/Secretaries in-Charge of Panchayats, Proceedings and Papers, Ministry of Rural Development, Government of India, 3 July 1993, pp. 74.

'Gram Sabhas Put the Agenda of Social Development Before the Gram Panchayats', report of the outcome of the meetings of gram sabhas organized by the Empowerment and Sustainable Development Initiative during 2004.

Gupta, V.S., *Rural Press: Problems and Prospects,* New Delhi: Press Institute of India, 1989, p. 78.

Mahi Pal, 'Gap Between Availability and Requirement of Training Infrastructure Under Panchayati Raj', *Journal of Rural Development,* April–June 1994, vol. 13, no. 2, pp. 159–79.

———, 'Haryana: Capacity Building of Panchayats: Task Ahead', *Economic and Political Weekly,* vol. 38, no. 6, 8–14 February 2003, pp. 507–10.

'Mid-term Appraisal of the Ninth Plan', Planning Commission, Government of India, October 2000.

Panwar, Manju, 'Using Folk Media for Panchayati Raj', *Panchayati Raj Update,* New Delhi: Institute of Social Sciences, 2003, p. 5.

Parameswaran, M.P., 'Role of Kerala Sastra Sahitya Parishad in the Movement for Democratic Decentralisation', paper presented in the International Conference on Democratic Decentalisation, 23–7 May 2000, Thiruvananthapuram.

'Proceedings: All India Conference on the Role of the Voluntary Sector in

National Development', held on 20 April 2002, Planning Commission, Government of India.

Report of the Committee for the Concept Paper on Panchayati Raj Institutions, Department of Rural Development, 1986, p. 22.

Report of the Task Force on Panchayati Raj Institutions, Planning Commission, Government of India, 2001, p. 133.

Varghese, A.V., 'Volunteers to Help People's Planning', *Deccan Herald*, 20 May 1997.

CHAPTER 6

The Decentralization Mechanism in France: An Overview

LUCY BAUGNET

Although the founding principle of the French Republic as enshrined in its Constitution has the State as the only custodian of political power, over the last twenty years or so, France has witnessed a relatively discreet transformation—decentralization. The process consists of transfer of power from the State to specific institutions: 'collectivités territoriales' or local bodies that thenceforth avail of a certain autonomy in decision-making and in making their own budget (principle of administrative freedom) under the surveillance of a State representative (the regulatory institution), which controls its legality. Therefore, the term 'collectivités territoriales' refers to 'local bodies' as administrative structures distinct from those of the State—mainly 'Communes' (Municipalities), 'Departments' and 'Regions', which, apart from their specific powers, also enjoy decision-making powers relating to themselves and a legal personality that enables them to appear in judicial proceedings.

Since the first decentralization laws were instituted in 1982–3, various local entities have been called upon to make use of their powers in matters falling under their jurisdiction with relative autonomy.[1] The principle of freedom of administration of local bodies by councils composed of elected representatives grants them regulatory rights to make use of their specific powers, as laid down by the Constitution (and confirmed by the constitutional amendment of 28 March 2003), while maintaining the concept of a unitary State.

The explicit objective of this transfer of power is to promote the adoption of responses better adapted to local conditions, characterized by their diversity and specificity.

Thus, one of the expected consequences of this move towards decentralization is increased democracy. In other words, the transfer of new powers to locally elected representatives should lead to responses that are closer to the citizens, in the sense that their expectations and needs can be better taken into account. The aim is, therefore, to strengthen local bodies and by doing so, take the democratic process towards greater effectiveness and adequacy of representation.

The relevance of the project lies within a much broader process concerning European countries, and more generally, one which is being taken up as a strategy in the face of globalization, economic globalization, in particular (in the sense of the integration and reorganization of production systems).

The secondary objective would be to expect local democracy—strengthened in this way—to encourage the management of tensions between two different dimensions: the local dimension, on the one hand, with its heritage and customs, rooted in an actual if not real specificity, transmitted over the years, and on the other hand, the global dimension, with its emerging culture, its new practices of mobility, instant communication and networking. The idea is that networks or systems can be supported by local resources, while the systems feed them in turn. In other words, the aim would be to favour a certain regulation between different levels and thereby take part in the redefinition of social links and citizenship in general. Faced with globalization, which is affecting all levels, local bodies are being presented as theoretically appropriate responses. In other words, the establishment of empowered territories or jurisdictions which are no longer conceived as abstract entities more or less arbitrarily carved out for the purpose of administrative management, but rather designed as effective and responsive organic entities in which the local dynamic stands out since it favoures its own interests and values, *would open* a new way supposedly far from any form of tribalism or notability.

In fact, the conception of territory as reflected in the decentralization process in France is far removed from the various objectives of 'territorialization' that came before it, though without doing away with them. These were added-on during the process of territorialization of the French State. The first objective, administrative in nature, is deeply entrenched since the 1791 Constituent Assembly. It certified the principles of Republican equality and local body autonomy and affirmed its controlling and regulatory functions. The second objective—both statistical and electoral—divided territories into strata of different sizes and types with their own methods of functioning with regard to elections. A third one—financial, proceeded with the task of sectoral zoning with different priority levels. A fourth one, also for the purposes of administration, divided French territory into regions and areas more or less arbitrarily. Some of the regions were relatively coherent and well-built historically, while others were more like an artificial assembly not based on any well-affirmed regional identities.

Decentralization for the benefit of local bodies not only tended to promote administrative deconcentration but also granted the local bodies powers that gradually clarified and favoured the revitalization of citizenship practices and involved the concomitant reconciliation of territorial management, participatory democracy and socio-economic forces.

The new division of powers related to specific skills and abilities between the State and the different levels of local bodies has undoubtedly had to face rough patches and irregularities in its implementation. The multiplication of power structures and the complexity of procedures treated their own problem. The mechanism set up for dividing and granting powers to the various bodies called for many adjustments. This lead on the one hand, to overlaps in power and the need for interactions and, therefore, for principles to govern such interactions, both between different levels (for instance, the principle of subsidiarity) and at the same level (horizontal federal bodies).

We shall now present the various phases of the process to show how the mechanism developed and grew gradually in order to promote the achievement of these objectives. The last part of this paper will question the implementation process, arguing that instituting a process does not amount to creating new practice.

THE STAGES

The process took place in different stages, briefly summarized below:

Regions were creaed in 1982,[2] with executive powers vested in the President of the Regional Council and not in the person of the prefect, who remained the representative of the State. The creation vested the Regions with a status comparable to that of the Communes with their mayor, and to that of the Departments, with the President of the General Council. This allows an 'organic' independence *vis-à-vis* central authority, thereby creating establishing in France three levels of local structures. Members of the local deliberating assemblies are elected by direct universal franchise.

The years between 1983 and 1986 witnessed the first transfer of powers[3] to the Regions: economic planning, common services, construction and maintenance of schools. The Departments were to look after social welfere and education colleges. The Communes were to be responsible for administration of closeness and urban development.

Adequate decision-making powers and resources were guaranteed through financial autonomy and autonomy in recruitment and personnel management.[4] The Constitutional Council also drew certain important limits. For instance, the implementation of a law affecting the exercise of public liberty could not fall under a local body and had to apply equally within the State's entire territory. The State decided the obligatory expenditure that the local bodies had to undertake and also determined the resources of the local bodies, with the understanding that no transfer of powers could take place from the State to local bodies without the corresponding resources. External budget control fell under the Regional Chambers of Accounts (CRC or 'Chambres Régionales des Comptes').

Different levels of local bodies did not all enjoy the same status or functions, nor did they have the same operating rules.

The process of decentralization seemed to have slowed down in the years 1986–92, without compromising the progress achieved so far.[5] But it took off once again with the promotion of local democracy and 'Intercommunalité' (Intercommunality): granting citizens the right to information, participation in local political decision-making,[6] and granting rights to elected representatives in the minority in General and Regional Councils in order to improve the adequacy of representation of local assemblies.[7]

In 1992, the law on 'Intercommunality'[8] promoted the development of cooperation between Communes: Communities of 'Communes',[9] advisory boards (associations, elected representatives and minorities).

A 1995 Pasqua Law introduced the notion of local areas or 'Pays', as well as the notion of territorial development plans for better local coherence and coordination. The Voynet Law[10] pursued the same objective and officially established 'Pays' as a project area for the development of the entire country. 'Pays', were created based on common heritage, since this made local identification possible and promoted an ontological security in a context characterized by loss of political and social reference points. Subsequently nine collective specialist service plans were drawn up. The delegation for territorial planning and regional action *Délégation à l'Aménagement du Territoire et à l'Action Régionale*, or DATAR) established 42 'Pays' (specific groupings of approximately 66,000 inhabitants). The 1999 Voynet Law's objective was to coordinate local initiatives, increase the effectiveness of public services and promote sustainable development.

A redefinition of the notion of 'Pays' as a coherent entity from the geographic, economic, social and cultural point of view could only be based on the agreement of all the local actors involved: Municipalities, inter-Commune bodies and the General Council. The objective was not to short-circuit existing authorities, but to involve them and promote the appropriation of the decentralization process by the people. In the experimental phase, it gave birth to a series of 'Test Local Areas' ('Pays tests'). Long-term planning on the basis of nine thematic public service plans (higher education, transportation, culture, energy, information, communications, natural and rural spaces, sports and health services) was aimed at building consistency *vis-à-vis* the plans drawn up by each region with regard to major facilities and services in the public interest.

The 1999 Chevènement Act clarified the modalities for inter-commune cooperation by proposing three types of 'Intercommunalité' (Intercommunality), each with its own specific dimensions and activities:

- 'Association of Communes' (with a minimum of 5,00,000 inhabitants), acting in the field of social and economic development, environmental design, city policies and management of public services;
- 'Conglomeration of Communes' (with a minimum of 50,000 inhabitants) for economic development, space and habitat layouts, city policies and three other fields to be selected from a list that includes, in particular, water purification and sanitation, sports facilities and the environment;
- 'Communities of Communes' (smaller in size), for economic development, cultural or sports facilities and school facilities.

In 2000, the SRU Act specified that townships (agglomerations) were at the heart of urban development and sustainable development policies. Public housing had to be better distributed and rail transportation had to be 'regionalized' in compliance with the SCOT ('Schéma de développement territorial' or territorial development plan). At present, the regions are entirely responsible for rail transportation (Euros 1.5 billion budget transfer).

The 27 February 2002 Act on 'Democracy of Proximity'[11] aimed at strengthening citizens' participation and proposed a fresh transfer of powers, in particular to the regions.

The 28 March 2003 constitutional amendment has given the implementation of the decentralization process a fresh impetus: 'l'organisation de la République est décentralisée' or 'the Republic's organizational structure is decentralized' (Art. 1). The amendment:

- Raises the constitutional status of Regions to that of local bodies (Art. 72)
- Lays down the principle of financial autonomy of local bodies (Art. 72–2)
- Proclaims the right of local bodies to experiment (Art. 72)
- Institutes local decision-making referendums and the right of petition for voters (Art. 72–1).

The 13 August 2004 Act on local liberties and responsibilities provides for several transfers of power.

THE IMPACT

Several questions still remain to be answered today:

1. *Have French citizens understood and assimilated this top-down decentralization process instituted by legislative mechanisms?*

This issue refers to the assertion that society cannot be changed by decrees (Bourdieu) and fundamentally calls for an intensive work on the conditions of its efficacy. Undoubtedly, transformations occur over a period of time, and they require a communication policy adapted to the needs of the public. However, the question is still open as to in what ways the measures taken facilitate give way to social representations by different target groups and whether they are able to fulfil expectations. More fundamentally, can the expected coherence of these actions be conceived without constructing spaces that are psychologically, socially and politically relevant? Only under such circumstances can the mobilization of these measures by local actors for 'common good', the desired local democratization, and the articulation between these different competences and different levels of application be achieved.

It must be understood that within France's centralized framework, the aim is not to promote the creation of 'imaginary communities', but rather to take into account the existing practices and representations in their anchoring process that more or less intensely punctuate, validate and legitimize the project's establishment. Let us take Anderson's counter-example of the nation as an imaginary community (1996). According to him, nationalism is born at the very instant that powerful world-level forces and different factors meet (1996: 19). There is no doubt that, *mutatis mutandis*, the creation of local bodies—Communes, Departments and Regions—can be explained, as we have mentioned earlier, through a broader context in which different types of logic come into play. However, contrary to the nation, they are far from being 'imaginary and imagined political communities that are intrinsically limited and sovereign' ('communautés politiques imaginaires et imaginées, intrinsèquement limitées et souveraines', Anderson, 1996: 19). While the nation State in France may be presented as the 'archetype centralized organization' ('l'archétype de l'organization centralisée', see Olivier Giraud's contribution to this collection), accompanied by a colourful imaginative world bolstered by historical constructions and reconstructions conveyed through language and images all through the socialization and enculturation process, this task is far from having been done for territorial entities. As we have mentioned earlier, although some Regions have a foundation based on traditions and are accompanied by a strong feeling of regional identity, several of them have been carved out on the basis of apparently more arbitrary criteria, without the feeling of belonging or collective awareness. Nor is it clear that those Regions that have been historically constructed as entities with a strong sense of identity are the ones where the process of participation in political and economic decisions is most noteworthy, nor do they prove to be the most suitable to develop relevant strategies in the context of globalization. The objective is not so much to promote micro-nationalisms or develop forms of communitarianism, but to be able to incorporate everything that goes into the social bond in the process. Social links in practice generate peculiar common social representations as forms of social thoughts that assume the feeling of belongingness to the same decision-making psychosocial space. In other words, implementing decentralization in France through local democracy enterprises means that its components—endowed with civil powers and responsibilities, more autonomous in their choice and imbued with the desire of coming closer to individuals—have to make sense for the individuals concerned. That is a prerequisite for their appropriation and for citizens' participation.

Moreover, within the framework of the new provisions, the decentralization process is not strengthening the units to which the French are most attached, i.e. the Communes (see the barometric surveys conducted by the 'Observatoire Régional du Politique OIP', or Regional Political Observatory). Indeed, they would probably be more disturbed or at least more confused by the creation of urban communities (see the contributions of François Rangeon and Nathalie Sanson in this collection).

As a paradox, while the process of decentralization is still appearing to many ordinary people as an abstract, distant and complex concept—quite expected in a top-down institutionnal implementation process—various forms of bottom-up participative democraty do exist in France. The associative world is widely spread and applies to infinite objects such as consuming, environment protection, neighbourhood comities, and so on. To provide them a meeting point in the frame of the decentralization process would reinforce the political dimension of local democracy, as it has been viewed by some political leaders as a stake for presidential elections.[12]

Local democratization also means that everyone has to make greater use of their skills and take on greater responsibilities, along with developing stronger links. In other words, attachment to one's region is not an indispensable requirement for a feeling of identification with decentralization; networks at micro levels can be articulated to institutional process if not institutionalizing them.

There is no doubt that the efforts made by the Regions in the field of institutional and political communications for the public and for the business community do take the desire for greater visibility and noteworthiness into account, but the image-building policy seems to be pursuing more general objectives. Rather than a 'top-down' strategy and a mechanism for a closer monitoring of the expectations and needs of different actors and citizens, and greater attention to economic, political and cultural community networks would undoubtedly enhance participation in this mechanism.

2. *In that case, what is the impact of decentralization on French politics?*

Decentralization has certainly had an impact on French politics, and France's political classes undoubtedly believe that major stakes are involved in the process (see the contributions by François Rangeon and Nathalie Sanson in this work). The scenario has undoubtedly changed for France's political actors, but has the democratization of power at the local level really taken place as was expected? A political answer could be found for the question of how this mechanism promotes local democracy, but the answer is necessarily incomplete. In fact, decentralization does set out to revitalize public action (see Catherine Agulhon's contribution in this collection). It's logic is both one of civic involvement, contractualization and rationalization in order to serve the market, without being reduced to it. All these characteristics together are expressed in the notion of concerted action, in accordance with the principle of governance, and has shown concrete results, in particular in the fields of education, vocational training and the environment (see the contributions by Catherine Agulhon and Florence Jamay in this collection). On the one hand, the attribution of specific powers to different levels of decentralization and, on the other hand, its counterpart, i.e. contractualization, can lead to certain discrepancies due to the heterogeneity of sometimes rival initiatives, calling for regulations whose legitimacy still remains to be established. Continued State control on the one hand and the strengthening of citizens' contrôl on the other hand can potentially guarantee the effectiveness of the decentralization process (see Florence Jamay's contribution in this collection).

It is very clear, therefore, that the notion of governance as the ability to govern oneself through institutions—one of the underlying principles of decentralization—and as the contractualization of public action leads one to question the notion of 'public interest' or 'common good' itself, whereas it is the nodal point of the democratic process.

The different texts presented in this work broach diverse dimensions of the decentralization process in France and its implications for local democracy.

NOTES

1. Thus, in the educational field, the Department—not the national Ministry of Education—would decide and supervise the construction or restoration of the necessary colleges within its jurisdiction. It could even take over their ownership, with the 13 August 2004 Act on local rights and responsibilities.
2. There are twenty-two regions in Metropolitan France and four regions in Overseas Territories (TOM—'Territoires d'Outre-Mer'). During the 28 March 2003 Constitutional Amendment, Regions and Overseas Territories were 'raised' to the rank of local bodies, and were enshrined in the text of the Constitution itself.

3. 7 January 1983 and 22 July 1983 Acts.
4. As of 1984, the five-year plan contracts between the state and the regions in which the other local bodies also took part started being drawn up and marked the beginning of territorial civil service (26 January 1984 Act).
5. The 13 July 1987 Act strengthened local executive bodies by augmenting their nomination powers.
6. 6 February 1992 Act.
7. 19 January 1999 Act, amended by the 11 April 2003 Act.
8. The 6 February 1992 Act. This Act promotes the development of several links between municipalities or 'communes' (called 'Intercommunalité' or Intercommunality). The 12 July 1999 Act, called the 'Chevènement Law', is aimed at strengthening and simplifying this cooperation.
9. The number of 'intercommunality associations' in France rose to 894 in 1996.
10. 25 June 1999 Act.
11. 27 February 2002 Act.
12. We are referring to the notion of 'participative democracy' which has been the core of Ségolène Royal's campaign. She was the President of the Poitou-Charentes Region and the socialist candidate in the 2007 presidential elections.

CHAPTER 7

Decentralization in France and India: A Comparison[*]

OLIVIER GIRAUD

This paper is a comparative study of the paths to decentralization taken by two very different countries—France and India. It calls for an explanation of the methodology applied for the comparison of two extremely different cases, an in-depth reflection on the decentralization phenomenon itself, as well as observation of the two different styles of decentralization adopted by these two countries. This reflection on the whole leads to a renewed questioning of the notion of decentralization itself as presented in comparative literature, which often compares Western countries only.

Among other mechanisms, globalization leads to a drastic increase in interdependences (economic, social, environmental, health, security) between countries, as well as a growing awareness of such interdependence (Schimank, 2005). From this perspective, globalization could be understood as a change in scale of the way public problems are understood, analysed and dealt with (Giraud, 2005a). International bodies such as the World Trade Organisation and supranational systems and protocols to save endangered species or to fight against global warming allow the deployment of global regulations that explicitly correspond to this 'upward' change in scale. The awareness of interdependence quite logically results in the understanding that an ever-increasing number of public problems go

*I would like to express my gratitude to Christian Azaïs, Julien Etienne and François Rangeon for their encouraging remarks on the first version of this paper.

beyond national borders and that these global problems require similar regulatory approaches.

However, the change in scale also results in a major 'downward' regulatory repositioning, towards the territorial, regional or sub-regional levels. For many decades, economic debates have evidenced that local bodies seem to be able to successfully fill the lacunae created by deficient and at times inefficient systems established by the State. The well-known works on the 'third Italy' have been quite revelatory (Putnam et al. 1994). Today, we observe an increase in the 'demand' for greater decentralization in the political and institutional spheres. Most countries with traditionally centralized structures—the United Kingdom, Italy and even France—have gradually chosen to change over to more decentralized systems. Federal nations such as Belgium, Switzerland and Canada have all opted for intergovernmental arrangements reinforcing decentralization and revitalizing federalism.

Initially an outcome of comparative analyses of economic performances, the 'territorialization' debate is currently being extensively imported into the global institutional realm. Territorialized political and institutional systems are praised for their ability to produce a 'positive public' action (Czada and Schimank, 2000; van Waarden, 1989), much better than national systems. Generally speaking, wedged in a compact geographical area and focusing on areas that are vehicles of collective identities, public problems appear to lead to more efficient formulations or initiate coordination that is just as efficacious. From this perspective, in a world enslaved by the globalization movement that crushes the individual and muddles traditional collective identities—be they cultural, ideological, religious—decentralization offers the advantage of bringing individuals closer to the seats of power. Finally, and this is undoubtedly a conclusive argument, decentralization is the corollary of territory-wise social differentiation, which is both socially and politically valued. The differences involved may be linked to the margin of adaptation to diversified local realities, but they also constitute available spaces for competition between territories. Such competition can give rise to social and political experimentation. The identification of best practices and their dissemination are public action tools that were enshrined long ago in the Bible of the federal State, that is the European Union. On the other hand, the norm of decentralization can take the form of competition between territories. Decentralization's competitive aspects—such as debates in terms of fiscal federalism, for instance—are centred on redefining solidarity norms between components of the same political entity (Braun, 1996).

Extensive changes in the organization of political systems are incidental to decentralization in both France and India. The changes affect fields as diversified as education, health, economic development, cultural action and social action, which are then called upon not only to reorganize their governance practices, but also their modes of organizing services.

Insofar as two very different countries are involved in pushing forward the decentralization process of political and social action systems, the paths they follow are also just as different. The State-controlled, centralized French system, founded on a strongly integrative approach of citizenship (Republican *à la française*), has initiated rather slow and far from ambitious—though real—changes in the past twenty years towards the decentralization and territorialization of public action. On its part, India's centralized federalism, which provides for extensive diversity in its conception of citizenship as a relationship between social groups and the State, also faces different movements challenging centralization, both in urban and rural areas.

What then is the common ground between the decentralization movements in France and India and how are we to compare the two? Are the dynamics in the two countries different since they are based on mechanisms that can't be compared?

This paper's format would not be able to do justice to all the aspects of comparison in these two particularly distinct and complex cases. Therefore, I intend to begin with a reflection on presumptions and conditions of comparison for a seemingly similar phenomenon —decentralization, analysed in two dissimilar contexts: France and India. From this perspective, the reflection will follow three phases that would challenge the category of decentralization itself as it is normally understood in European debates.

The first part is devoted to questioning what can be expected from a comparison between the two different systems. In fact, the comparison of these two most different systems (*Most Different Systems Design* or MDSD) stems from a thought-provoking research tradition aimed at producing targeted knowledge, but while laying down special conditions for the researcher.

In the second part, the reflection shall focus on the phenomenon under scrutiny—decentralization. This will mean the formulation of a definition and a basic analytic framework for decentralization.

In the third and final part of this study, these frameworks and definitions lead to questioning the specific contours of decentralization in France and India, and also to questioning the fact that these different forms of decentralization stem from social mechanisms that are similar enough to be compared. What social structures are involved in the decentralization phenomenon? Can shared aspects of 'belonging' and relevant communities of public action be matched? How can we decode their respective relationships with the various dimensions of decentralization?

HOW AND FOR WHAT REASON ARE WE COMPARING THESE TWO CONTRASTING SYSTEMS?

International comparisons fulfil different functions. For some authors, they are a way of importing scientific experimentation into the social sciences. By selecting systems that differ from each other only with regard to a single variable—presidential system *versus* parliamentary system; leftist government *versus* rightist government; centralized system *versus* decentralized system, and so on—the causes can be identified and, if necessary, the laws can be demonstrated (Kriesi, 1994). For other authors (Passeron, 1991), on the other hand, the development of societies involves so many factors that we would be deluding ourselves if we believe that we can reproduce experimental conditions into the social sciences, to whatever degree it may be. The 'cases' that serve as the basis for international comparisons are unique historical entities. Thus, these cases can neither be reproduced nor adapted at will as 'variables' that can be controlled.

However, the American historical sociology tradition says that the comparison logic of national systems makes it possible to study the styles of these systems. The different variables under scrutiny are then either present or absent in one case or the other. Therefore, the comparison is limited to a few specific cases. The relevant variables that are examined and form the basis for hypotheses are understood in their specific context. Their 'variance'—the absence or presence of a strong communist party, landholding system, forces of religious schisms, etc.—can thus be checked within a Weber framework that justifies the complexity an internal logic of each of these systems (Leca, 1992).

Whether little or great interest is shown in the complexity and commonalities of the two cases, the logic that drives a comparative strategy based on MDSD is above all an experimental one and is based on an accepted strategy of comparison in social sciences (Landman, 2000).

MDSD's demonstrative logic consists of a combination of the method of comparison '*of agreement*' and '*of difference*', which were both developed by John Stuart Mill (1865). The '*of agreement*' method consists of selecting cases in which most of the characteristic traits are different, but which also offer a 'crucial similarity' that can be split into independent variables—common causal factors—and also into a common dependant variable—the phenomenon to be explained. On the contrary, the method '*of difference*' consists of selecting systems that are similar, but which diverge—'crucial difference'—with regard to one factor within the entire set of interdependent variables, and also with regard to the dependent variable (cf. Table 7.1). The block with a crucial difference is constituted by the relationship between the causal factor and the phenomenon to be explained. For instance, the method '*of agreement*' would consist of studying a group of very different countries in terms of their economic and social structure, but which would have the shared characteristic of a high level of unemployment. We would then discover that amongst the independent variables, each country presents an identical variable, perhaps the causal variable, which could be the type of public employment service, wage earners' qualification structure, or the scale of an economy's

TABLE 7.1: COMPARATIVE METHODS '*OF AGREEMENT*' AND '*OF DIFFERENCE*'

	Method '*of Agreement*'		Crucial differences/ similarities	Method '*of Difference*'		Crucial differences/ similarities
	System A	System B		System A	System B	
Dependent Variable (*to be explained*)	High unemployment rate	High unemployment rate	SIMILAR	High unemployment rate	Low unemployment rate	DIFFERENT
Independent Variable 1 (*explanatory*)	Service economy	Industrial economy	DIFFERENT	Service economy	Service economy	SIMILAR
Independent Variable 2	Weak trade unions	Strong trade unions	DIFFERENT	Economy open to foreign trade	Economy open to foreign trade	SIMILAR
Independent Variable 3	High degree of employee qualification	Low degree of employee qualification	DIFFERENT	High level of government expenditure	High level of government expenditure	SIMILAR
Independent Variable 4	High interest rates	High interest rates	SIMILAR	Passive employment policies	Active employment policies	DIFFERENT

openness to foreign trade. A comparative strategy in terms of the method '*of difference*' would, on the contrary, consist of studying two countries whose economic and social configurations are basically similar, but which have very different unemployment levels. This difference in the dependent variable would be found in one of the independent variables, which would constitute the similarity between the cases.

Similar to the method '*of agreement*', the MDSD method consists of selecting exceptionally contrasting cases. But as in the method '*of difference*', it also consists of selecting either cases that contain the same independent variable, or one or two similar interveners, which could even be tested. The 'crucial similarity' then no longer constitutes a block split into dependent and independent variables, but is clearly located within the phenomenon to be explained. In the same way the 'crucial difference' is located amongst the decisive factors of independent variables. In a way the 'crucial similarity' allows the definition of a relevant family of cases to be examined—because all of them present an identical phenomenon to be studied—and the 'crucial difference' allows us to isolate the cases on which to work: the cases taken up for study would be those that are as different as possible with regard to this crucial difference.

Clifford Geertz' work on *Islam Observed* (Geertz, 1971) is undoubtedly the best illustration of such a research study. In this path-breaking work, Geertz raises the issue of how world cultures sharing the common denominator of being a part of the Islamic world face modernity. In order to scientifically test Islamic cultures, Geertz selects the most divergent cases possible from the Islamic world: Morocco, situated in North Africa, the western-most land in the Islamic world; and Indonesia, located in South-East Asia, the eastern-most part of the Islamic world. In their classic article on putting comparative strategies into perspective in historical sociology, Theda Skocpol and Margaret Somers (Skocpol and Somers, 1980) also quoted from James Lang's work, *Conquest and Commerce* (Lang, 1975). In this work, James Lang studies the diversity of approaches and contributions from European countries that have taken root in American soil. Choosing the cases of England and Spain while ignoring France and Portugal, the author selects most different cases from the viewpoint of the categories that he finds of interest. In fact, he compares the idea of European projects in America for the purposes of conquest, control and political exploitation with the notion of European presence in America for purposes of trade. Spain's presence clearly corresponds to the first motivation and England's to the second. The Portuguese and French presence do not offer clear-cut contrasts as regards these two categories, and hence do not truly represent the diversity of the situations present.

The aim of the most contrasted cases' comparative strategy is twofold: to attempt to isolate representative cases of situational diversity and secondly, to work on cases that offer clearly-read situations, which offer the opportunity to apply tests convincingly. In fact, the selection of these 'extreme' cases—Morocco and Indonesia, for instance—stems above all from a resource-saving strategy. Researchers seek such extremely different cases to unearth causal factors or a configuration of specific factors that make it possible to 'neutralize' the variables related to the phenomenon of the maximum. There is no doubt that Morocco and Indonesia are two Muslim countries, but hidden behind this common factor is the shadow of a great number of dissimilarities that gradually emerge from the common identity encountered at first sight. The dissimilarities are especially welcome in this case since they have the potential to reveal a host of unexpected causal factors. The geopolitical contexts, development levels, histories and institutions inherited from colonial powers, and the countries' cultural and political traditions have the potential to emerge as indispensable elements for the definition of the different paths taken by these countries.

France and India constitute a pair of cases that offers the possibility of comparing most contrasted cases. Decentralization—which puts these two countries in the same class as parts of the same whole—is a phenomenon to be explained or analysed in these cases. However, among all the countries that share this characteristic, France and India undoubtedly represent almost the maximum level of dissimilarities, especially as regards crucial factors for a decentralization analysis. The institutional architecture, the size of the two countries, their levels of economic development, but above all, their social, religious, ethnic, linguistic and political homogeneity levels appear to be decisive factors for analysing the different paths chosen by these countries.[2] If we take these aspects into consideration, for all practical purposes, France and India are located as far away from each other as possible amongst the group of contemporary democracies. France represents the archetypal centralized, Western, developed, medium-size Nation State with a strong, ancient tradition of political and cultural integration. On the other hand, albeit more-or-less centralized, India is a developing federal State covering a large territory and above all ridden with deep schisms: in terms of social status with the caste system, economically, linguistically, ethnically and in terms of its religions. Although since the last quarter of the twentieth century, France, like many other European countries, may have witnessed considerable churning due to socio-political differences—religious and ethnic minorities, renewed growth of social inequalities, rise of regional identities, emergence of new forms of identities, and so on—there is still a clear and strong contrast between the country's overall homogeneity and the situation in the Indian Union, within which the high number of schisms can and do lead to violent clashes.

In accordance with the tenets of this theory, the selection of France and India clearly roots the comparative perspective in the strategy of most different cases. These two countries are undergoing the decentralization process, as is the case in a number of democratic countries. In this respect, they do belong to the same category, though it is a large one, with a number of countries. But within this category, and in the light of relevant factors for the analysis of decentralization, these countries represent a very high degree of diversity. Hence they exemplify the diversity that exists within the group of contemporary democracies that are dealing with decentralization. Centralized countries undergoing the decentralization process, such as Sweden, the United Kingdom or Italy, could have in a way substituted France. Huge federal but centralized nations that have recently switched over to democratic systems and are ridden by numerous and deep schisms, like Russia, Brazil and Argentina could have been chosen over India. However, France and India are the 'winners' in their respective category for a comparative study in terms of the *Most Different Systems Design.*

WHAT DOES DECENTRALIZATION MEAN?

Decentralization belongs to the family of concepts that has been rendered so meaningless that it is often used without really being defined. Hence the digression to define decentralization accurately becomes imperative in my attempt to compare this process in France and India. The definition provided here has been inspired by analytical debates on this phenomenon, especially comparative ones, in Western countries. However, international comparisons, among other things, help us to distance ourselves from concepts that are too endogenous or that concern situations that are too close (Dogan & Pelassy, 1980). The comparison of these most different cases gives us the propitious opportunity to re-examine the categories commonly used in the context of comparisons between Western countries. Hence, decentralization as defined at this stage of analysis ought to be re-examined after a comparison of these two cases.

In fact, decentralization signifies a movement devolving powers held by Nation States to a lower-rung political community. This shift implies the delegation of powers in favour of elected representatives. Hence, in general terms, decentralization is synonymous with political democracy. It is a form of delegation of power that is often associated with political communities contained in a territorial context. However, it can also be applied to other groups formed on bases that are not territorial in nature. One example is the case of the Belgian federation. Apart from Walloon, Flanders and Brussels, formed on the basis of territorial divisions, linguistic communities —the French community and the Flemish community—are also recognized as relevant communities entitled to delegation of powers, in matters pertaining to culture or schooling, for example. In the tradition of communitarian politics, especially the Anglo–Saxon model, political communities are considered relevant on the basis of the vicinity principle, religious or ethnic affiliation, or even on the basis of a group action—*self-help*—or yet, on the basis of an identity attributed to—rather than claimed by—age, gender or sexual minority groups (van Gunsteren, 1994). These contemporary forms of communitarian politics often culminate in empowering these groupings to execute limited public policies—social policy measures, justice of the peace courts or other types of conflict resolution bodies, or powers for community organization. At times, in the case of local democracy, they bolster the democratic process in moments of crisis (Blondiaux & Sintomer, 2002).

Decentralization creates problems with regard to the relations between the centre and the periphery or, in general terms, problems with regard to the relations between the political system and its components. As is often the case in politics, the oft-repeated issues of 'integration with system' and 'integration of the system' are raised (Habermas, 1973, Jobert & Muller 1987). Decentralization considers both these as interdependent courses and proposes to lower the system integration level—by increasing the autonomy of its components—in favour of the integration within the system of communities, regions, groups or individuals that do not recognize themselves in an overly integrated and too distant a system.

There is a wide spectrum of institutional forms available—from unitary states, confederations of independent states and decentralized states to federal states, etc.—and this palette makes different modulations of the arrangements between the facet of the integration of the system and that of integration with the system. The various available forms could be seen as so many arrangements between envisaged policies, which are supposed to be translated into the national framework.

The gravest crises these institutions have to weather are civil wars. Nations are then created, also within a limited geographical area, and claim their independence from the centre. Ethnic, religious, regional, etc., conflicts are also strong destabilizing factors for the integration of the system. The nature of political, cultural, social, linguistic, religious schisms within a political system therefore become basic factors to understand the relationship between integration with the system and the integration of the system.

The four relevant qualities of the decentralization of political power are participation, differentiation, delegation and accountability, which are oft repeated reasons cited for this democracy reform movement.

(i) The renewal and strengthening of democratic contracts are objectives that are frequently mentioned to explain decentralization's contemporary destiny. Decentralization, which brings citizens closer to decision-making bodies, is purported to favour *participation* and give a boost to the legitimacy of political processes. Decentralization ought to awaken new forms of community action, as it is fostered in socially constituted territories and more so because it breaks with traditional hierarchical forms. From this perspective, forms of governance aimed at social mobilization are privileged instruments for implementing new forms of community action.

(ii) The logic of *differentiation*, experimentation and even creating inter-territorial competition are key factors for transforming the contemporary political forms of institutional organization. Territory-based community action then becomes the vector and developer of specific community action logic. The national framework is increasingly called into question as a 'natural' interdependent community. The logic of positive emulation in the national context is encouraged by the multiplication of indicators and other assessment practices.

(iii) The real driving force behind decentralization is the *devolution* of power. Decentralization systematises the transfer of power to communities, which gain autonomy; thus it leads to capacity creation. The identities, community action and mobilization that emerge in the political communities defined find that the devolution of power constitutes a constructive achievement. The delegation of power, at the local level, entrusts an interactive mission to stakeholders organized at the territorial level.

(iv) Community *accountability* should be seen as an important counterpart to the devolution of power. The entire ambiguity of the *empowerment* logic can be found here. The logic behind the delegation of power vests the beneficiaries of such a transfer with autonomy, but in most cases the transfer is accompanied by compensations. Hence, the new public action is not a simple withdrawal of central power but in fact a re-deployment of this power.

These four aspects fall within the framework of diverse political orders of reference. Therefore, they generate a variety of norms and values in contemporary political systems, which are related to these different political orders. They are associated with different aspects of integration with the system and integration of the system.

Participation is a classical method for analysing democracy. This is an aspect that alludes to the republican concept—in the Greek sense of the term, or as it was restated by Hannah Arendt. Above all, integration with the system is aimed essentially at the individual. The individual is considered to be actively integrated with the system through his political participation and his contribution to society. *Differentiation* refers to the idea of a continuous dynamic that makes society as well as economies work. Institutional and political systems have to be flexible and realistic *vis-à-vis* these dynamics. The norms regarding the system's integration have to be able to adapt to these dynamics. The *delegation* or *devolution* of power stems from present-day thinking on activating political communities and society at large. The system's integration and integration with the system are not seen as contradictory but rather as congruent in nature. Motivating individuals caught in their privileged framework also helps in achieving the political system's aims on the whole. Finally, community *accountability*, the counterpart to the devolution of power, alludes to the system's integration. A principle of the order of things is devised with increasing precision in contemporary political systems: the granting of new powers, rights, funding, etc., are always accompanied by new responsibilities.

DIFFERENT FORMS OF DECENTRALIZATION: FRANCE AND INDIA

On the one hand, comparing such different cases as France and India enables us to take up representative cases of a variety of situations present and on the other, to submit the same phenomenon—decentralization in this case—to examination by potentially explanatory and highly differentiated variables.

The study of the decentralization phenomenon in France and India undertaken here can only be stylistic and exploratory in nature.

I shall begin by giving a summary outline of decentralization as it exists in the French political system first, followed by the same for India, and shall compare the isolated dynamics in each case in my concluding remarks.

DECENTRALIZATION—FRENCH STYLE: LESSONS INCOMPLETE

France classically represents the complete nationalization of the political space. The state was founded not only on the will to shape a unified and integrated linguistic, historic and political space (Thiesse, 2001), but also on a citizenship concept that disallows collective identity based on regional culture or religion. The French national framework thus constitutes a particularly effective, classical outcome of the major functions of politics. Thus, the central national space is both an area for the construction of public problems and a space for national democratic debate; a space for the resolution of public problems; centralized administrative structure; as well as a space for political socialization—construction of political subjects (Giraud, 2005a). However this vision, focused on the political space, ignores the social structures and schisms that prevail in French society and its political system.

The decentralization debate has changed significantly since the 1980s when the first successful initiatives were taken. In the 1980s, decentralization was considered a revolutionary move, representing a complete break with the past, not unlike the move that sounded parliamentary domination's death-knell in French politics (Mabileau, 1977). Decentralization, seen as an invitation to territorial differentiation, was considered an experiment whose results could not be foreseen. The centre/periphery relations that had developed in the French context were well known and generally worked fairly well (Grémion, 1976). Based on cross-regulation between the State's departmental administrative hierarchy and powerful local representatives in the political parties' arena, the system eventually evolved a complex control system that gave the deciding vote to the local authority through partisan politics.[3] Moreover, the system enabled dual coordination—or integration—between two important dimensions of the French political system: the arena defining centre/

periphery relations as well as the one regulating inter-partisan relations.

The progress made in decentralization since the proclamation of the 1982 and 1983 Acts, the reforms initiated by important legislations such as the 1993 Five-Year Plan on Employment and the 13 August 2004 Act on the second stage of decentralization led to significant changes in the regulation of the French regime's centre/periphery relations (Duran and Thoenig, 1996). Firstly, these changes introduced a high degree of uncertainty in the French system. The increase in the number of sources of legitimacy, the immense importance given to networks—to the hierarchy's detriment—the esteem granted to 'voluntary' coordination (partnerships) and other forms that enable territorial community action to see the light of day were all elements that impeded, and continue to impede, a clear understanding of the French system, post-decentralization. On the other hand, French-style decentralization and the instruments of public action that it valorizes aim at mobilizing and integraing new social groups into the process of deliberation and the implementation of concrete decisions. These groups can be economic or professional associations, individuals, or the target groups of public action. The uncertainty prevailing in the power equations between State administrations and decentralized authorities or even the local or regional specificities in the organizational capacities of interest groups are both manifestations of all that still remains to be learnt in France's transition towards greater decentralization. But they are also a manifestations of the disparities in territorial community actions—disparities that are most often revealed only by the decentralization process. The decentralization of vocational training is a particularly illustrative example of the current situation (Dubouchet and Bel, 2005; Giraud and Mériaux, 2003).

Recent studies on decentralization in France reveal the magnitude of prevailing misconceptions regarding local power systems, extended to social players in the perspective of public action (Négrier). Exchanges between local representatives and external State services have indeed been modified by the laws of decentralization. At the same time, the vision of power systems has been extended to encompass social players too. This territorial networking is currently still under study.

DECENTRALIZATION—INDIAN STYLE: REALITY BEFORE REFORMS?

The Indian political sphere still remains deeply scarred by colonial and post-colonial history. Recent political changes represent, on one hand, the telescoping between myriad traditional Indian political systems, built on hierarchies and social, cultural, religious and other schisms, governed by multiple scattered power systems. On the other hand, there is also a Western power system centred on norms of standardization, uniformity and rationalization of power. The deep-rooted maladjustment between the nature of social and cultural structures and the fundamental norms of the politico-institutional system inherited from the British represents the entire gamut of the subcontinent's political organization (Mitra, 2001). To be more precise, centralizing trends within the Indian federation stem, above all, from the magnitude of central funding, the supremacy of central expertise and an extensive use of emergency measures that can suspend the democratic powers of the union's member states (Vaugier-Chatterjee, 1999).

In this context, the Congress party's strategy was to build a 'client' (vote-catching) democracy within a centralized federal structure—at times termed authoritarian (Rajashekara, 1997)—prone to changes in the seat of power at the regional or local level this could be interpreted as an attempt to establish a system for integrating the political system, threatened by numerous schisms and tensions between different and sometimes even hostile rationales (Jaffrelot, 2004). The weakness of the national political space as a public space, the deep divide between the north and the south—for instance in the matter of the integration of the caste system within the political system—or the profound differences in the level and rhythm of economic development between different member states of the Indian Union are indicators of the specificities of the role of politics, as the grammar of the incorporation of the system within the Indian context.

Thus, Steven Wilkinson has demonstrated, in a very captivating manner, how the implementation of consociation measures, of sharing and allocation of power—especially to representatives of ethnic or religious groups—was a major factor in the rise in inter-ethnic conflicts in the 1970s and 1980s (Wilkinson, 2000). Contrary to the famous theory put forward by Arend Lijphart (Giraud, 2005b; Lijphart, 1968, 1979, 1984 and 1999), in the case of India, the practice of delegation of power to groups based on strong identities did not engender a culture of compromise, harmony and cooperation, but on the contrary, led to the hardening of identities, the mobilization of groups and the radicalization of the stands taken by different groups.[4]

More recently, three occurrences pertaining to the country's partisan regime demonstrate the fragility of the national political space: the break-up of the Congress party; the extensive heterogeneity within the party—its constituents in one state could turn out to be its fiercest opponents in another; and the weakness of opposition parties at the national level (Chhiber and Petrocik, 1989). Analyses of the regime's democratization emphasize the practically incommensurate regional differences in this regard (Heller, 2000). The exemplary success of Kerala, one of the southern states, is characteristic of the fragmentation of the forms of power within the subcontinent. Moreover, the unrelenting advance of globalization has led to new forms of destabilization that affect the modes of subjectivation and reinforce inequalities among social groups and between territories, while also triggering new forms of destabilization (Assayag, 2005; Bayart, 2004).

It is evident therefore that there is no common single perspective of decentralization in India. In the Indian context, the notion refers to an entire series of phenomena. Viewed according to the standardized, institutionalized, Western concept, decentralization has made very little progress in the Union and its member states in India. Based on the same ethno-centric concept of decentralization, now applied to India's member states, the phenomenon appears to have made real progress only in the southern part of the country—in the states of Kerala and Karnataka (World Bank, 2004). On the other hand, if we look at the reality of the power phenomenon from the viewpoint of its specificities, its wide differentiation, the host of systems of allegiance, the strong impact of caste on the structure, the social hierarchies, and the local and regional aristocracy and clergy, then the decentralization of power appears to be the primary reality in India. The failure of the Congress party's attempt at national integration and the inability of centralized federalism to progress either in integration with the system or the integration of the system are indicators of this situation.

CONCLUSION

Comparing the forms of decentralization in France and India has above all allowed us to take stock of the diversity of the phenomena involved in decentralization. Therefore, our initial definition has to be reviewed and, in fact, expanded. In our initial perspective, centred on the Western institutional context, decentralization was associated with a phenomenon that was democratic in nature and could, above all, be summarized as a procedure of delegation of power to communities, incorporated within a well-defined political *ensemble*. Political integration and participation within territorial, religious or other communities were at the very basis of integration with the system. The founding understanding of decentralization thus consists in lowering the level of integration of the system in order to reinforce integration with the system.

Furthermore, the initial definition of decentralization focused on strong modalities of articulation between provincial and central powers. These articulations are not only an integral part of democratic practices, but are also directly linked to mechanisms for the rationalization and standardization of the organization of power in Western societies, as advanced by Max Weber (Weber, 1976). In the Indian context, decentralization is first and foremost associated with forms of power-structuring that are closely linked to local political, cultural and religious contexts. Power concentration and rationalization mechanisms are therefore very loosely connected to the national system. Thus, decentralization refers more to juxtaposed forms of decentralization rather than facets of power sharing.

The vertical segmentation of power levels found in the Indian context should not lead solely to the relativization of the way democracy is played out in this country. This observation should also provoke a critical review of the relevance of the procedures of articulation between the central and provincial power-sharing arrangements in Western countries. Decentralization and federalism cause breaks in political systems, which create access points for social players (Mayntz and Scharpf, 1995). The latter—trade unions, employers' associations, organizations of medical professionals, environmental protection movements, and so on—sometimes avail of more integrated structures than the entire range of public action processes. For example, in the case of vocational training governance in Germany, unions are involved in steering decisions on federal interprofessional and sectoral norms; they are present in the *Länder* management arena, and also find representation in their companies (Giraud, 2003). In the face of the strong continuity at different stages of political decision-making and implementation, political power is segmented and at times divided, and, in specific cases, it is limited to providing a space for negotiation. However, contrary to the host of fragmented forms found in the Indian case, social interests in Western countries play almost the same tune, and this holds true even in sectors where they are more powerful than the political system. In this way, despite the variations that lend a meaning to the very use of decentralization, shared power systems directly contribute to the fundamental mechanisms of integration with and of the system.

At this stage, while the comparison of institutional forms does draw attention to important issues, it also evidences its limitations. Power does not always manifest itself in institutions. On the contrary, it always applies to social forces. A comparative analysis in this matter ought to help define the relation between principles of order that are likely to be meaningful to society. The comparison of municipal powers, applied, for instance, to marketing, the grant of building licences or the organization of local law and order systems would provide highly stimulating case studies on local combinations of institutions and relevant social forces in each of the contexts.

NOTES

1. I shall take up this issue again in the second point devoted to decentralization.
2. Incidentally, Gerhard Lehmbruch's work has explained German coordination mechanisms between the institutional sphere (the federal structure) and the partisan sphere, which strikes almost the totally opposite note. The *Bundesrat*, which is supposed to represent the interests of the *Länder* within the federal structure, is in fact mainly used by political parties to veto federal government decisions. Therefore, the dominant streams of logic are expressed mainly within a centralized space.
3. G. Lehmbruch, *Parteienwettbewerb im Bundesstaat—Regelsystem und Spannungslagen im Institutionengefüge der Bundesrepublik Deutschland*, Opladen: Westdeutscher Verlag, 1998.
4. The definition of the inter-state boundaries of the Union's member states on the basis of culture or language barely raised any problems in the south, whereas it led to disorder and radicalized the stands taken in the northern states, especially in Punjab (Vaugier-Chatterjee, 1999: 30).

REFERENCES

Assayag, J., *La mondialisation vue d'ailleurs - L'Inde désorientée*, Paris: Le Seuil, 2005.

Bayart, J-F., *Le gouvernement du monde - Une critique politique de la globalisation*, Paris: Fayard, 2004.

Blondiaux, L.Y. Sintomer, 'L'impératif délibératif', *Politix*, 15, 2002, pp. 17–35.

Braun, D., 'Der bundesdeutsche Föderalismus an der Wegscheide, Interessenkonstellationnen, Akteurskonflikte und institutionnelle Lösungen', *Staatswissenschaften und Staatspraxis*, 1996, pp. 101–35.

Chhibber, P.K. and J.R. Petrocik, 'The Puzzle of Indian Politics: Social Cleavages and the Indian Party System', *British Journal of Political Science*, 19, 1989, pp. 191–210.

Czada, R. and U. Schimank, 'Institutionendynamik und politische Institutionengestaltung: Die zwei Gesichter sozialer Ordnungsbildung', in R. Werle and U. Schimank (eds.), *Gesellchaftliche Komplexität und kollektive Handlungsfähigkeit*, Francfort sur le Main: Campus, 2000, pp. 24–43.

Dogan, M. and D. Pelassy (eds.), *La comparaison internationale en sociologie politique—Une sélection de textes sur la démarche du comparatiste*, Paris: Librairies Techniques, 1980.

Dubouchet, L. and M. Bel (eds.), *Décentralisation et formation professionnelle—Réflexions pour le futur*, Paris: Editions de l'Aube, 2005.

Duran, P. and J.C. Thoenig, *L'Etat et la gestion publique territoriale. Revue Française de Science Politique*, 46, 1996, pp. 580–623.

Geertz, C., *Islam Observed: Religious Development in Morocco and Indonesia*, Chicago: Chicago University Press, 1971.

Giraud, O., *Fédéralisme et relations industrielles dans l'action publique en Allemagne: la formation professionnelle entre homogénéités et concurrences*, Paris: L'Harmattan, 2003.

——, 'Nation et globalisation. Mécanismes de constitution des espaces politiques pertinents et comparaisons internationales', in J.C. Barbier and M.T Letablier (eds.), *Politiques sociales—Enjeux méthodologiques et épistémologiques des comparaisons internationales*, Brussels: Peter Lang, 2005a, pp. 97–118.

——, 'Négociation et action collective en politique—Les institutions et la culture du compromis politique face à la mutation des formes de la conflictualité sociale', in M. Nachi, M. de Nanteuil (eds.), *Eloge du compromis—Pour une nouvelle pratique démocratique*, Brussels: Académia-Bruylant, 2005b, pp. 287–306.

Giraud, O. and O. Mériaux, 'France et Allemagne: décentralisation et capacité de régulation des systèmes d'acteurs régionaux', in M. Bel, P. Méhaut, O. Mériaux, *La décentralisation de la formation professionnelle—Quels changements dans la conduite de l'action publique?*, Paris: L'Harmattan, 2003, pp. 43–67.

Grémion, P., *Le pouvoir périphérique. Bureaucrates et notables dans le système politique français*, Paris: Le Seuil, 1976.

Habermas, J., *Legitimationsprobleme im Spätkapitalismus*, Francfort sur le Main: Suhrkamp, 1973.

Heller, P., 'Degrees of Democracy: Some Comparative Lessons from India', *World Politics*, 52, 2000, pp. 484–519.

Jaffrelot, C., *Inde: la démocratie par la caste*, Paris: Fayard, 2004.

Jobert, B. and P. Muller, *L'Etat en action—Politiques publiques et corporatismes*, Paris: P.U.F., 1987.

Kriesi, H., *Les démocraties occidentales—Une approche comparée*, Paris: Economica, 1994.

Landman, T., *Issues and Methods in Comparative Politics*, London: Routledge, 2000.

Lang, J., *Conquest and Commerce: Spain and England in the Americas*, New York: Academic Press, 1975.

Leca, J., *Postface: la sociologie historique retombe-t-elle en enface? Ou 'quand la sociologie abandonne devant l'histoire'. Revue Internationale de Sciences Sociales*, 1992, pp. 453–65.

Lehmbruch, G., *Parteienwettbewerb im Bundesstaat—Regelsystem und Spannungslagen im Institutionengefüge der Bundesrepublik Deutschland*, Opladen: Westdeutscher Verlag, 1998.

Lijphart, A., 'Typologies of Democratic Systems', *Comparative Political Studies*, 1, 1968, pp. 3–44.

——,'Consociation and Federation: Conceptual and Empirical Links', *Revue Canadienne de Science Politique*, XII, 1979, pp. 499–515.

——, *Democracies: Patterns of Majoritarian Consensus Government in Twenty-One Countries*, New Haven: Yale University Press, 1984.

——, *Patterns of Democracy: Government Forms and Performance in Thirty-six Countries*', New Haven: Yale University Press, 1999.

Mabileau, A., *Les génies invisibles du local: faux-semblants et dynamiques de la décentralisation. Revue Française de Science Politique*, 47, 1997.

Mayntz, R., and F. Scharpf, *Gesellschaftliche Selbstregelung und politische Steuerung*, Frankfurt: Campus, 1995.

Mill, J.S., *A System of Logic: Ratiocinative and Inductive: Being a Connected View of the Principles of Evidence, and the Methods of Scientific Investigation*, London: Longmans, Green & Co., 1865.

Mitra, S.K., *'Langue et fédéralisme: le défi de la multi-etnicité'*, *Revue Internationale des Sciences Sociales*, 2001.

Négrier, E., 'French Regulatory Path? State, Economy and Territory', *Tijdschrift voor Economische en Sociale Geografie*, 91, 2000, pp. 248–62.

Passeron, J.C., '*Histoire et sociologie—Identité sociale et identité logique d'une discipline*', in J.C. Passeron (ed.), *Le raisonnement sociologique—L'espace non-poppérien du raisonnement naturel*, Paris: Nathan, 1991, pp. 57–88.

Putnam, R.D., R. Leonardi and R.Y. Nanetti, *Making Democracy Work: Civic Traditions in Modern Italy*, Princeton: Princeton Press, 1994.

Rajashekara, H.M., 'The Nature of Indian Federalism: A Critique', *Asian Survey*, 37, 1997, pp. 245–53.

Schimank, U., *Weltgesellschaft und Nationalgesellschaften: Funktionen von Staatsgrenzen. Zeitschrift für Soziologie*, 2005.

Skocpol, T. and M. Somers, 'The Uses of Comparative History in Macrosocial Inquiry', *Comparative Studies in History and Society*, 22, 1980, pp. 174–97.

Thiesse, A.M., *La création des identités nationales—Europe XVIIIe XXe siècle*, Paris: Editions du Seuil, 2001.

van Gunsteren, H., 'Four Conceptions of Citizenship', in B. van Steenbergen (ed.), *The Condition of Citizenship*, London: Sage, 1994, pp. 36–48.

van Waarden, F., 'Territorial Differentiation of Markets, States and Business Interest Associations: A Comparison of Regional Business Associability in Nine Countries and Seven Economic Sectors', in W.D. Coleman and H.J. Jacek (eds.), *Regionalism, Business Interests and Public Policy*, London: Sage, 1989, pp. 13–58.

Vaugier-Chatterjee, A., *Le fédéralisme entre centralisation et décentralisation. Pouvoirs*, 1999, pp. 25–41.

Weber, M., *Wirtschaft und Gesellschaft–Grundriss der verstehenden Soziologie [5e édition révisée par J. Wincklemann]*, Tübingen: Mohr, 1976.

Wilkinson, S.I., 'India: Consociational Theory and Ethnic Violence', *Asian Survey*, 40, 2000, pp. 767–91.

World-Bank, 'India: Fiscal Decentralization of Rural Governments', *Document of the World Bank/South Asia Region*, January 2004.

CHAPTER 8

Local Democracy and New Territories in France

FRANÇOIS RANGEON

The question of local democracy is today being raised at the global level. In many countries, one is in fact witnessing a renewal of local democracy, in a great variety of forms and degrees (Nakata, 2003). This renewal affects both urban and rural areas,[1] the central question being that of the place of the citizen in the processes of territorial rearrangement, in the constitution of 'new territories'. Economic and social changes are transforming territories ('metropolization', the multiplication of transactions between urban and rural territories); this is leading public authorities to attempt to reorganize the administrative and political structures of local bodies.

Thus, since the 1980s, France has witnessed a strong move towards decentralization, translated into the redistribution of powers and responsibilities to the benefit of local bodies. This new redistribution of powers is taking place not just to the benefit of traditional, local territorial bodies (Communes, Departments and Regions), but also to the benefit of new territories, in particular urban agglomerations, rural areas countries and 'Communities of Communes'. 'Intercommunality'—understood in France to mean voluntary cooperation among Communes and not their authoritarian mergers—has seen considerable expansion, with practically the whole of the French territory being covered by 'public establishments for inter-commune cooperation' (EPCI, *Etablissements Publics de Co-opération Intercommunale*). The transfer of power from the state to local territories was accompanied by territorial restructuring, which raised the issue of local democracy in France in new ways.

Traditional territories relied on representative democracy, each of them—Commune, Department and Region—being managed by a deliberative assembly elected through universal suffrage and itself expected to appoint the local executive from within: mayor, president of the general or regional council, and their deputies.

While representative democracy appears nowadays to be an inadequate response to the democratic aspirations of the people and while participatory democratic experiences are multiplying, has the institution of new territories contributed to the invention of new modes of practising local democracy? In order to answer this question, it would first be necessary to analyse territorial dynamics in France (i) as much in urban areas (built-up areas and metropolises) as in rural ones (the various 'countries' and inter-communality or inter-municipal bodies). The institution of these new territories reveals a considerable participatory democracy deficit (ii), decentralization having reinforced the power of local elected officials rather than developed citizens' capacities to participate in public debate. Nevertheless, the transfer of power and the creation of new territories have profoundly transformed the modes of operation of local government (iii). The shift from local government to territorial governance thus raises the question of the future of local democracy in France.

TERRITORIAL DYNAMICS IN FRANCE

The French territory is characterized by two contradictory phenomena: urbanization and municipal fragmentation. While a century ago only 10 per cent of the population used to live in cities, today 80 per cent of France's population (75 per cent of the European population and 50 per cent of the world population) is concentrated in urban and peri-urban zones. Yet, France is the European country with the highest number of Communes, a very large majority of them being lightly populated rural ones (less than 1,000 inhabitants). In order to try and resolve this paradox and to render rural and urban territories more dynamic, the authorities have, via successive small steps, redesigned the French landscape while refashioning the structure of agglomerations and rural spaces.

AGGLOMERATIONS AND METROPOLISES

There are around 150 urban areas in France (continuously urbanized territories) with more than 50,000 inhabitants each. Nearly all of them are organized either as urban inter-municipal communities (all the Communes of a single urban area containing, in principle, more than 5,00,000 inhabitants),[2] or as agglomeration or metropolitan inter-municipal communities (urban areas comprising between 50,000 and 5,00,000 inhabitants).[3] The three principle French cities, Paris, Lyon and Marseille, have a special status and are divided into city districts or *arrondissements* (31 December 1982 Act).

For a long time, 'big cities' constituted a privileged space of modernity and a laboratory of social change (The Chicago School). Areas of concentration of wealth and activities, they also engender exclusion and disengagement with respect to the political system.[4] It is in the agglomerations and metropolises that the universalist character of citizenship is most called into question in the name of the demand for the recognition of differences among social groups and communities. The big city thus appears emblematic of the divorce between the political sphere and civil society.

That is why, since the 1970s, governments have focused their efforts, with varying degrees of success, on the development of participatory democracy in agglomerations and metropolises. The direct participation of inhabitants in the life of their city is supposed to constitute the preferred means of renewing distended social ties and arousing the civic spirit. Unfortunately, 'this enchanted vision of local democracy doesn't stand up to the test of the facts' (Jouve, 2005: 324, '*cette vision enchantée de la démocratie locale résiste mal à l'épreuve des faits*'). The so-called 'democracy of proximity' Act of 27 February 2002 tried hard to impose the creation of city-district consultative councils in the big cities. In reality, although they may be open to all, the actual levels of participation of inhabitants in these councils are very low (less than 5 per cent) and, most often, elected officials control their functioning very firmly. As to policies against exclusion in the urban environment—called 'city policies' in France, since the 1980s, they invoke the participation of inhabitants in an incantatory fashion but hardly provide the means for effective participation (Rangeon, 1994).

Whether representative or participatory, local democracy is in crisis in agglomerations. Like decentralization, the process of political construction of agglomerations was essentially the doing of elected officials, and the population was hardly associated with it. The increasing complexity of metropolitan stakes (Jouve, Lefebvre, 2004), the rise to power of big cities as economic actors and the development of urban expertise have doubtless gone against the constitution of a public space of local democracy. In fact, forums for the participation of civil society in French agglomerations of more than 50,000 inhabitants, in particular 'development councils' instituted by the Voynet Act of 25 June 1999, have been quasi-monopolized by local notables and have hardly provided space for the direct expression of citizens' voices.

As against numerous European cities that have demonstrated innovation with regard to local democracy, 'the French case is characterised above all by the weakness of such initiatives' and by a strong 'centralisation of power around the mayor and his deputies' (Le Galès, 2003: 341).

If urban concentrations have distanced citizens from the locii of decision-making, one could think that the future of local democracy lies in small communities where proximity appears to favour the practice of democratic debate. But are rural areas indeed the privileged terrain of democratic renewal?

The 'Countries' Rural Areas and Intercommunality

Due to the impact of multiple factors—economic, demographic and institutional—rural territories have been transformed in France over the last thirty years. Agriculturists represent but a small minority of inhabitants of rural areas, with more and more of them working in the city, and inter-commune cooperation has largely remedied municipal decay. Nearly all villages are henceforth grouped within intercommunality organizations or 'Communities of Communes' (there are about 2,000 of these in France, each bringing together 10,000 inhabitants, on average).[5] For ten years now, and in a more informal manner, rural inter-municipal bodies are being urged to gather together within the 'countries'—spaces of economic, geographic or cultural solidarities favourable to local development initiatives (Portier, 2002).

Less known and less covered by the media than urban inter-commune bodies or those of metropolises, rural inter-commune bodies account for no less than 80 per cent of French inter-municipal cooperation and cover a vast majority of the national territory. Their success can be explained in two ways. On the one hand, they have not called the existence of communes into question and have not undermined the municipal freedoms to which elected officials remain extremely attached. On the other, they have made it possible to offer inhabitants services and facilities that the communes would not have been able to provide on their own.

The problem with rural inter-commune bodies—but also with urban and metropolitan inter-municipal bodies—lies in the absence of any direct election of their representatives by the population. In fact, the members of the inter-municipal assemblies are appointed by the municipal councillors of member municipalities. Intercommunality thus remains the business of elected officials and does not directly concern citizens.

The 'countries', of more recent creation, are not witnessing the same success as inter-municipal bodies for the moment. These are territories sufficiently vast to permit the implementation of sustainable development projects. There are currently 360 of them on French territory. The majority have signed a development convention with the State and with their Region. Moreover, some of them benefit from the financial support of the European Union. With the goal of involving populations in the preparation of development plans, the 25 June 1999 Act envisaged the establishment of a 'development council', a consultative body representing civil society. In practice, the members of these organizations are chosen by elected officials, who most often nominate notables, and who remain entirely free to follow or not follow the opinions rendered by these assemblies (Moreau, 2005).

The functioning of the 'countries' is therefore hardly more democratic than that of intercommunality bodies. In both cases, proximity does not appear to be an adequate condition for democracy. Indeed, to the contrary, the establishment of these new territories is revelatory of the democratic deficit of decentralization in France.

THE DEMOCRATIC DEFICIT OF DECENTRALIZATION

Decentralization has often been analysed as 'the consecration of notables' (Rondin, 1986), that is to say as a reinforcement of the power of big local elected elites rather than as the progress of local democracy. It is true that although it may be directly concerned by its effects, the general population has barely been involved in the process of the transfer of power from the State to the local bodies. Until recently, public opinion was openly broadly favourable to decentralization (Percheron, 1992). The last decentralization reform (13 August 2004 Act) did not meet with the same support from public opinion, and numerous difficulties are being faced in its implementation (Marcou and Wollmann, 2004).

But decentralization is not reducible to a transfer of powers; equally, it engenders a new territorial apportionment of public action. Has the emergence of new territories favoured a renewal of local democracy?

Local Democracy and Inter-Commune Cooperation

Inter-municipal cooperation in France suffers not only from a deficit in the democratic legitimacy of its representatives, but also from a lack of transparency and an insufficiency of public debate about the principal stakes involved. Even as the powers and budgets of inter-commune establishments continue to grow, citizens are very poorly informed about their functioning and about the decisions taken by their representatives. They are not involved in the making of essential choices. In most public establishments for inter-commune cooperation, in urban as much as rural areas, decisions are taken by commissions or boards, by a small number of representatives elected. Divergences between member Communes are handled before the official meetings of the deliberative assemblies, where the opposition is weakly represented, and which are often reduced to the role of a recording room. 'Democracy on the sly, bureaucracy in the shadows' (*'démocratie en catimini, bureaucratie de l'ombre'*) are expressions that clearly illustrate the limits of inter-commune democracy (Le Saout, 2004: 67).

Two solutions were envisaged by the public authorities in order to overcome this democratic deficit. The first consisted of introducing universal suffrage for the election of inter-commune assemblies. The government has proposed this reform several times, but the Parliament has so far opposed it. Parliamentarians, in particular the senators—the vast majority of whom are also local elected officials—fear that the election of inter-commune assemblies will call the legitimacy of mayors and general councillors into question and eventually lead to the disappearance of Communes and Departments.

Another solution consisted of reinforcing citizens' powers by giving them the right to express themselves via referendums. Instituted at the municipal level in 1992 and the intercommunality level in 1995, local referendums were extended to all local bodies by the constitutional amendment of 28 March 2003. In addition, the legal value of referendums has been reinforced by the last reform, at least at the local body level, to the exclusion of inter-commune establishments. Nevertheless, the decision to turn to a referendum was entrusted to local elected officials alone, referendums at the people's initiative being proscribed.[6] Furthermore, the law raises several obstacles against the organization of local referendums: limitations concern both the nature of the questions allowed to be raised and the period in which a referendum can be held. In sum, these difficulties make the institution of local referendums far from effective. In practice, the number of local referendums that have been effectively organized is very small, in particular at the inter-municipal level. The failure of the reform can be explained by the reluctance of locally elected officials to make use of a procedure that could potentially call their decision-making powers and legitimacy into question. Another explanation for this failure lies in the weak identity of inter-commune territories, considered less likely to evoke feelings of belonging and electoral mobilization around their principal stakes.

Inter-commune democracy thus appears to have been confiscated by the locally elected elite. The history of the relations between the State and local bodies in France remains one of a 'long refusal of local democracy' (Deyon, 1999: 13). Nevertheless, for several years now, the debate on local democracy has shifted towards the question of participatory democracy and the theme of 'democracy of proximity' has invaded political discourses (Le Bart and Lefebvre, 2005).

What Kind of 'Democracy of Proximity'?

The idea of proximity is inherent to that of decentralization, because the latter aims to bring decision-making closer to the citizens. But the proximity of decision-making is not in and of itself the proof of democracy; what is also required is for citizens to be involved in the preparatory and implementation processes.

The belief according to which citizens are the main architects of the success or failure of a public policy has led local decision makers to multiply peoples' consultation and participation procedures. Traditionally, local representative democracy relied on the hypothesis according to which elected officials, with the help of experts and technicians, were the best placed to know what was good for citizens, and therefore to decide in their place and in their name.

This hypothesis is no longer accepted today. In France, as in a number of other countries, the last two decades have been marked by the rise of the participatory imperative, in particular in urban contexts (Bacqué Rey and Sintomer, 2005: 121). However, the institution of participatory democracy is most often rooted in a desire on the part of elected elites to search for a new legitimacy, rather than in real demands by citizens. This explains the limited success of participatory forums, the low mobilization of inhabitants, the disappointments and resulting frustration.

Since the 1990s, urban mayors have multiplied participatory

democracy initiatives by organizing city-district committees and councils in their towns, holding regular meetings with the population in different parts of the city, implementing new ways of informing and consulting inhabitants, while explaining the main development projects. . . . The development of new communication technologies has been particularly marked in major cities—with the possibility of dialogues with elected officials over the internet, the broadcasting of local assembly debates, visual presentations of town-planning projects and so on. But above all, such communications is essentially aimed at gaining media coverage for the elected elite and improving the public image of their community, rather than favouring citizens' representations (Gerstlé, 2004: 244).

Within the framework of city politics, the neighbourhood has been recognized as a relevant space for public debate, and in 2002 the government raised the issue of proximity as a priority for public action.[7] The same year, the legislature adopted a law 'relating to the democracy of proximity' that provided for the obligation to create 'neighbourhood councils' in cities of more than 80,000 inhabitants.[8] Nevertheless, the implementation of this law has not lived up to the hopes of its initiators. On the ground, locally elected elites have remained in charge: they freely define the boundaries of the neighbourhoods, the composition and powers of their neighbourhood councils, as well as the resources at their disposal. Studies conducted on the functioning of neighbourhood committees and councils show that they contribute as much to enabling the local establishment of elected elites as to giving voice to the population (Rangeon, 1999: 329). Members of such councils frequently express their disappointment at barely being heard by elected officials. The local press reports on these frustrations: 'The Neighbourhood Committee Feels Wronged' (*Courrier Picard*, 8 March 2003), 'Stormy Meeting at the Neighbourhood committee' (*Courrier Picard*, 11 April 2003), 'The Neighbourhood Committee is Fed Up' (*Courrier Picard*, 3 October 2001). The representatives of these committees feel that their place in the decentralization process is not sufficiently recognized and that they are rarely consulted on projects that exceed the neighbourhood level and concern the entirety of the agglomeration.

The gulf between the political discourse on the importance of the theme of proximity and the reality of everyday practises on the ground stands revealed as extremely wide. Although some innovative experiments in participatory democracy have been conducted in several cities (Hannoyer and Leblanc, 2004: 17) and although the demand for democracy is growing among the general population (Sorbets, 2002: 16), broadly speaking, it remains no less true that democracy of proximity appears to be a fuzzy concept, with often-disappointing effects.

For all that, local government is witnessing major transformations today, which make it possible to envisage new developments in local democracy in the future.

TRANSFORMATION OF LOCAL GOVERNMENT

The foundations on which local public action rests have evolved considerably over the last few decades. The state has lost its monopoly over public interest and local bodies have been granted powers to participate in its definition and implementation (Rangeon, 2005a: 45). The relationship between the State and local bodies is no longer one of subordination, but of contractual cooperation and partnership.

Becoming economic actors, local bodies no longer confine their actions to the public sphere but engage equally in the private and commercial spheres.[9] In particular, regions and big cities are active on the international scene where they tie-up numerous economic, cultural and higher-educational transactions.

In such a context, local government changes its character and increasingly resembles territorial governance, which leads to a reconsideration of the issue of local democracy.

From Local Government to Territorial Governance

By local government, one generally means the powers held by elected representatives of local bodies to elaborate on and implement public policies by deploying their own human, financial and technical resources. Local government equally evokes a mode of public action modelled on the State model—i.e. centralized, strictly framed by legal rules, founded on the mechanism of representation and the principle of the supremacy of public over private interest.

On the other hand, territorial governance refers to a flexible and negotiated form of public action, practised in an enlarged territorial frame, based on a vast redistribution of powers and on public–private partnership. Taking the form of a managerial process based on project orientation, programme-wise funding and a continuous evaluation of actions, territorial governance claims to break away from traditional methods of administrative functioning. Decentralization, by encouraging local bodies to revise their modes of action, has enabled them to become aware of their capacities for innovation and experimentation which, in many spheres, have proved to be superior to those of the State. In such sectors as personnel management, drafting contractual policies and public–private partnership, local bodies today constitute the locii of experimentations in administrative modernization.

More generally, the French Constitution of 4 October 1958 (Constitution of the Fifth Republic) established the right to local experimentation in 2003, thus introducing a breach in the principle of uniformity that traditionally governed the status of local bodies. Likewise, the new constitutional principle of territorial subsidiarity, according to which 'the purpose of territorial bodies is to take decisions concerning the entire gamut of powers that can best be deployed at their level' (Constitution, Article 72, Para 2), henceforth allows for the easing and regulation of multi-level cooperation.

In the context of globalization and European integration, local bodies thus become privileged spaces for coordination between various forms and the levels of regulation.[10] The multipolarity of actors and of decision-making forums, the expansion and diversification of partnership types and the tendency of the main local bodies (Regions, Departments, and Metropolises) to ascribe a general jurisdiction over their territory to themselves has considerably enlarged the field of possibilities and increased the room for original initiatives, to the benefit of local authorities. That is how the world is witnessing the 'comeback of European cities', which have become 'a laboratory for the reinvention of politics in Europe'

(Le Galès, 2003: 389). We are also witnessing the gradual emergence of the Europe of regions, regional power having been recognized by the Treaty of Maastricht in 1992, and European regions having since multiplied their exchange and cooperation networks (Pasquier, 2004).

Yet, the diversification of the actors and forums of decision-making does not necessarily signify the progress of local democracy. On the one hand, territorial governance is reinforcing the professionalization of public action through the increasing recourse to expertise and the arbitrage of local, elected 'big men'. On the other, it is rehabilitating the role of citizens, recognized as being capable of blocking or modifying big urban planning projects, through their mobilization. Meeting the expectations of users is increasingly emerging as a decisive criterion—if not *the* decisive criterion—for measuring the success of a public policy. In this sense, territorial governance opens up new potentialities for local democracy.

Towards a Renewal of Local Democracy?

The renewal of local democracy may be envisaged not only in the context of decentralization—transfer of power provides a chance to reorganize public action and grant inhabitants new powers—but also in the context of 'the new urban question' (Donzelot, 1999: 87). Big French cities have in fact been facing a deepening crisis for thirty years now. They confront three major phenomena: the gentrification of city-centres, the flight of the middle classes towards peri-urban zones and the relegation of the underprivileged classes to the suburbs. This segregation, at once social and spatial, impedes the cities' ability to fulfil their traditional role of integration. The image of the city as cradle of politics (Athens) and a school of democracy (Tocqueville) is tending to get effaced by a logic of fragmentation instead—of an inward communitarian withdrawal, conflicts and violence.

Since the 1970s, local democracy has been generally presented as one of the remedies that could help in attenuating the effects of urban segregation. Yet, during this period, the democratic deficit in cities has increased relentlessly: the rise of electoral abstention, in particular in the suburbs, the growing disinterest of inhabitants in local political life, the decline of the sense of belonging to the city, etc. The initiators of the new 'city policy' and the decentralization policy have enhanced their efforts to enable the blossoming of a new urban citizenship. However, the results have not measured up to the ambitions proclaimed.

Despite numerous reforms aiming to spread the rights of local citizens in the field of information and participation, and in spite of the multiplication of initiatives in numerous cities (establishment of Committees of Experts, Youth Councils, Economic and Social Committees, etc.), the notion of local citizenship remains to be constructed. Neither at the political nor judicial level does the notion of 'local citizenship' show any true consistency (Hardy, 1994: 116).

We are nevertheless witnessing a real growth—albeit disorderly and often fleeting—of the practice of participatory democracy, which contributes to the creation of a new equilibrium between representative and participatory democracy at the local level (Andrieu, 2004: 154). Citizens are recognized as constituting a valuable force for contesting, proposing and assessing local public policies, particularly in the fields of urban planning, security and environmental protection. But in no case is this participatory democracy—which remains under the tight control of elected elites—likely to question the legitimacy of representative democracy. Local participatory democracy has not managed to set itself up as a countervailing power and, most of the time, it is being reduced to a decision-making aid for the elected elites.

Studies conducted in cities on the functioning of citizen participation bodies reveal a dual paradox. On the one hand, the stronger the separation between the elected elite and citizens and the wider the gap between different population categories, the more alive and dynamic does participatory democracy appear. It is as if the strengthening of urban segregation and the malfunctioning of representative democracy were producing an increased need for participation (Jacquier, 2004: 102). On the other hand, 'it is strange to note that the local level can be perceived simultaneously as a natural sanctuary for political participation and a democratic desert' (Blondiaux, Marcou and Rangeon, 1999: 5). Thus, theoretically, cities should constitute privileged spaces for participatory democracy, but it would nevertheless remain very largely mythic in practice. This dual paradox perhaps explains the hybrid nature of local participatory democracy, at once an instrument for the legitimization of elected elites and a factor for challenging their power.

Recent developments in decentralization have moreover led to a diversification of democratic practices, each city having the tendency to invent its own model of local democracy. Given the decline of the principle of territorial uniformity and the fading of national public policy models, local democracy can be seen to be a lever for change. In fact, local elected officials try to rely on citizens' participation in order to appropriate and implement the principle of differentiation.

Thus, two stages in the recent evolution of local democracy may be distinguished. Until the end of the 1990s—with the 2002 'Democracy of Proximity' Act constituting without doubt the latest example—the State attempted to impose a uniform model of local democracy on all local bodies. Today, these local bodies have liberated themselves and, often through a process of imitation and cross-hybridization, they are defining their own instruments of participatory democracy. While increasing the exchange of experiences across the numerous national and European networks in which they participate, cities are in the process of reinventing a new local democracy, practised in reconfigured territories.

Finally, the relationship between local democracy and new territories is actually undergoing deep-set transformations in France. It would undoubtedly be premature to evaluate the magnitude and sustainability of these changes. Will they lead to the real and durable progress of participatory democracy, or, indeed, will the representative system take over these innovations? The dominant trend appears to point to an 'Americanization' (Hoffmann-Martinot, 2004: 62) of local democracy in France because of a triple evolution—the reinforcement of urban segregation, the decline of participation in local elections and, together with this, the increase in the media-profile of elected elites, the challenging of local fiscal systems that are considered opaque and unjust, and a rising scepticism about the effectiveness of local public policies. But isn't this Americanization of local democracy one of the manifestations of a more general trend towards the Americanization of French politics in general?

NOTES

1. See, for example, in India, the renewal of village councils (panchayats) since the end of the 1970s. B. Ghosh and G. Kumar (ed.), *State Politics and Panchayats in India*, New Delhi: Manohar and Centre de Sciences Humaines, 2003.
2. Urban inter-municipal communities were instituted by the 31 December 1966 Act. There are currently 14 of them.
3. Metropolitan inter-municipal bodies are the result of the 12 July 1999 Act. There are more than 130 of them today.
4. Thus, it is in urban areas that one notes the highest rates of electoral abstention. See C. Ysmal, *Le comportement électoral des Français*, Paris: La Découverte, 1986, p. 72.
5. Instituted by the 6 February 1992 Act, inter-municipal bodies take responsibility for the management of space and economic development, as well as, optionally, roads and transport, sanitation, educational, cultural and sporting facilities, and environmental protection.
6. More exactly, a referendum can be organized if so demanded by at least a fifth of the registered voters of the community concerned. But the deliberative assembly remains free to accept or refuse such demands. Administrative Court of Appeals, 22 February 2005, *Association les amis de la terre du val d'Ysieux, Actualité Juridique Droit Administratif*, issue no. 19, 2005, p.1052.
7. J.P. Raffarin, Prime Minister, Declaration of the Governments General Policy, National Assembly, 3 July 2002.
8. The 27 February 2002 Act, *Journal Officiel* (Official Gazette) of 28 February 2002. See S. Guérard, *'La démocratie locale en questions'*, *Revue de Droit Public*, issue no. 5, 2004, p. 1291.
9. See the call for a partnership between companies, local bodies and universities made by the president of the Chamber of Commerce and Industry of Paris, Pierre Simon, in *Le Nouveau Courrier*, April 2005, p. 5.
10. *La régulation. Nouveaux modes ? Nouveaux territoires ?'*, *Revue Française d'Administration Publique*, issue no. 109, 2004; also see J. Chevallier, *L'Etat post-moderne*, LGDJ, 2nd edn., 2004.

REFERENCES

Bacqué, M.H., H. Rey and Y. Sintomer, *La démocratie participative urbaine face au néo-libéralisme* ('Urban Participatory Democracy Confronted by Neo-liberalism'), *Mouvements*, issue no. 39/40, 2005, p. 121.

Blondiaux, L., G. Marcou and F. Rangeon (eds.), *La démocratie locale*, Paris: Presses Universitaires de France, 1999.

Chevallier, J., *L'Etat post-moderne*, Librairie Générale de Droit et de Jurisprudence, 2nd edn., Paris, 2004.

Deyon, P., *Le long refus de la démocratie locale* ('The Long Refusal of Local Democracy'), in L. Blondiaux, G. Marcou and F. Rangeon, *La démocratie locale*, Paris: Presses Universitaires de France, 1999, p. 13.

Donzelot, J., *La nouvelle question urbaine* ('The New Urban Question'), *Esprit*, issue no. 11, 1999, p. 87.

Gerstlé, J., *La communication politique*, Paris: Armand Colin, 2004.

Ghosh, B. and G. Kumar (eds.), *State Politics and Panchayats in India*, New Delhi: Manohar and Centre de Sciences Humaines, 2003.

Guérard, S., *La démocratie locale en questions* ('Local Democracy in Questions'), *Revue de Droit Public*, issue no. 5, 2004, p. 1291.

Hannoyer, F. and N. Leblanc, *Participation, démocratie et expérimentation* ('Participation, Democracy and Experimentation'), *Territoires*, issue no. 447, 2004, p. 17.

Hardy, J., *Citoyenneté, citoyennetés locales* ('Citizenship, Local Citizenships'), *Pouvoirs Locaux*, issue no. 23, 1994, p. 116.

Hoffmann-Martinot, V., *Vers une américanisation de la démocratie locale* ('Towards an Americanisation of local democracy?'), *Pouvoirs Locaux*, issue no. 62, 2004, p. 62.

Jouve, B., *La démocratie en métropoles: gouvernance, participation et citoyenneté* ('Democracy in Metropolises: Governance, Participation and Citizenship'), *Revue Française de Science Politique*, issue no. 2, 2005, p. 317.

Jouve B. and C. Lefèvre (eds.), *Horizons métropolitains*, Lausanne, 2004.

Le Bart, C. and R. Lefebvre (eds.), *La proximité en politique*, Rennes: Presses Universitaires de Rennes, 2005.

Le Galès, P., *Le retour des villes européennes*, Paris: Presses de Sciences Po., 2003 (English edn. Oxford University Press).

Le Saout, R., *Intercommunalité et démocratie* ('Inter-municipal Cooperation and Democracy'), *Pouvoirs Locaux*, issue no. 62, 2004, p. 67.

Marcou, G. and H. Wollmann (eds.), *Annuaire 2004 des collectivités locales*, Paris: Centre National de la Recherche Scientifique, 2004.

Moreau, F., Le pays, un nouvel outil pour le développement durable des territoires', thesis for a Master's in 'Public Policy Assessment', Université de Picardie Jules Verne, Amiens, 2005.

Nakata, M. (ed.), *Building Local Democracy: A Sociological Study of Community-based Organisation among Eleven Countries,* Tokyo: Jitiai Kenkyu-sya, 2003.

Pasquier, R., *La capacité politique des régions. Une comparaison France/Espagne,* Rennes: Presses Universitaires de Rennes, 2004.

Portier, N., *Les pays,* Paris: La Documentation Française, 2002.

Rangeon, F., *Réflexions sur la politique de la ville* ('Reflections on City Policy'), in J. Wòdz, *Vie politique locale,* Slask, Katowice (Poland), 1994, p. 175.

———, *Les comités de quartier, instruments de démocratie locale* ('Neighbourhood Committees, Instruments of Local Democracy?'), in L. Blondiaux, G. Marcou and F. Rangeon (eds.), *La démocratie locale,* Presses Universitaires de France, 1999, p. 329.

———, *Peut-on parler d'un intérêt général local ?* ('Can One Speak of a Local General Interest?'), in C. Le Bart and R. Lefebvre (eds.), *La proximité en politique,* Rennes: Presses Universitaires de Rennes, 2005a, p. 45.

Rondin, J., *Le sacre des notables. La France en décentralisation,* Paris: Fayard, 1986.

Sorbets, C., *Démocratie locale, citoyenneté et participation : des formes et des processus en questions* ('Local Democracy, Citizenship and Participation: Forms and Processes in Question'), *Annuaire 2002 des collectivités locales,* Paris: Centre National de la Recherche Scientifique, 2002, p. 16.

Ysmal, C., *Le comportement électoral des Français,* Paris: La Découverte, 1986.

CHAPTER 9

Mayors in France: What Lies Ahead?

NATHALIE DEVEZE-SANSON

Commune-level institutions boast of a long and rich history beginning with the Middle Ages. Since Communes were awarded both legal and political recognition, they merely needed to set-up different bodies to represent them—variously over time as called peers, municipal magistrates, or councillors. The end of the Middle Ages was marked by a spirited commune movement, with cities in the north liberating themselves from feudal power and laying the foundations of proper municipal power.

A significant amount of stability characterized the geographical structures of the French territorial administration. The current map of Communes very closely resembles the one that was drawn up by the revolutionaries at the end of the eighteenth century, which Bonaparte barely touched on. The Revolution of 1789 transformed the former parishes of the 'Ancien Régime' into Commune and the 14 December 1789 Act recognized the right of all communities of inhabitants to turn into administrative cells at the grassroot level:[1]

> The revolution standardised the organisational structure— all communities of inhabitants, irrespective of their size, were given the status of a Commune (44,000). Active citizens had to elect a municipal body, presided by the mayor. The only institutional difference between communes lay in the number of members in the said municipal body, which was established according to the size of the population it represented. (Dupuis, Guéden and Chrétien, 2004: 255)

In 1882, the principle of electing a mayor gained acceptance. Thus, mayors entered into France's day-to-day political life and turned into the most familiar figures, closest to the citizens. Having become a part of recorded history a long time ago, communes constitute the local administrative level. In its Article 61, the 5 April 1884 Act affirmed the principle—still in force today—of the general competence of communes '*le conseil municipal règle, par ses délibérations, les affaires du ressort de la commune*' ('The Municipal Council rules on affairs that fall within the purview of the commune, in the light of its deliberations'). This is a fundamental Act, as it establishes the current municipal organization system, which was taken up by the *Code général des collectivités territoriales* (CGCT or General Territorial Communities Code).

Section XII of the 6th Republic Constitution, dated 4 October 1958, called '*Des collectivités territoriales* (About Territorial Communities)', and Article 72, revised in 2003, specify that, '*Les collectivités territoriales de la République sont les communes, les départements et les régions, les collectivités à statut particulier et les collectivités d'outre mer régies par l'article 74*' ('Republic's territorial communities are: Communes, Departments and Regions, Special Status Communities and Overseas Communities, as governed by Article 74'). '*Dans les conditions prévues par la loi, ces collectivités s'administrent librement par des conseils élus* . . . ('Under the conditions stipulated by law, these communities administer themselves freely through elected Councils. . .'). Since then, Communes —legal entities established in public interest—have acquired certain bodies of their own, such as elected municipal councils, with mayors at their head.

The local elected representative may be defined as an intermediary between the centre and the periphery, in charge of the implementation of state or national norms at the local level and of transmitting local complaints to the authorities at the centre. He is the mediator who establishes communication between the various networks within local society, and enjoys popularity and the confidence of his voters: 'Compared to Ministers, Members of Parliament and other political figures, French mayors enjoy amazing popularity. In fact, the head of the municipal executive's popularity has never flagged—not since the Liberation, at least' (Le Bart, 2003: 9). As Bachelot-Narquin (2001) noted, the French vote overwhelmingly for mayors attributed with all sorts of virtues: availability, proximity, realism. A study conducted by SOFRES[2] in October 2000 and published in *Le journal des maires* indicated that 70 per cent of the French have 'complete' or 'some' confidence in their mayors, as against 29 per cent who have no confidence in them. Other elected representatives do not enjoy the same level of faith, as indicated by other comparative studies. The corollary to this kind of attachment to mayors who are close to their voters is the latter's attachment to the commune, a territory perceived to be familiar. The relations the French enjoy with their commune are fairly emotional. As Vandelli (2000) mentioned:

> The commune represents the first line of public institutions, it's the closest terminal to its citizens, who maintain direct and constant contacts with it since it accompanies them all through their lives, from the very beginning (when the birth certificate is drawn up) to the very end (when the death certificate is prepared and a burial plot in a cemetery is assigned). Thus, citizens perceive the commune as a family institution. (pp. 5–17)

However, the heterogeneous character of communes cannot be forgotten. In fact, great diversity lies behind the term. What could be the common features between a rural commune with 200 inhabitants and an urban commune with 140,000 inhabitants or more? Today, France has 36,679 communes, of which 32,000 (90 per cent) have less than 2,000 inhabitants; there are 500,000 municipal councillors.

The status of a local elected representative applies to a very diverse category and gives rise to certain powers, required and mobilized by various representatives depending on the size of their commune. Close to his fellow-citizens and also competent, willing to listen but also able to solve the problems brought before him, a mayor is the 'conductor' of the municipal orchestra. However, this ideal portrait has to be qualified and is undergoing major changes. Some authors have observed a drift towards a certain municipal 'presidentialism': 'In communes, a "personalisation of power" often takes place in favour of the mayor' (Becet, 1996: 45–50). Thus, local affairs would be managed by the mayor, thereby reducing deputies to playing a token role and conducting Municipal Council meetings

TABLE 9.1: DISTRIBUTION OF FRENCH COMMUNES BY DEMOGRAPHIC STRATA

Demographic Strata	No. of Communes	No. of inhabitants
0 to 500 inhabitants	21,038	46,94,522
500 to 2,000 inhabitants	10,900	105,32,582
2,000 to 3,500 inhabitants	1,994	52,36,198
3,500 to 5,000 inhabitants	813	33,70,462
5,000 to 10,000 inhabitants	1,003	6,740,852
10,000 to 50,000 inhabitants	802	156,48,408
50,000 to 100,000 inhabitants	82	49,35,267
> 100,000 inhabitants	37	90,88,113
Total	36,679	601,86,184

Source: INSEE, 1999 General Census.

authoritatively, without any real debate on matters of interest to the Commune. The role of the municipal majority is therefore limited to validating projects imposed by the mayor.

With the implementation of the 6 June 2000 Act on equal access for women and men to elective positions, another change came about in the March 2001 municipal elections. In order to compensate for the absence of women in local political life, women have been thrust upon municipal councils by the implementation of this law. But gender parity did not play any role in elections to the posts of deputies, as men dominated town halls and continued to occupy most executive posts.

The growth of inter-commune structures and the implementation of significant transfers of power from Communes to these Government Establishments for Inter-Commune Cooperation (*EPCI*, or *Etablissements Publics de Coopération Intercommunales*), threw the distribution of local powers into disarray, along with the deeply ingrained image of a powerful mayor in French minds, one who focused exclusively on 'his town hall'. Indeed, would the development of inter-communal interactions pose a threat to the mayor's prerogatives and eventually compromise his very existence?

The current status of mayors and their fulfilment of their functions shall be analysed in the first part of this paper. This will lead us to examine the evolution and drift towards municipal 'presidentialism'—i.e. the emergence of an autonomous authority, henceforth in the hands of an independent local political elite, though one that is essentially masculine. We shall subsequently widen the analysis to envisage the mayor's role within the framework of inter-commune bodies and question the potential consequences of this development: a shift of local powers from communes to the EPCI.[3] Eventually, we will see the termination of the real or symbolic powers vested in mayors.

CURRENT STATUS OF MAYORS

What are the necessary conditions to become a mayor? What are the powers that mayors enjoy? Although the working world has opened up considerably to women, has the same occurred in local politics in France? What is the proportion of women mayors? Has the implementation of the 6 June 2000 Act led to the feminization of the municipal executives?

According to some authors, exercising the powers vested in mayors could lead to pernicious effects and, in particular, the risk of 'municipal presidentialism'. Indeed, the post of 'mayor of a French commune' hides different realities. In fact, a rural mayor elected as the head of a Commune of about a hundred inhabitants, retired, with a town hall secretary helping him for a few hours every week, carries out extremely different tasks and does not have much in common with a big city mayor, who is a professional politician and manages his city with the help of a local administrative set-up, employing several hundred persons. Thus, the category of mayors is heterogeneous in nature: 28,000 mayors administer Communes with less than 1,000 inhabitants, while more than a hundred are head cities with more than 50,000 inhabitants. However, some homogeneity can nonetheless be observed: a shared legal standing applicable to all mayors, irrespective of the size of the commune they head. This homogeneity relates to the legal status and powers of mayors, municipal elections that take place on the same day everywhere in France, the same ceremonials from one

Commune to another (the red, white and blue sash, the bust of Marianne, etc.) and the Annual Congress of the French Mayors' Association (*AMF* or *Association des Maires de France*).

Thus, it is important for us to specify the current status to which the French mayors are subject.

Assuming a Mayor's Responsibilities

There are several elements that constitute a Commune or local government: its name; its territory, which can be of variable sizes, from several thousands of hectares to a much more modest area and; finally, its population. The last one is particularly important as the number of bodies placed at the head of a Commune as well as the mode of election of municipal elected representatives vary depending on the population size.

Municipal Elections and Mayoral Powers

Each Commune has a municipal corps consisting of a municipal council, mayor and one or several deputies (Dupuis, Guédon and Chrétien, 2004: 255). The mayor is elected by the municipal council and not by the electors directly. But the likelihood of confusion stems from the presence of the future mayor at the head of the list during campaigning. The municipal council has 9 to 69 councillors, depending on the Commune's population, except for special cases like Paris, Marseille and Lyon, which are not examined here.[4] Municipal councillors are elected (Articles L.228 to L.239 of CGCT) by universal suffrage for a renewable term of six years. Different conditions must be fulfilled to be able to contest as a candidate: one needs to be a French national, be at least 18 years of age, and one's name must be included in the Commune's electoral lists or one must be a taxpayer from the Commune. Since 1992, the right to vote and eligibility to contest elections granted to certain categories of foreigners, right to vote and eligibility to contest elections have been granted more precisely, 'to (European) Union citizens residing in France'. However, they cannot be elected mayor or deputy mayor, nor can they elect the senators (Article 88–3 of the 5th Republic Constitution).

The 19 November 1982 Act established a system of differentiated designation for municipal councillors depending on the commune's population. The electoral system varies with the size of the Commune. Thus, there are three Commune sizes: those with up to 2,500 inhabitants, those with a population between 2,501 and 3,499 inhabitants and Communes with more than 3,500 inhabitants.[5] For Communes with 2,500 inhabitants or less, an election system of two rounds by majority vote is in force, with the necessary flexibility to enable the election of individual candidates (full lists or not, isolated candidatures, possibility of electors voting for candidates from different lists).

For Communes with a population between 2,501 and 3,499 inhabitants, the election system of two rounds by majority vote has been established, with the possibility of cross-party voting, i.e. votes can be cast for candidates from different lists, names can be deleted, thus allowing for incomplete lists.

For Communes with more than 3,500 inhabitants, a combined system amalgamating elections by majority vote and proportional representation has been selected, which straightaway grants the majority of seats, plus one, to the list that receives the majority of votes. The rest of the seats are then distributed on the basis of proportional representation (for lists having received at least 5 per cent of the votes), and the list enjoying the majority of seats is also included in this distribution[6] (Vital-Durand, 2004: 29). The selected system thus favours the list that receives the majority of votes and allows a reinforced majority to be established within the council.

The municipal council is the Commune's deliberating assembly. It 'decides on the Commune's affairs through its deliberations' (Article 2121–29 of the CGCT), and therefore, in principle, enjoys overall powers. The mayor and deputies are elected by the municipal council from among its members (Article L.2122 and following of the CGCT)—with a restriction of 30 per cent of the council's legal strength—by secret ballot and the absolute majority of members constituting the municipal council for the first two ballot rounds. If required, a third round may be held on the basis of a relative majority and, in the event of a tie, the eldest candidate is elected

(Article L.2122–7 of the CGCT). Thus, contrary to certain preconceived ideas and the mayoral candidate's placing at the head of the list in an electoral campaign, the Commune's inhabitants do not elect the mayor directly. It is always possible for a councillor's name to be proposed spontaneously as a candidate during the election of the mayor and his deputies. Once elected, the mayor acts as an interface, as he is both a state official and the 'conductor' of the Commune's administrative orchestra. As a state official, the mayor fulfils duties that are administrative in nature (execution of general safety measures, publication of acts and regulations, organization of elections and censuses). He is also the registrar and the law enforcement officer. The mayor's post is also that of the Commune's executive. He is responsible for the preparation and execution of deliberations within the municipal council, over which he presides. Once elected, he acts under the municipal council's control (Article L.2122–21 of CGCT). He represents the Commune (power to represent the Commune in court, conclude contracts and enter into contracts on behalf of the Commune). He prepares and executes the budget and governs the municipal heritage. The mayor designates individuals to fill the posts created by the council. Finally, he enjoys his own powers by virtue of his post with regard to the administrative police, i.e. he can take measures 'aimed at ensuring law and order, security and public health' (Article L.2212–1&2 of CGCT), without the municipal council's authorization. The mayor is also competent in matters of special policing (lifeguards, traffic) and as the head of the Commune's administration, he is hierarchically superior to the Commune's officials and can take the regulatory measures necessary for the proper functioning of the various departments.

The traditional concept of a local mandate as brought up by Montaigne when he spoke of the mayor of Bordeaux, 'the office (of the mayor) is all the more attractive as it involves neither any rent nor gain, other than the honour of fulfilling the post' was reaffirmed in 1884 with the rejection of the idea of remunerating those who devoted some of their time and energy to the town. This concept, according to which only notables or prominent individuals could in fact devote their time to managing the town's affairs still continues. Local elected representatives are still largely 'perceived through the figure of the notable—both unchanging and changeable, probably as it is undefined for the most part' (Garraud, in Fontaine and Le Bart, 1994: 29). Let us recall how Max Weber had defined notables: 'persons who, because of their economic status, are in a position to effectively run and administer a grouping continuously, without any salary, as a secondary profession' (Weber, 1971: 298). While the notion of a notable is losing steam today in major cities, it often continues to be prevail in smaller communes, where a family's reputation, socio-professional status and renown remain major criteria in the choice of mayor. The desire to give an elected representative a certain status aims at enabling various socio-professional categories to invest themselves in municipal life and thereby reconcile their professional life and local mandate.

The 3 February 1992 Act on conditions for the exercise of local mandates, followed by the 27 February 2002 Act concerning close-at-hand democracy made it possible to indemnify the mandate exercised and obtain training adapted to the complexity of situations to be managed. Henceforth, local elected representatives were granted a status that enabled them to enjoy a certain number of benefits (credit hours, etc.). The right to training was instituted and legal credit for hours worked[7] was offered to salaried elected representatives, but it is rarely used, as it is often ill-perceived by employers. Parliamentary debates preceding the vote on the 27 February 1992 Act indicated the desire—shared by the government—not to professionalize local representatives but to improve the guarantees necessary for them to exercise their mandates.[8] It is also pertinent to point out that elected representatives do not receive a salary but compensation, which reinforces the desire to reject professionalization of any kind. The 5 April 2000 Act reassessed the compensation for mayors (Article L.2123-23 of CGCT), varying on the basis of eight demographic strata and fixed as a percentage of a civil service index.[9] It may vary between € 612 and € 5,227 per month.

The politicians' desire to establish their influence through dual national and local legitimacy, for instance, by getting elected as parliamentarians and mayors, often reveals that the local mandate is neglected in favour of a deputy's seat. This practice often leads to dissatisfaction on the part of their constituents, who are critical of their mayor's absence. That is why the 5 April 2000 Act provided for a restriction on dual mandates. Thenceforth, no one could hold more than two local mandates: mayor and chairperson of a regional or general council (Article L.2122-4 of CGCT). The parliamentary mandate was incompatible with fulfilling the duties of more than one local mandate. Legislators want to prevent the mayor's post from being monopolized by a certain category of the population, which reflects a desire for openness, not just quantitative but also directed at new socio-professional categories with a limited representation among elected municipal representatives, as shown in Table 9.2. In fact, the accumulation of personal resources (municipal fame, trust) takes time and fulfilling a local mandate calls for a significant amount of availability and accessibility. These criteria are often difficult to meet in the case of more modest social categories, such as women and youth, thereby *de facto* excluding them from the *res publica*. The incentive offered by the limitation of mandates was thus aimed at 'opening up' access to local elective posts, as although a change in the socio-professional composition of mayors could be noted between 1977 and 2001

TABLE 9.2: DISTRIBUTION OF MAYORS AS PER SOCIO-PROFESSIONAL CATEGORIES

(*in per cent*)

Socio-Professional Categories	1977	1989	1995	2001
Farmers and farm labourers	39.5	28.5	19.9	18
Commercial and industrial professions	12.7	9.8	9.3	7
Private sector employees	12.5	14.6	12.9	19
Professionals	5.5	5.2	4.6	5
Teachers, civil servants and government employees	11.5	14.5	12.1	15
Retired and others	18.3	27.4	32.5	36

Source: Ministry of the Interior.[10]

(Table 9.2), it remained limited. While the number of farmer-mayors has been declining constantly since 1977, associated with a fall in agricultural activity, conversely, retirees are increasingly 'seizing power', as indicated by Table 9.3. In fact, the decrease in the retirement age allows them to have free time earlier than before and they are increasingly investing themselves in municipal life. Such an investment therefore constitutes an extension of their professional life and removes the notion of inactivity, which is sometimes difficult to bear. For them, a municipal mandate constitutes a means to extend their activity, one that can bring them recognition and social esteem. Private sector employees too have increased in number, encouraged by the fact of obtaining the status of a local elected representative, with the advantages associated with it.

Table 9.3 confirms the analysis carried out and shows that age is an important factor in access to a mayor's post. In fact, the young—aged less than 40 years—are largely absent as they accounted for just 5.3 per cent of the mayors in the municipal elections in 2001.

The comparative Table 9.4 shows the growth in the percentage of women mayors, but the number is still marginal, thus indicating a low representation of women as heads of the municipal executive. It must also be said that women mayors are essentially to be found

TABLE 9.3: DISTRIBUTION OF MAYORS BY AGE GROUPS (2001)

–40 years	40 to 60 years	+ 60 years
5.3 %	66.2 %	28.5%

Source: Association des maires de France (Mayors' Association of France).[11]

TABLE 9.4: TRENDS IN THE PROPORTION OF WOMEN AMONG ELECTED MAYORS

1977	1989	1995	2001
2.3 %	5.5 %	7.6 %	10.9 %

Source: Association des maires de France (Mayors' Association of France).[12]

in Communes with less than 500 inhabitants; in 1995 not a single Commune with more than 100,000 inhabitants was headed by a woman.

This assessment led us to question how far elected representatives were able to meet the specific needs of certain categories of people and, in particular, those of the youth or working women (who represent 46 per cent of the working population), and their ability to incorporate these demands in the Commune's priorities: setting up a drop-in day care centre or a crèche in a village, creating a basketball field or a roller-skating rink, for instance.

The Imposition of Women in Politics

At the end of the twentieth century, French politics remained a male bastion, often impregnable and filled with 'cooptation'. In fact, while women involved themselves in the working world and most practised some professional activity, their access to politics remained very difficult. While they accounted for 53 per cent of the French electorate, the feminization of politics was extremely limited and experienced very slow progress, as the analysis of trends in the percentage of women mayors (Table 9.4) has shown us. The percentage of municipal women councillors rose from 14 per cent in 1983 to 17 per cent in 1993. However, while there was confirmed progress in each municipal election, it remained limited. With the mobilization of women playing a decisive role in political democracy, the need was felt to allow women's entry into politics. The 1990s were marked by an increased awareness of the inequality between men and women, and the term 'parity in politics' was coined. It was felt that if things were left as they were, the feminization of politics would be extremely slow. France has been fairly backward in this aspect compared to other European countries. In fact, it comes second-last among European countries, just before Greece, with 10.9 per cent of women elected to parliament.

According to the *laissez-faire* idea, local life was not closed to women. However, in reality, men had put up barriers (women being nominated by a political party only in an impregnable constituency, for instance). Only an aggressive policy could straighten this situation. Parity may be defined as 'a means by which political society would remove obstacles that prohibit or limit women's access to political and, in particular, elective responsibilities' (Gaspard, 1996: 21–34). The 8 July 1999 Constitutional Act amended Article 3 of the 5th Republic's Constitution, according to which, henceforth: '*la loi favorise l'égal accès des femmes et des hommes aux mandats électoraux et aux fonctions électives*' ('the law promotes equal access to women and men in electoral mandates and elective posts'). But it has been noted that there is still a wide gap between laws and existing practices. The 6 June 2000 Act '*tendant à favoriser l'égal accès des femmes et des hommes aux mandats électoraux et aux fonctions électives*' ('is aimed at promoting equal access to women and men in electoral mandates and elective posts'). This so-called Gender Parity Act introduced what years of politics had failed to establish.

Women, who had long sat discreetly on the benches of parliament, regional and municipal councils, could thenceforth be active in politics. The Act came was applicable to all communes with more than 3,500 inhabitants; '*sur chacune des listes, l'écart entre le nombre des candidats de chaque sexe ne peut être supérieur à un. Au sein de chaque groupe entier de 6 candidats dans l'ordre de présentation de la liste doit figurer un nombre égal de candidats de chaque sexe*' ('in each list, the gap between the number of male and female candidates cannot be of more than one. Within each group of 6 candidates in the list's order of presentation, there should be an equal number of men and women'). Political parties had to submit lists with 50 per cent each of women and men (plus/minus one) during municipal, regional, senatorial (in departments where the list system was applicable) and European elections, as well as those to the Corsican Assembly. However, there was no strict alternation between men and women in the lists' composition, which would have led to women occupying the top positions in the municipal executive, but it was implemented in groups of six candidates. In practice, it has often been seen that women occupied the last three positions in each group.

The 6 June 2000 Act was enforced for the first time in the municipal elections held on 11 and 18 March 2001 in the 2,669 Communes with more than 3,500 inhabitants. The idea upheld by Lionel

Jospin, the prime minister, was to modernize political life and revitalize the political classes. As is often the case, the Act aroused qualms. Some of the elected representatives who wished to stand for elections again did not easily accept giving up their place to women, especially when they had not proved themselves unworthy. Such an action was seen as 'real heartbreak' (Sanson, 2001).

The 6 June 2000 Act had indirect effects too. Parity enabled all the candidates to give a younger, more diversified look to their lists. 'A large number of outgoing mayors even admitted to having used this constraint (gender-based vote splitting of lists) as an excuse to give their list a younger look and get rid of councillors deemed troublesome' (Lehingue, 2001: 3–32).

While the 6 June 2000 Act strove to achieve the intended objective, i.e. the promotion of equal access for men and women to municipal posts in particular, it did not have a spill-over effect in terms of equal access to the head of the municipal executive.[13] Women have been imposed in politics and men will have to make a place for them in a sphere that they had appropriated for centuries as if it were their exclusive prerogative.

PERNICIOUS EFFECTS OF THE CURRENT STATUS OF FRANCE'S MAYORS

Any organized human activity triggers pernicious effects, i.e. consequences that are contrary to participants' intentions (Crozier, 1979: 11). This definition, given by Michel Crozier, can be matched with the equally illuminating one by Raymond Boudon: 'Pernicious effects occur when two (or more) individuals, while striving for a given objective, trigger a state of affairs that was not sought after and could even be undesirable from the perspective of either both the individuals or of one of them' (Boudon, 1979: 20). However, can the continuance of male domination despite the enforcement of the 6 June 2000 Act and the observation of a drift towards 'municipal presidentialism' in the way mayoral duties are fulfilled be described as pernicious effects? While the 6 June 2000 Act demonstrated the desire to feminize municipal politics, the consequences that emerged, i.e. the continued predominance of men in mayor's posts, were actually contrary to the outcome expected from the enforcement of parity, and, in fact neutralized it. Finally, while the 1992 Act had endowed elected representatives with a certain status and granted them special allowances with the desire to open up municipal posts to a much greater range of socio-professional categories, isn't 'municipal presidentialism' an outcome contrary to what the legislators wished for?

CONTINUANCE OF MALE DOMINATION

'*La femme investit la mairie mais l'homme garde les clés.*'[14] ('Women have occupied the town hall, but the keys remain with the men.') This eye-catching headline in the newspaper *Libération,* sums up the situation on the morrow of the 11 and 18 March 2001 municipal elections fairly well. Women candidates in these elections did get elected, so it could be said that the objective of feminizing municipal life had been attained. But the marked increase in the number of elected women candidates did not really translate into the feminization of posts of responsibility in the Commune's executive. More women might have been municipal councillors but the numbers of women mayors or deputy mayors were not much higher than in 1995. Thus, it is be the election of women to the head of Communes that would demonstrate the real feminization of posts. In fact, while the 6 June 2000 Act introduced gender parity in municipal election lists, it remained silent on the actual distribution of the posts of deputies after the elections. There was no legal obligation to impose parity in the distribution of posts. Gilles de Robien, deputy mayor of Amiens in 2001 and current Minister of Education, was in favour of the application of post-municipal election parity in the allocation of deputies' posts. He had sponsored a bill to that effect in March 2001, but the bill was not adopted. The parliament, with a majority of men who were also elected local representatives, rejected the bill, since it would have reduced the extent of their local power.

However, what really happened in practice? Did elected representatives play the game of parity or on the contrary, did parity produce 'unlooked-for effects'. One of the Act's damaging effects could be seen in the exclusion of women from true municipal power, i.e. access to the posts of mayor or first deputy. By selecting eighteen women deputies as compared to fifteen male deputies and appointing Anne Hidalgo as the first deputy mayor, Bertrand Delanöe demonstrated that in Paris, women henceforth would share power formerly reserved for men. But this example has not spread to other municipal executives. In fact, the 2001 municipal election results showed marginal feminization of the mayor's post, 10 per cent as against 8 per cent in 1995[15] (Table 9.4). It must be pointed out that 95 per cent of women mayors only governed small rural Communes, with limited stakes. The continued gender inequality observed in politics often relates to inequality *vis-à-vis* power. Over 90 per cent of France's town halls continue to be governed by men and male domination persists, with women remaining municipal councillors for the most part. True municipal power still lies in the hands of men. Having had to yield their place as municipal councillors, the men have more easily been able to keep their hold over cities, since they enjoy greater political capital here (fame, seniority, etc.). Such discrimination is much clearer in the 36 Communes that have more than 100,000 inhabitants—only four women were elected mayors. As Sineau (2001: 267) noticed,

> The 'slow' revolution that Lionel Jospin had hoped and prayed for did take place. The 6 June 2000 Act was an effective tool for engendering political equality among men and women. However, the spirit of parity failed to get much play in mayoral elections—indirect elections about which the Act had nothing to say.

While women have entered the municipal councils as of 2001, it would be interesting to see whether the significant penetration of women at the executive level and, more particularly, their access to the post of mayor continues in the next municipal elections in 2008.[16]

Another negative effect in the fulfilment of the mayor's mandate can be noted in the monopolizing of power by certain elected representatives. Indeed, personal power is appropriated, which certain authors define as 'municipal presidentialism' (Sorbets, 1982: 105–15; Mabileau, 1992: 67–78).

Towards Municipal Presidentialism?

The recognition of the status of elected representatives and the fixing of an allowance for mayors and their deputies by virtue of their posts went hand in hand with the professionalization of local politics. Further, by granting greater autonomy to municipal executives and doing away with state supervision, the decentralization policy applied by the state since 1982 resulted in the concentration of power in the hands of mayors, who turned into the actual local political decision makers enjoying the status of municipal notables.[17] The notion of a 'notable' has evolved over the last few years. While a family's reputation and social position (associated with practising one profession or another) continue to be important factors leading to the description of such citizens as notables, the widening of the field to include new professions (civil servants, association, union or professional leaders) has changed the conditions of access to local mandates. However, while the composition of this class of notables may have changed, they continue to occupy the central position in local systems. Indeed,

> Notables reached their zenith with decentralisation, which turned them into the actual leaders of the local politico-administrative system by granting them decision-making powers hitherto reserved for State officials and by attributing specific powers over the communities over which they now had control. (Rondin, 1985)

Roselyne Bachelot-Narquin, former Minister of the Environment and also a elected local representative, came up with the same analysis:

> Today, every second French person lives in a municipal system in which democracy has been confiscated and every day decisions concerning his life are taken without consulting him or even considering his opinion. The entire system has been developed to assure the reigning mayor absolute power. (Bachelot-Narqin, 2001: 15)

This 'confiscation' of power by a few elected representatives has contributed to the idea of male municipal presidentialism. (This becomes apparent from the start of the electoral campaign itself, during which the posters used by the candidates' list often present just 'the future mayor'. Indeed, this reflects personalization of power in which other councillors on the list are completely overshadowed.)

From the outset, the voting system contributes to the reinforcement of the position of the Mayor. His list of nominees for succession carries more weight and eventually with the additional votes that some of his nominees receive from other sources contributes to the final election of the new Mayor. Moreover, municipal council meetings often reveal mayors who lead the debates, with the councillors of the party in power often relegated to a role of assenters, silent 'extras' who merely raise their hands to approve of decisions taken by the mayor in the solitude of his office. The mayor is no longer perceived as the 'conductor' of the municipal orchestra, but as a one-man orchestra. The confiscation of power by a few elected representatives has contributed to the idea of municipal presidentialism. Jacques Chaban-Delmas, mayor of Bordeaux from 1947 to 1995, and, much closer home, Georges Frèche, elected mayor of Montpellier in 1977, with their powerful personality and the authoritarianism are but two examples. Their longevity in their posts makes it possible for mayors to gain control over the municipal organization and accumulate resources that then enable them to consolidate their position in the local political arena. However, this observation has to be qualified because elected representatives who devote all their time to their mandate and for whom this is the main source of remuneration are just a handful. In fact, 90 per cent of communes have less than 2,000 inhabitants. Thus, the compensation mayors receive is low and can no longer be the sole source of income. Professionalism, while it is quite widespread among mayor-parliamentarians, remains limited for the holders of a single mayoral mandate in a small commune. Thus, the concentration of power in the hands of mayors could emerge as a pernicious effect of decentralization; decentralization, whose objective, ironically, is to grant greater autonomy to territorial communities and ensure true democracy.

French mayors, elected by municipal councils, are representatives of the grassroot territorial community. As mentioned earlier, the French are attached to their mayor, who is considered to be close to the citizens and attentive to their concerns. But there is great disparity in this post.[18] The title of mayor, despite identical attributes (tricolour sash, etc.) actually hides very different realities.

This analysis of the status of mayors now makes us take interest in the role of mayors within the framework of territorial restructuring. In fact, the decentralization policy actively followed by the state for the last twenty years or so and reaffirmed in 2003 by the Decentralization 'Act II' aims at providing greater autonomy to local authorities[19] and the development of inter-commune structures indicates the desire to take certain local needs into consideration, beyond the territory of each commune.

What are the impacts of the changes wrought by decentralization with regard to the post of mayors, in particular with the creation of inter-commune structures?

MAYORS FACED WITH TERRITORIAL RESTRUCTURING

As François Rangeon pointed out, 'Since the early 1990s, the dynamism of decentralization, progress achieved in building Europe and the revival of urban planning led to a spectacular resurgence in inter-commune cooperation. (Rangeon, 1997: 5). '*Inter-communalité*' as the new inter-commune dynamic is called, may be defined as cooperation between bordering or neighbouring Communes, based on their free will to jointly carry out a certain number of development or town planning projects, or to jointly manage a certain number of their responsibilities. It has taken the form of a host of structures, which have progressed considerably over the last few years. The EPCI (*Etablissements Publics de Coopération Intercommunale* or Public Establishments for Inter-Commune Cooperation) have developed significantly both in major urban cities (in the Amiens metropolis, for instance), as well as in rural villages, and have led to the transfer of some Commune-level responsibilities to communities of Communes or towns. However, such transfers could possibly undermine the authority of municipal representatives, who could be divested of their powers and of a significant part of their means. Does this spell the death of the municipal mandate and the post of mayors?

Growth of Inter-Commune Bodies

Inter-commune bodies are the consequence of an aggressive practice of Communes 'that strive to promote their individual interests through a joint project and a common structure' (Rangeon, 1997). It not only designates 'cooperation between pre-existing territories but also the desire to build new territories, new solidarities and implement new forms of action' (Rangeon, op. cit.). The 6 February 1992 framework law, called ATR (*Administration Territoriale de la République* or Territorial Administration of the Republic), and the 12 July 1999 Act concerning the strengthening and simplification of inter-commune cooperation laid down the conditions for the implementation of inter-commune activities, while the 1999 Act laid down a new form of inter-commune cooperation in towns—town communities.

Summary Presentation of Various Inter-Commune Bodies

The Union of Communes is an association of municipalities for the pursuit of a shared objective. Governed by Articles L-5212-1 to L-5212-34 of the CGCT, it is the oldest form of inter-commune body. Communities can take two forms:

Community of Communes: Created by the 6 February 1992 Framework Act, it is governed by Articles L-5214-1 to L-5214-29 of the CGCT. It is composed of a minimum of two Communes and represents inter-commune cooperation in rural areas.[20] Set up by a prefectoral bye-law after the agreement of the municipal councils of the concerned Communes, its powers are fixed by the CGCT. The Community of Communes enjoys two blocks of compulsory powers, area development and economic development activities with regard to the entire community. It enjoys one optional power, which it can select from the following: environmental protection and development, housing and environment policies, creation, development and maintenance of road networks and lastly, the construction, maintenance and operation of cultural, sports and pre-elementary and elementary education facilities.

The Community of Communes demonstrates the ability of small town mayors to federate peripheral mayors for a specific project. Thus we see the rare case—if not the only one in France—of a Community of Communes located both in the Somme Department, i.e. the Picardy region, and in Maritime Seine Department, an Upper Normandy region, which involves the collaboration of two departments, two regions and two prefectures. It is being financed either through additional taxation (property tax, housing tax) from member communes, by EPCI taxation or TPU (*taxe professionnelle unique* or the single professional tax).

Town Community (*communauté d'agglomération*)*:* The establishment of this EPCI by the 12 July 1999 Act made it possible to group a host of Communes with more than 50,000 inhabitants around one central Commune with more than 15,000 inhabitants, in one single block. Governed by Articles L-5216-1 and 5216-10 of the CGCT, there were 155 town communities on 1 January 2004, including 2,632 Communes. Within the Community Council, each Commune is represented by a minimum of one seat.

The mission of each of these Communities is to ensure economic development, and they have been granted four compulsory responsibilities (Article L-5216-5 of the CGCT): economic development, community area development, housing policies and town policies. Further, they have to take on three of the following five responsibilities: road networks of interest to the community, sanitation, water, environment policy and cultural and sports facilities. For resources, Town Communities collect the TPU by right, along with receiving State subsidies and grants.

Urban Community: Governed by Articles L-5215-1 to L-5215-42 of the CGCT, it represents the most integrated form of inter-commune cooperation. The 31 December 1966 Act created four urban communities as of 1 January 1968: Lille, Bordeaux, Strasbourg and Lyon. Eight such voluntary groupings have come up since: Dunkirk, Creusot-Montceau-les-Mines, Cherbourg, Mans, Brest, Nancy, Alençon and Arras. The 12 July 1999 Act instituted urban communities as a mode of inter-commune cooperation by right for single-block town groupings with no enclaves and with over 500,000 inhabitants. Today, there are fourteen urban communities because Marseille, Nantes, Toulouse and Nice joined up with existing Urban Communities.

Within the Community Council, communes are represented by one seat and a distribution system fixes the number of delegates in accordance with the town's population. It is interesting to note that the operating rules are similar to those of communes: a Community Council '*règle par ses délibérations les affaires qui sont de la compétence de la communauté*' ('governs the affairs that fall within the purview of the community on the basis of its deliberations') (Article L-5215-19 of the CGCT). The executive consists of a president and four to twelve vice-presidents who constitute the board. 'The Community Council elects its President and Board for six years; the relations between the President and Community Council are comparable to those between a Municipal Council and its Mayor' (Auby, Auby and Noquellon, 2004: 116).

The powers are quite extensive and require a mandatory transfer: urban development, housing and work/business site development, educational premises, urban transport, sanitation, domestic waste, road network and parking. For resources, it collects services charges and receives its own taxes (TPU) as well as increased allocations from the State.

Constant Development of Inter-Commune Bodies

The 12 July 1999 Act on the strengthening and simplification of inter-commune cooperation marked a significant step in the development of inter-commune activities. It has essentially taken the form of increasingly marked transfers of municipal powers to the EPCI as well as the devolution of fiscal powers to these establishments. Inter-commune cooperation is no longer something to shy away from, and is perceived today as a prerequisite for the commune's development. Communes fight with each other to ensure that attractive inter-commune facilities are located within their commune.'Thus, mayors use inter-commune cooperation to enhance the effectiveness of their own actions. They make the most of opportunities in the form of financial incentives, without legitimizing the inter-commune relationship as such' (Le Bart, 2003: 104). Unlike communes, the inter-commune territory does not exist as an identity-related territory and inter-commune representatives remain elected representatives of a commune. However, the growth of inter-commune activities does raise several issues and, eventually, it would raise the question of the mode of designation of inter-commune representatives elected by direct universal suffrage. Moreover, the shift of a significant portion of a commune's powers[21] to inter-commune bodies does raise the issue of the future of municipal mandates and, more particularly, that of the mayor's post.

Development of New Power Stakes

The development of inter-commune activities, which are no longer purely management-related in nature (pooling of existing activities), but are being transformed into projects (the construction of a swimming pool, a stadium, etc.) emerges as a potential threat to municipal leadership. Indeed, the inter-commune movement has shifted from the mere construction of facilities whose cost was prohibitive for one commune alone to the designing of joint development projects. Inter-commune relations with their own taxation system (Community of Communes, Town Communities) have witnessed a spectacular growth over the last ten years or so and in a large number of fields, communes are no longer the relevant territorial units for public action.

After years of reticence, even hostility, before the pooling of certain responsibilities and powers, local representatives became aware of the stakes associated with these structures and understood the personal benefits they could draw from making their commune an EPCI member. Thus, the latter have become new local power centres. Given this state of affairs, hasn't the mayor's position weakened?

Shift in Power from Communes to Government Establishments for Inter-Commune Cooperation

'Henceforth, it is clear that communes are on the decline because all that comprised the substance of their activities has been taken away. How hypocritical it is to invite electors to the polling booths to select municipal councils that will no longer have anything to do?' (Bachelot-Narquin, 2001: 52). This clear-cut position expresses the fears of certain mayors of being elected to administer empty shells, with the majority of the commune's powers having shifted to the EPCI.

'Inter-commune bodies and activities endeavour to engender both a new distribution of power and a reconstitution of territories. Without directly challenging a mayor's authority over his commune's territory, inter-commune bodies are bringing about a redistribution of powers, means and responsibilities' (Rangeon, 1997: 9). While it may not seem as if the mayor's post will disappear, it has nonetheless evolved and mayors are emerging as mediators. 'The natural trend for the mayors of central communes is to use the inter-commune institution to expand their public territory and thereby consolidate their monopoly position. They can directly chair such structures' (Le Bart, 2003: 35) Gilles de Robien, the current Minister of Education in Villepin's government, is one such example. Nominated the Minister of Transport in Raffarin's government in 2002, he was constrained to resign his post as mayor of Amiens, which he had held since 1989. Indeed, the limitation on concurrently holding several mandates did not allow him to hold the post along with a ministerial portfolio, but the same does not apply to inter-commune institutions. Hence, while Gilles de Robien had to 'reluctantly' leave his post as mayor, he was elected head of the Amiens Metropolis and continues to *de facto* preside over not just the destiny of his commune, in which he enjoys a significant presence, but also those of the town community with extended powers.

While small commune mayors may be concerned about their commune's future and the reality of their powers,[22] mayors of larger communes—administrative centres of cantons, cities and central communes—have a clearly distinct perception of inter-commune activities, having understood the interest they can draw from their presence within such inter-commune institutions.

Use of Inter-Commune Structures by Mayors: From the Continuance of Male Executives to the Rejection of Elections by Universal Suffrage

With inter-commune structures widening the scope of their powers, mayors have realized the new stakes of power. Their election to the post of an EPCI president enables them to demonstrate to their voters how essential the role they play is, not just within the commune but also within the greater framework of the Community of Communes. Mayors thus emerge as influential local representatives. Playing the role of mediators—intermediaries between voters and their needs, which these inter-commune bodies try to fulfil—mayors are anxious to control the development of the inter-commune system and to occupy decision-making posts: 'The responsibilities fulfilled at the helm of an inter-commune body play an increasing role in the way local political careers grow'(Rangeon, 1997: 10). Hence, mayors—at least some of them[23]—are turning this development to advantage and making the most of situations that might otherwise be unfavourable to them. While the development of inter-commune activities may undermine some of their powers, some mayors have been able to turn the situation to their advantage. Thus, the growth of EPCIs has enabled mayors to get round two handicaps: the application of equal access to elective posts as imposed by the 6 June 2000 Act and the limitation on the concurrent holding of several mandates, which does not apply to EPCI executives—whence their hostility to elections by direct universal suffrage to EPCI executive posts.

Practice has shown that executive levels very often remain a male bastion. Indeed, the advent of women in local politics would seem to coincide with the development of inter-commune structures and the consolidation of their powers. In a way, the opening-up of politics to women did not make up for inequalities—in fact, it reinforced them. Haven't men given up their seats to women and shared their benches within municipal councils, while saving all power (by co-option) within EPCIs almost exclusively for themselves, fully aware of the fact that the latter would become the real local power centres of tomorrow with the expansion of their powers and financial resources? Indeed, since the law has not imposed parity in these structures, women only occupy 5 per cent of EPCI chairmanships: 'Women are entering Municipal Councils at a time when strategic power is shifting from communes to towns' (D. Dulang, *Le Monde*, 27 March 2002). Women are totally absent from inter-commune responsibilities. In fact, out of 14 urban communities, not a single one is chaired by a woman. In Strasbourg, Robert Grossmann relinquished the mayor's post to Fabienne Keller in 2001, but he soon moved on to chair the urban community, as also illustrated by Amiens. On the contrary, this quick analysis demonstrates the legitimacy of a coercive rule imposing parity-based recruitment. It would be interesting to observe the composition of municipal and inter-commune executives in 2008, in order to verify whether the penetration of women in 2001 has developed into their sustained establishment at the level of executives.

The rejection of elections by universal suffrage by inter-commune structures also illustrates how the whole inter-commune dynamic has been used by mayors to their advantage. Currently, commune representatives within these structures are designated by the commune and not by elected representatives, which presents several disadvantages. First and foremost, there is a democratic deficit as they represent the interests of a commune without being directly elected by its inhabitants. Inter-commune bodies are devoid of any democratic character as their members are not selected by direct universal suffrage, but through a second-degree designation by municipal councils. Voters have no direct control over inter-commune bodies. Representative assemblies had exerted pressure against the election of representatives of inter-commune bodies by direct universal suffrage, fearing a loss of control over such institutions.

Actually, such elections had been provided for by the Act of 4 February 1995.[24] During the parliamentary debate preceding the vote on the 12 July 1999 Act (Chevènement Act), the National Assembly had been in favour, but the Senate opposed it, with the government coming round to the Senate's position. Ministers were already or were soon to assume the position of local representatives, so they therefore went along with them.

Based on the observation that there was likely to be a '*généralisation de l'intercommunalité*' ('widespread application of inter-commune collaboration') by 2007, the commission for the future of decentralization presided by Pierre Mauroy expressly provided for '*la reconnaissance de l'échelon intercommunal par le suffrage universel*' ('the election of the inter-commune echelon through universal suffrage'). The report entitled, '*Refonder l'action publique locale*' ('Reorganizing Local Public Action')[25] was handed over to the prime minister in November 2000. The report's Proposal No. 7 lays down the principle of '*l'élection en 2007 au suffrage universel direct des conseillers des intercommunalités à fiscalité propre*' ['the election of councillors to inter-commune structures with their own taxation by direct universal suffrage in 2007']. But the Senate opposed it by invoking two arguments: the development of inter-commune collaboration in itself was not yet sufficiently advanced to envisage elections by direct universal suffrage and the specific modalities of the electoral system had not been fixed. These arguments did not seem to be very convincing, but were more of an attempt to gain time, and appeared to be more of a delaying tactic than a solid legal line of argument.

> Being elected indirectly, the leaders of such grouping have got accustomed to settling inter-commune issues among themselves, safe from any immediate electoral sanctions, while being able to invoke democratic legitimacy. It is understandable that this relative comfort is an additional reason for many to oppose the idea of electing EPCI council members by direct universal suffrage.
>
> (Gaxie, in Rangeon, 1997: 25–49)

The SOFRES survey conducted between 25 and 27 July 2000 on the '*Les français et l'avenir de la décentralisation*' ('The French and the future of decentralization')[26] demonstrated that 54 per cent of those questioned wanted the president and representatives of inter-commune councils to be elected by universal suffrage by all the citizens of the concerned communes.

But from 'one missed opportunity to another' (Muller-Quoy,

2002: 283–90) the attempt to establish the principle of the election of members of deliberative bodies seemed to be pushed to a later date—more precisely to the next municipal elections in 2008.

To the question of whether the municipal mandate is doomed, 'Experts on inter-commune collaboration respond in the negative, so strong is the ability of commune representatives to occupy the inter-commune terrain' (Le Bart, 2003: 35). The law is in their favour as it does not provide for the designation of the members of inter-commune bodies by direct universal suffrage, and the mayors would not face any concurrent political legitimacy issue at the inter-commune level. Indeed, a natural tendency on the part of central commune mayors to use the inter-commune institution to expand their political territory and consolidate their monopoly position has been observed. Thus, mayors are able to use inter-commune structures to their benefit. The above-cited example of Gilles de Robien is a good illustration.

Local politics remains centred on mayors and the latter's legitimacy has been able to withstand the inter-commune revolution. But the continuance of this predominance could be questioned if the election procedure for EPCI members is modified. In addition, municipal communications (newspapers, bulletins, guides, TV) promote the mayors' activities while inter-commune bodies are only just starting to do so and therefore have an image problem. In fact, they are not well known, either with regard to their powers or to the men constituting them.

CONCLUSION

The 1982 decentralization laws have changed the organizational rules for local public intervention. Local elected representatives are no longer mere 'communication channels'. Some are no longer content to just manage their towns but have turned into real entrepreneurs, endeavouring to find local solutions to trying problems, particularly tensions associated with living conditions in towns, social aid for the elderly, and so on. The example of Jean-Louis Borloo, as mayor of Valenciennes and the way he revitalized his city, or that of Gilles de Robien, in Amiens, who brought town halls closer to the citizens are experiences that have since been repeated at the national level.

While the mayoral role is changing, sociological analysis still reveals a distinct lack of representation of women in this post. The 6 June 2000 Act imposed what years of free political process had not been able to check—the under-representation of women in political life.

It is interesting to draw a parallel between the feminization of French and Indian municipal politics. The functioning of Indian society is still characterized by the caste system; the vast majority of Indians are categorized into innumerable castes and sub-castes, according to their occupation and region of origin. The caste system and the caste-based politics associated with it enable one caste (essentially brahmins) to control the village panchayat (local government) and exert enormous political influence over lower caste villagers, as the upper caste is also that of moneylenders and all the villagers are indebted to them. This observation must, however, be qualified, because it has been noted that

> the old logic of 'clientelism' (caste-based politics), which made indebted peasants and workers vote for rural notables is crumbling. Instead, lower caste parties, who have been encouraged to mobilise themselves through measures of positive discrimination in their favour, are taking off and assuming power throughout North India.[27]

India is one of the many democracies that took the path of quotas. Thus, the 73rd and 74th Amendments of the Indian Constitution, passed in 1993, requires all the states to reserve one-third of seats for women in the panchayati raj system—a three-tiered local governance system (village, intermediary level and district). Composed of members directly elected by the villagers, panchayats enjoy decision-making powers in several fields: agriculture, health, employment and primary education. In a very short span of time, women have shown their ability to exert effective power at the village level and defy regressive traditions. Thus, as quoted by Pande:

> a meeting was organised by the Madhya Pradesh Chief Minister with women representatives. Chairs were organised for the ministers and mats were placed on the ground for the women representatives. One of them spoke up and said, 'You

speak of equality for women politicians and quotas that must be reserved for them. We are women politicians now—elected by the people. Is there a shortage of chairs in your town?' A hundred years ago, such a woman and her family would have been hanged for such audacity. Instead, the chief minister thanked her for raising the issue and the next day, there were chairs for everyone. (Pande, 2000).

These women are also fighting to increase access to power for the most marginalized sections of society and thereby try and limit the role of the male elite that currently holds power.

Thus, both in France and India, the access of women to political posts and local power remains quite difficult without recourse to quotas or legislative incentives favouring parity, despite the agreement in principle in this regard, as expressed by men politicians for the past several years.

NOTES

1. See also L. Fougere, J.P. Machelon, F. Monnier, '*Les communes et le pouvoir. Histoire politique des communes françaises de 1789 à nos jours*', Paris: PUF, 2002.
2. *Société française de sondages et d'études de marchés* (French surveys and market studies company). Set up in 1963, it essentially conducts opinion polls.
3. EPCI: *Etablissement Public de Coopération Intercommunale* (Government Establishment for Inter-Commune Cooperation).
4. In fact, a special system has been provided for these three communes by the 31 December 1982 Act. Their originality lies in the existence of a sub-commune structure with its own organs: the 'arrondissement' or district (Article L.2511-3 and following of the CGCT). These three communes are divided into 'arrondissements' (20 in Paris, 16 in Marseille and 9 in Lyon). In Paris, each 'arrondissement' has a council and a mayor, whose powers are limited to the civil state, compulsory schooling and national service. The 'arrondissement' council functions according to modalities that are comparable to those provided for other municipal councils.
   J.B. Auby, J.F. Auby, and R. Noguellou, '*Droit des collectivités locales*', Paris: PUF, coll. Thémis—Public Law, 2004, pp. 128–9.
5. Articles L.1, L.118-3, L.225, L.270, L.273 of the electoral code.
6. Hence, communes with less than 100 inhabitants have a nine-member municipal council, those between 3,500 and 4,999 inhabitants have

27 seats and those with more than 300,000 inhabitants have 69 seats. Article L.2121-2 of the CGCT presents a detailed table of the number of seats in accordance with different demographic sizes.

7. These 'credit hours' are paid in a lumpsum every quarter. The sum is fixed with reference to the weekly work duration. It varies according to the size of the commune and the post held (mayor, deputy mayor or municipal councillor). For instance, for mayors of communes with less than 10,000 inhabitants, the credit hours are equal to three times the legal weekly work duration. Article. L.2123-2 and following of the CGCT.
8. *Journal Officiel* (JO—Official Gazette), *débats Assemblée National* (National Assembly Debates), 11 December 1991, p. 7596.
9. On 1 January 2004, it amounted to € 612 per month for mayors of communes with under 500 inhabitants, € 1982 for those of communes with 3,500–10,000 inhabitants, € 5227 for mayors of communes with over 100,000 inhabitants.
10. Ministry of the Interior, Domestic Security and Local Freedoms, '*Les collectivités locales en chiffres 2004*', Paris: La Documentation française, 2004, p. 108.
11. Ibid.
12. E. Vital-Durand, op. cit., p. 38.
13. Since March 2001, the representation of women is as follows: 10.9 per cent of mayors—i.e. 3,946 out of a total of 36,679 communes and 47.5 per cent of municipal councillors in communes with over 3,500 inhabitants. Indeed, access to the post of mayor still remains very difficult for women.
14. Newspaper *Libération*, 31 March–1 April 2001.
15. *Source:* Ministry of the Interior, op. cit.
16. The date of the municipal elections initially schedule for March 2007 will be postponed to 2008. In fact, to avoid an overcrowding of elections in 2007, essentially due to the presidential elections, a bill submitted to the Council of Ministers on 2 August 2005 for their (municipal elections) postponement to March 2008.
17. '*Le notable est perçu comme celui qui occupe durablement le pouvoir, le monopolise par la pratique du cumul des mandats et la longévité élective*' ('Notables are seen as the ones who occupy the seat of power sustainably, monopolize it through the practice of accumulating terms of office and elective longevity'), Ph. Garraud, op. cit., p. 30.
18. In fact, retired rural farmer-mayors, well-established in their communes of 500 inhabitants for generations, have concerns and responsibilities that weigh heavily on their post, which differs from that of the 'entrepreneur-

mayors', elected in large ambitious cities and surrounded by a chief of staff and heading a very large number of municipal staff. A. Faure, '*Le village et la politique. Essai sur les maires ruraux en action*', Paris: L'Harmattan, 1992.

19. Let us quote, for instance, the revised Article 1 of the Constitution of the Vth Republic, which specified the Republic's '*l'organisation décentralisée*' ('decentralized organization') from then on; Act no. 2004-809 of 13 August 2004, authorizing different experimentations at the local level.
20. On 1 January 2004, we counted 2,286.
21. In particular, sports facilities, road networks and waste management.
22. S. Vignon, *Les rétributions inégales de l'intercommunalité par les maires ruraux*', in R. Le Saout, and F. Madone (dir.), *Les effets de l'intercommunalité*, Rennes: Presses Universitaires de Rennes, 2004, pp. 17–38
23. In fact, mayors of rural communes with less than 3,500 inhabitants are not very involved in this kind of instrumentalization since the 6 June 2000 Act does not affect them. Moreover, their communes often benefit from inter-commune ties without their mayors playing a key role in these bodies, which are often headed by mayors of larger communes.
24. S. Cals, *De la simplification des structures intercommunales: entre échecs et espoirs*', RFDA, 2004, pp. 31–41.
25. P. Mauroy (under the chairmanship of), '*Refonder l'action publique locale*', Report to the Prime Minister by the Commission on the Future of Decentralisation, Paris, La Documentation française, 2000.
26. SOFRES, '*L'état de l'opinion 2001*', presented by O Duhamel, Ph. Mechet, and Seuil Paris, 2001, p. 100.
27. Ch. Jaffrelot, 'Inde', in P. Perrineau, D. Reynie, *Dictionnaire du vote,* Paris: PUF, 2001, pp. 515–18, see also Jaffrelot, 'Inde: *la démocratie par la caste*', Paris: Fayard, 2005.

REFERENCES

Auby, J.B., J.F. Auby and R. Noguellou, '*Droit des collectivités locales*', Paris: Presses Universitaires de France (PUF), collection. Thémis – Public Law, 2004.

Bachelot-Narquin, R., '*Les maires : fête ou défaite?*', Paris: A. Carrière, 2001.

Becet, J.M., 'Les compétences de la commune', in *Les collectivités locales en France,* Paris: La Documentation française, 1996, pp. 45–50.

Boudon, R., '*Effets pervers et ordre social*', Paris: PUF, 1979.

Cals, S., '*De la simplification des structures intercommunales: entre échecs et espoirs*', Paris: RFDA, 2004, pp. 31–41.

Crozier, M., '*On ne change pas la société par décret*', Paris: Grasset, 1979.

Dupuis, G., M.J. Guédon, and P. Chrétien, '*Droit administratif*', Paris: A. Colin, 9th edn., 2004.

Faure, A., '*Le village et la politique. Essai sur les maires ruraux en action*', Paris: L'Harmattan, 1992.

Fontaine, J., Ch. Le Bart (dir.), '*Le métier d' élu local*', Paris: L'Harmattan, *Logiques politiques*, 1994.

Fougere, L., J.P. Machelon and F. Monnier, '*Les communes et le pouvoir. Histoire politique des communes françaises de 1789 à nos jours*', Paris: PUF, 2002.

Ph. Garraud, '*Le métier d'élu local : les contraintes d'un rôle*', in *Le métier d'élu local*, Paris: L'Harmattan, *Logiques politiques*, 1994.

Gaspard, F. (dir.), '*Les femmes dans la prise de décision en France et en Europe*', Paris: L'Harmattan, 1996.

Gaxie, D., 'Stratégies et institutions de l'intercommunalité', in *L'intercommunalité*, Paris: PUF-CURAPP, 1997.

Jaffrelot, Ch., 'Inde', in *Dictionnaire du vote*, Paris: PUF, 2001, pp. 515–18.

———, '*Inde: la démocratie par la caste*', Paris: Fayard, 2005.

Le Bart, Ch., '*Les maires. Sociologie d'un rôle*', Villeneuve d'Ascq, Presses Universitaires du Septentrion, *Espaces politiques*, 2003.

Lehingue, P., '*Faire parler d'une seule voix? Les scrutins municipaux des 11 et 18 mars 2001*', *Regards sur l'actualité*, no. 270, Paris: *La Documentation française*, 2001, pp. 3–32.

Le monde, Newspaper D. Dulong, 27 March 2002.

Le Saout, R. and F. Madone (dir.), '*Les effets de l'intercommunalité*', Rennes: *Presses Universitaires de Rennes*, 2004.

Libération, Newspaper 31 March–1 April 2001.

Mabileau, A., '*L'élu local: un nouveau professionnel de la République*', *Pouvoirs*, no. 60, Paris, 1992, pp. 67–78.

Mauroy, P. (under the chairmanship of), '*Refonder l'action publique locale*', Report to the Prime Minister by the Commission on the Future of Decentralisation, Paris: *La Documentation française*, 2000.

Ministry of the Interior, Domestic Security and Local Freedoms, '*Les collectivités locales en chiffres*', Paris: *La Documentation française*, 2004.

Muller-Quoy, I., '*L'élu local: un nouveau statut, nouveau droit*', Paris: AJDA, 2002, pp. 283–90.

Pande, M., '*Le laboratoire des panchayats*', UNESCO, 2000.

Perrineau, P. and D. Reynie (dir.), '*Dictionnaire du vote*', Paris: PUF, 2001.

Rangeon, F., '*L'intercommunalité. Bilan et perspectives*', collective workes, Paris: PUF, CURAPP, 1997.

Rondin, J., '*Le sacre des notables, la France en décentralisationi*', Paris: Fayard, 1985.

Sanson, N., '*La femme imposée en politique. Enjeux et effets pervers de la parité: le cas des élections municipales des 11 et 18 mars 2001*', Amiens, DEA Administrative and political science thesis, University of Picardie Jules Verne, 2001.

Sineau, M., '*Profession femme politique*', Paris: Presses de Sciences Po, 2001.

Sofres, '*L'état de l'opinion 2001*', presented by O. Duhamel and Ph. Mechet, Paris: Seuil, 2001.

Sorbets, C., '*Est-il légitime de parler d'un présidentialisme municipal?*', Paris: *Pouvoirs*, issue no. 24, 1982, pp. 105–15.

Vandelli, L., '*La cellule de base de toutes les démocraties*', Paris: *Pouvoirs*, issue no. 95, 2000, pp. 5–17.

Vignon, S., '*Les rétributions inégales de l'intercommunalité pour les maires ruraux*', in *Les effets de l'intercommunalité*, Rennes: Presses Universitaires de Rennes, 2004.

Vital-Durand, E., '*Les collectivités territoriales en France*', Paris: Hachette, 2004.

Weber, M., '*Economie et société*', Paris: Plon, 1971.

CHAPTER 10

The Division of Powers between the State and Local Bodies in France

ISABELLE MULLER-QUOY

Whereas in a federal state it is the constitution which defies precisely be distribution of power,[1] in a unitary, decentralized state such as France,[2] it is statute that restricts the autonomy of local bodies to administrative freedom. Local bodies are merely administrative institutions although they are the outcome of universal suffrage and are representative of the local population's interests. According to Article 72 of the 1958 Constitution, '*les collectivités locales s'administrent librement par des conseils élus dans les conditions prévues par la loi . . .*' ('local bodies are freely administered by councils elected under the conditions provided by the law . . .'). The notion of administrative freedom applies at two levels: it has an organic, structural, representative aspect, and a functional element of freedom in the implementation by these bodies of their powers. But the freedom of self-administration can only be exercised in conditions provided by law. Actually, though administrative freedom allows for the free management of their interests by local bodies, it cannot be identified with independent government: '*si la loi peut fixer les conditions de la libre administration des collectivités territoriales, c'est sous la réserve qu'elle respecte les prérogatives de l'État*' ('while the law can establish the conditions of administrative freedom of local bodies, it is on condition that it respects the State's prerogatives').[3] This necessary recognition of the autonomy of local bodies by the State illustrates the relationship of subordination to the State (the primary institution) of secondary institutions, which the State contains within itself. Any institution that has a limited purpose is secondary, for the group that it represents is more limited and the interests it defends are less extensive than those of the State. The operating criterion is therefore that of the worth or value of the public interest being upheld. The State can control local public interest because it defends the general interest that it expresses through laws (the law being the expression of the public will). For their part, local bodies define collective interest, limited in space by the human group that they represent, and an interest that is subordinate to the general interest, and therefore subordinate to the law. In the system of unitary, decentralized States that we are familiar with, local bodies are not independent but simply autonomous. The autonomy of local bodies should therefore be understood as the realization of local powers by the representative authorities of the local institution, be they general or delegated powers, within the framework of the limits set down by the principle of legality.

Legislative empowerment is therefore required for local bodies to be able to exercise these powers. Such empowerment may be general, in which case it is defined by the general power-giving clause, according to which Councils govern their community's affairs through their deliberations.[4] This necessary condition for decentralization was recognized as early as in the 1871 Departmental Charter and by the 1884 Commune Charter, which established genuine decentralization in France by recognizing this power, peculiar to local bodies. But the power to act can also be precisely defined by legislators, which is the main objective of the recent waves of decentralization successfully given shape by the 7 January and 22 July 1983 Acts relating to the division of powers between the State and Communes, Departments and Regions,[5] and the 13 August 2004 Act relating to local liberties and responsibilities.[6] These two forms of legislative authorization to act are not exclusive of one another. The preise definition of powers, i.e. determined by national legislators, does not eliminate the local margin for manoeuvre in defining its own interests, although it may limit its scope, for local budgets are not unlimited.

Whereas in a federal State, the federated bodies hold exclusive powers, determined and guaranteed by the Constitution,[7] in a unitary State, in principle, no specific criteria are fixed for dividing powers between the State and decentralized local bodies. But the question has obviously been raised, especially since 1983, when decentralization was considerably strengthened in France. What would be the best criteria to use for the division of powers. What method? What powers should be given to each local body level and how? France has five levels of administration, if one includes Europe, as well as the State, Region, Department and Communes, and its public establishments for 'intercommunality' (EPCI, or *établissements publics de coopération intercommunale*) also need to be taken into account. Without qualifying as local bodies as such, the latter represent an additional local administration level and therefore wield local powers. The division of powers is aimed at stating whether the State or local bodies should have the most important place. It is at the heart of the dialectics between unity and diversity and is a question that is political in nature. However, being unable to respond to this question clearly by laying down some principle for the division of powers (I), French legislators have been more modestly committed to setting out a method for the division of powers. The response has been by nature more technical, more judicial and has seemed very modest, but has nevertheless been very important, for it has expressed the reality of local bodies in today's France (II).

I. ABSENCE OF A CLEAR PRINCIPLE FOR THE DIVISION OF POWERS AMONG LOCAL BODIES IN FRANCE

Till 2003, there was no reference to this question of general principle in the Constitution, the constituent body having restricted itself to laying down legislators' powers to define local powers. The academic commutators had tried to find a criterion in vain (A). The constitutional revision of 28 March 2003 introduced a new approach to local bodies that has led to the modalities of the division of powers being called into question in France today. Indeed, it has laid down the principle according to which *'les collectivités territoriales ont vocation à prendre les décisions pour l'ensemble des compétences qui peuvent le mieux être mises en œuvre à leur échelon'* (local bodies have the role of taking decision in relation to all the issues that can be better addressed at their level). This formulation is now described as expressing a principle of subsidiarity. Thus resisting once again the issue of the position of different local bodies in implementing the general interest.

A. 'No Affairs are Local by Nature': The Impossibility of a Practical Definition of Local Affairs

Toute collectivité locale a une double nature. Institution de droit public, personne morale, elle est tributaire de la loi : le législateur en définit la nature et le statut, c'est lui qui détermine et fait varier le champ de ses compétences. Mais la collectivité s'entend encore d'un groupement humain solidaire, bénéficiant d'une vie propre, d'une sorte 'd'autonomie' spontanée. Cette seconde nature trouve dans la vieille notion d'affaires locales son expression juridique. (All local bodies have two facets. As institutions of public law and corpoate legal entities, they are creatures of statute: legislators define their nature and status, and determine and vary the scope of their powers. But local bodies are also understood as integral groups of citizens with their own life—a sort of spontaneous 'autonomy'. This second aspect finds legal expression in the old notion of local affairs).[8]

In substantive law, the notion of local affairs is reflected in a general clause attribtuing power to local bodies. Thus, Article L.2121-29 of the general code of local bodies (CGCT) envisages that *'le conseil municipal règle par ses délibérations les affaires de la commune'* ('the municipal council governs the commune's affairs through its deliberations').

While the general power-giving clause is effectively acknowledging the existence of a sphere of affairs peculiar to local bodies, these powers on the other hand, are 'absolutely, not inherent'.[9] Local bodies, henceforth incorporated within the unitary State, no longer possess natural rights as in the Middle Ages. It is the State that gives legal definition to their general role. For all that, while the State creates the possibility of governing local affairs through local bodies, it

> *ne crée pas leur substance, ni leur contenu, mais seulement leur autorité. . . Lorsque le législateur les consacre en les incorporant dans des droits juridiquement sanctionnés, il ne les crée pas, il leur donne la possibilité de s'exercer dans le cadre et sous la protection de l'ordre juridique existant* (does not create their substance [i.e. that of local affairs], nor their content, but only their authority. . . . When legislators establish them by incorporating them in laws that have been legally sanctioned, they do not create them, but enable them to be exercised within the framework of and under the protection of the existing legal order).[10]

Indeed, the law cannot define them, for '*le développement du droit est ici le reflet de la reconnaissance de la puissance propre de la personne et de sa volonté subjective*' ('Here, the development of law reflects a recognition of the local bodies' own power and of its subjective will').[11] The clause expresses the existence of a local body's own rights, and it is justified—by its flexibility, by its ability to adapt according to the demands of social groups, which are the substrata of the local body. But as a matter of fact the clause is only complementary, residual. While it determines a sphere of local powers, a product of local initiative, it only complements the powers that are legally ascribed. However, while the ambit of local affairs is effectively limited by the scope of legally determined attributions, it is nonetheless a source of overall power—a general role.

The notion of local affairs does not help to distinguish the national sphere from the local. Yet, the classical theory

> *a entretenu l'illusion qu'il existait un critère de détermination à la fois clair et favorable à l'autonomie locale, parce que reposant sur un domaine naturel reconnu par la loi* (maintained the illusion that that there was a determing criterion that was both clear and favourable to local autonomy, because it was based on the natural domain recognised by the law).[12]

This observation is derived from an error in interpretation by which local affairs are defined as '*un ensemble de matières, de travaux, d'activités qui seraient locaux par leur objet concret*' ('an ensemble of material, work and activities that would be considered local due to their specific purpose').[13] While until the nineteenth century, it was possible to identify the material content of intrinsically local affairs, it is no longer the same today. The development of public institutions, the integration of local bodies within the State apparatus, in a more global and complex public sphere, no longer allows the development of 'autonomous' local life (in the sense of a life outside of the State). In fact, the local interest no longer exists, for it is nationalized due to multiple factors: concerns about equality, solidarity, the imperatives of city and regional planning, of urbanization and economic development, as well as the effectiveness of public policies. The distinction became so invisible that local affairs lost their specific features. It then became practically impossible in principle to define what these affairs cover. '*si la formule d'affaires locales parait simple, c'est de la simplicité merveilleuse du passé administratif*' ('if the local affairs formula seems simple, it is due to the marvellous simplicity of the administrative past'). '*Dresser un inventaire des affaires locales*' ('Drawing up an inventory of local affairs'),[15] and defining them in concrete terms, leads to an impasse. There is no material domain reserved for local bodies.

The criterion for local affairs is not, as we have just seen, the subject matter, but the goals pursued. The law always understood local affairs with reference to local public interest. At the core, the notion of local affairs is a sociological datum, for it reflects the needs of the population residing within the local territory. Local affairs are not exclusive of one another. For example, a commune's interest is not exclusive of an intervention by a department of the same nature, for what is felt as a need in the commune could also be felt elsewhere. That is why the public water distribution service—traditionally described as a commune-level public service—was recognized as a departmental public service by the State Council in the 'Ville de Cayenne'[16] decree. By definition, this notion is barely legal, but is based on a variable and contingent sociological substratum. As such, it cannot be strictly defined once and for all, but allows for possible future changes. It is characterized by its 'dynamism'. It is

> *une incitation, pour chaque collectivité à continuel-lement inventer, créer, à aller au-delà de ce que fait l'État, de faire autre chose et autrement. C'est en quelque sorte le droit à la différence que consacre la clause générale de compétence au profit des collectivités locales* (an incentive, for each local body to continually invent, create, go beyond what the State does, to do other things in other ways. It is in some ways the right to be different that the general clause on powers confers, for the benefit of local bodies).[17]

In conclusion, the notion of local affairs should no longer be used for delimiting powers, which is based on a field of local intervention in opposition to other interests. Since the impossibility of providing a concrete definition of the notion of local affairs led to the inability to delimit the scope of local powers in relation to national powers, some scholars decided that the notion of local affairs was of no use. That is why it was described as 'a hollow notion, devoid of meaning', or better still as an 'outdated'[18] notion. Indeed, some authors argue the abandonment of the general clause in favour of the exclusive division of powers brought about by decentralization laws. However, the general clause on powers and the notion of local affairs '*méritent davantage d'être resituées qu'écartées*' ('deserve to be restored rather than set aside').[19] The notion of local affairs should be understood in terms of the fact that it gives local bodies the general role to intervene and not on what it does not give—which is a definite, guaranteed criterion for the division of powers.

B. What of the Principle of Subsidiarity?

The constitutional revision of 28 March 2003,[20] introduced the principle according to which '*les collectivités territoriales ont vocation à prendre les décisions pour l'ensemble des compétences qui peuvent le mieux être mises en œuvre à leur échelon*' ('the purpose of territorial governments is to make decisions in relation to all the powers that can be best implemented at their level') (Art. 72C). This refers to the issue of local affairs, although it may be differently interpreted today. The fact remains that it is quite blurry and indeterminate. What criteria should be used to assess progress? Is proximity to citizens to be taken into account, i.e. democratic logic or effectiveness, or the rationality of action in the logical framework of public performance? It is for the legislators and judges to give concrete shape to this objective.

Subsidiarity appears as a criterion that is '*plus prometteur que précis*' ('more promising than precise')[21] as '*une règle de bonne gouvernance plus qu'un véritable principe juridique*' ('a rule of good governance rather than a genuine legal principle'),[22] this is because the principle of subsidiarity formulates an objective to be attained but it cannot be directly invoked by local bodies before the judge.[23] Nevertheless, it manifests a new 'state of mind',[24] in that it indicates that the

> *législateur devra penser l'exercice d'une compétence par les niveaux inférieurs avant de songer à remonter son exercice aux niveaux supérieurs* (legislators will have to think of the exercise of certain powers by the lower levels before thinking of translating such a practice to higher levels).[25]

Thus, although this may only be symbolic and would not provide any concrete guarantees to local bodies, the formulation of the principle of subsidiarity *à la française*[26] in the constitution recognizes the equal dignity and legitimacy of local bodies in undertaking administrative functions.

Thus, instead of providing a constitutional guarantee of local powers as is the case in federal States, French Law inclines towards the search for an optimal method of dividing powers, i.e. towards a more technical problematic in the absence of a solution to the fundamental question of the State's and local bodies' respective places.

II. THE WILL TO DEVELOP METHODS FOR THE DIVISION OF POWERS

For wanting a definite criteria to serve as a guide for the division of powers, French legislators tried to develop a method for the division of powers in 1983. They decided to divide the power between 'blocks' at the local body level, granting each block a different subject specializations (A). At the time of the new Act strengthening decentralization, the results of this method were not assessed as very good. The 13 August 2004 Act relating to local liberties and responsibilities made a significant transfer of powers from the State to local bodies. However, it was characterized by a very realistic and pragmatic method (B).

A. 1983: Dividing Power Between Blocks

The 7 January and 22 July 1983 Acts had developed a power-division methodology by defining blocks of power at the local level, in order to avoid local overlapping and dual financing. But the consequence of these laws was that the citizens never got to know who did what, and more importantly dilution of responsibilities. The Act likewise laid down the principle excluding the tutelage of one local body over another (Art. l 111-3 CGCT), which means the equality of all local bodies, whatever their category (Commune, Department or Region) or size. Thus, Communes were assigned most powers in matters of town-planning and land licenses. Likewise, Departments held the main powers in matters of social action, health and safety, rural facilities and land development, to quote only the most important. Finally, Regions henceforth governed economic development activities, continued professional training and apprenticeship, schools, and so on.

But this enumeration of subjects—'power blocks'—proved very defective when put into practice. Some powers were shared in a structured manner, but by dividing the same block of subjects among different levels of local bodies. Thus, in the field of education, Communes governed pre-elementary and elementary education, Departments looked after colleges and Regions were in charge of secondary schools. This technique of specialization according to the level of the local body was not practical in all fields. Also, some domains covered areas that were the responsibility of several local bodies. Intervention in terms of aid to enterprises was undoubtedly the subject of harmonization by the Regional Council, but other levels of local bodies were not forbidden to take action. There were still numerous instances of double financing that hindered the system's legibility. Finally, a substantial number of powers were entrusted to all the levels of local bodies without any precise specification about their linkages, especially in the case of powers related to cultural matters. The desire for transparency (for the citizens especially) was praiseworthy, but utopian, for it was not possible to identify the relevant levels for the exercise of different powers. The relevance of the attribution of power to a given local body level was, indeed, based on objective factors, but tradition and lobbying also played a considerable role, as proved by the importance given to the Departments in the new transfer of powers that took place in 2004, since this level perhaps felt threatened by the competition it faced, from above by the Regions, and from below by the Communes.

B. 2004: A Pragmatic Step

The 13 August 2004 Act granted many new powers to local bodies. The State refocused on regalian missions (pertaining to their prerogative) and entrusted several powers to the local bodies closest to the citizens. Truly speaking, the 2004 Act[27] implemented Phase 3 of the decentralization process (after Phase 1 in 1871–84 and Phase 2 in 1982–3). But this time, it was in an age of pragmatism.

The power blocks designated in 1983 did not disappear; in fact, they were further entrenched. However, rather than power blocks that failed to correspond to a very complicated reality, the emphasis was now on 'leaders', on fields of competence in which a local body exercised its main powers although this may not have been its exclusive prerogative. Other powers that were shared either in a structured manner (for example education) or without any specific interlinkages (for example culture) were strengthened or rationalized. Finally, new fields were added.

Thus, the principal powers enjoyed by Regions in matters of economic development and professional training were intensified. As for Departments, the Act strengthened them substantially, thought it may have seemed as if this level had been put in the hot seat. Departments asserted themselves as leaders in social action, in that they 'defined and implemented social action policies', for which they were granted general coordination powers. Compared to the other levels, Communes were neglected by the Act, which reinforced the idea that the small size of French Communes and their dispersion (3,70,000 Communes, of which 90 per cent had less than 3,500 inhabitants) were obstacles to the strengthening of their powers. On the contrary, 'intercommunalities' in the form of public establishments for 'intercommune' cooperation asserted themselves as the obvious substitute level. Finally, although the law related to 'local liberties', the presence of the State was solidly reaffirmed. The State appropriated certain powers for itself (for instance, the fight against major diseases, epidemics, vaccinations, and the fight against cancer and leprosy). It could take for itself substitute powers in the context of the allocation of social housing, or in the absence of an agreement between Communes on the division of school expenses. The State's role as guarantor was reaffirmed.

Thus the 1984 Act referred to the national public service of education and mentioned that the State ensured consistency and efficiency in the local network.

The Act established a classification based on the scope of powers and not according to the level of the local body, and rightly so. The debate on the optimal method of the division of powers was deliberately set aside. It is easy to see that the sharing of powers was assumed as uncontroversial and that these new powers were not fixed once and for all by the legislators. Thus, this new transfer of powers offered three original features in that the powers were sometimes experimental (1), sometimes discretionary (2) and sometimes based on the application of the notion of the leading local body (3).

1. *Experimental Powers*

The sense of pragmatism one felt on reading the 1984 Act is strengthened by its evolutionary nature and the calendar of the division of powers it established, which would only come into effect in 2008, in particular because of the introduction of the practice of experimentation. Indeed, thanks to the new Article 37-al 1, introduced by the constitutional revision of 28 March 2003: 'for a limited purpose and duration, the Act and the regulations may include provisions of an experimental nature'. There were nine such so-called 'national' experimentations in the Act, as the legislators or governing powers (namely the executive) wanted them, and their aim was to test the validity and effectiveness of such a transfer of powers. They anticipated a time period at the end of which they would be null and void or generalized. But the time period varied, which led to a very complicated calendar. This new practice allowed the exercise of powers with a variable geometry in time and space, breaking with the principle of uniformity.

The Regions enjoyed powers in matters of economic development, management of community funds and the establishment of hospital facilities. Thus, Regions were principally but not exclusively concerned. Departments would be able to experiment with exercising their powers in the matter of legal protection of the youth, and Communes would be able to experiment with a new administrative organization for primary schools or with helping in rehabilitating unsound housing. The Constitutional Council admitted the validity of this procedure although it departed from the principle of equality before law, provided that legislators defined its aim and conditions quite precisely and they did not disregard other constitutional requirements.[28] The new procedure faces great uncertainty for, in order to make the transfer more acceptable or to have time to solve outstanding problems, in certain fields such as the management of civilian aerodromes, experimentation is referred to, whereas the transfer of power has already been generalized!

Furthermore, another possibility of so-called 'local' experimentation that had not yet been implemented was offered to local bodies. Thus, by virtue of Article 72, Paragraph 4 of the Constitution,

> *dans les conditions prévues par la loi organique et sauf lorsque sont en cause les conditions essentielles d'exercice d'une liberté publique ou d'un droit constitutionnellement garanti, les collectivités territoriales et leurs groupements peuvent, lorsque selon le cas la loi ou le règlement l'a prévu, déroger à titre expérimental et pour un objet et une durée limités aux dispositions législatives ou réglementaires qui régissent l'exercice de leurs compétences* (Under the conditions provided by the organic law and except when the fundamental conditions for exercising a public freedom or a constitutionally guaranteed right are in question, local bodies and their groupings can, when provided for by the law or regulations, depending on the case, depart from the legislative or regulatory provisions that govern the exercise of their powers, as an experiment and for a limited purpose and duration).

The 1 August 2003 Act relating to experimentation by local bodies[29] frames this new procedure in very strict terms, for it could lead to an infringement of national laws and regulations and create a dent in the principle of a single, uniform norm and, therefore, in the equality of citizens[30]—a 'sacrosanct' principle of the indivisible French republic. It actually means temporarily allowing local bodies to try solutions that are more specific and more appropriate given the diversity of situations and territories, and to break with uniformity. For all that, the procedure does not establish any normative autonomous power for local bodies, since an authorization from the State is required to implement it, with the State then having to take the decision to pursue, generalize or discard the experiment. The local experimentation procedure is interesting in principle due to its underlying concern for the effectiveness of government action and its visible relinquishment of theoretical responses to the transfer of powers. But one doubts that it is used very often, for the procedure is very unwieldy and tightly defined by the national authority.[31]

2. *Discretionary Powers*

Apart from experiments as such, the feeling of being in the presence of a 'patchwork of local powers' is strengthened by the importance given to voluntary action. Many of the powers that the State transferred to local bodies in 2004 were not transferred compulsorily but on a discretionary basis, as was the case with the transfer of powers at the request of local bodies or even with the delegation of powers. It was an '*à la carte*' decentralization that was instituted. Thus, for example, Article 145 of the 13 August 2004 Act affirmed that

> *à l'initiative de la région et du département ou à leur demande, les communes et leurs groupements peuvent participer à l'exercice de tout ou partie des compétences relevant de la responsabilité de l'une ou de l'autre de ces collectivités territoriales, dans des conditions prévues par une convention* (at the initiative of the Region or Department or at their request, Communes and their groupings can exercise all or part of their powers that fall under the responsibility of one or other of these local bodies, under the conditions provided for in an agreement).

Here, the Act gives way to a procedure of requsting powers, which means that a local body or group of local bodies may apply to collaborate in the exercise of powers vested in other levels of government. Such an appeal may be top-down—from a regional local body to a smaller local body or association—or bottom-up, at the latter's request. Furthermore, the delegation of powers—especially from Departments or Regions to public establishments for 'inter-commune' cooperation with their own taxation system (Art. 51)—enables activities on behalf of and for the benefit of the Department or Region. Such an association for exercising joint powers is put into concrete form by the creation of a conference of executives—a forum for consultation between Departments and Regions to promote better harmonization.

In all cases, such requests are voluntary and confirm contract-based solutions as the privileged method for establishing relations between local bodies, with the now well-known advantages and defects of this method of exercising powers.[32] Such voluntary action has become permanent, in that it does not have any fixed time limit. Indeed, twenty agreements that have been or will be concluded between Prefects for applying the Act can be counted. The Act has not, *a priori*, created an entire series of transferred powers, but the option of exercising them does exist. These are called 'alternative transfers'.[33] Such is the case for powers related to farming, the development of non-autonomous ports, or the public domain of rivers or even the transfer of ownership of classified buildings, attributed according to the principle of 'the highest bid', '*d'une mise aux enchères aux collectivités territoriales et à leur groupements de façon indéterminée*' ('of being put up for auction for local bodies and their associations in an unspecified manner'[34]). It is to be noted that legislators did not want to alarm 'intra-regional' local bodies by transferring often experimental powers to Regions or by formulating the powers that Regions could exercise with regard to other local bodies in a less directive fashion.

While the objective of clarity or legibility for citizens has become secondary with up 2004 Act, cooperation and partnership in the implementation of public policies between different levels of local bodies has become the key principle along with the requirement of effective government action. The last fact was also expressed, in particular, by the notion of the leading local body.

3. *The Notion of a Leading Local Body*

If a comparison is made between the 7 January and 22 July 1983 Acts, it must be emphasized that the division of powers was set down in principle—very far from the requirement of clarification and legibility—although the prime minister would have wished to, in his words, '*mettre un terme à la cogestion des politiques publiques*' (put an end to the co-management of public policies). The emphasis here was on associated action, partnership, and the alternative and discretionary nature of a fair number of transfers. Nevertheless, the concern for coherence and coordination was not absent. Without the word being used, the idea of a leading local body[35] was given concrete shape, especially to the benefit of Regions, although the prohibition of the tutelage of one local body over another was constitutionally reaffirmed at the same time. Thus, Article 72 of the Constitution calls for a re-balancing of something that initially appears to be irreconcilable, namely the prohibition of the tutelage of one local body over another, with the implementation of joint action and coordinated policies. According to this article,

> *Lorsque l'exercice d'une compétence nécessite le concours d'une ou plusieurs collectivités territoriales, la loi peut autoriser l'une d'entre elles ou un de leurs groupements à organiser les modalités de leur action commune* (When the exercise of a power necessitates the cooperation of one or several local bodies, the law can authorise any one of them or one of their associations to organise the form of their joint action).

A lot of uncertainty surrounds this possibility, which 'remains to be developed'.[36] This procedure for modifying the division of powers is not new. As early as in 1995, the Act on land use planning and development had provided that

> *collectivités pourront par convention désigner l'une d'entre elles comme chef de file pour l'exercice d'une compétence ou d'un groupe de compétences relevant de plusieurs collectivités* (local bodies could by agreement designate one amongst them as the leader for exercising a given power or group of powers falling under the jurisdiction of several local bodies).

But the Constitutional Council had censored this[37] on the grounds that only the law should intervene to determine the powers of local bodies. It could not allow the latter do so themselves. Now, the idea was taken up again and given concrete shape in the 13 August 2004 Act, which, rather than putting an end to power tangles, tried to rationalize them.[38] This is the case with the coordinator's role that Regions had to play in the field of economic development and Departments had to play in the area of social action. The Act provides very few details regarding the requirements for such consultations, but it has not been subject to a vote of censor on this point. No guarantee has likewise been provided as regards the sanctions the leader would have at its disposal in relation to other local body levels that prove to be reticent, for instance, by refusing to sign the joint action implementation contract.[39] The procedure remains very hazy in this regard.

The desire to grant greater powers to local bodies has been demonstrated clearly by the French Constitution and French legislators. But a great deal of uncertainty remains. First and foremost in relation to the reasons for, and the significance of, the affirmation of such subsidiarity. Is it a question of ordaining the proximity of the decision-making power as a 'school for democracy' or of improving the efficiency of government action, or even of the State shifting responsibilities to local bodies by equipping them to wield certain powers? Then, as for the modalities of such transfers of power, while sometimes, as in 1983, the legislators were looking for a certain visibility, they did so without really examining the necessity, the relevance or the usefulness of such transfers.[40] It is true that finding a solution to this issue seems quite difficult when France has four territorial administration levels.[41] A clear and coherent division of powers in terms of different territories/local bodies cannot be carried out and has not been carried out until today, as much for political reasons as for technical ones. In 2004, realistic legislators proposed a pragmatic, partnership-based notion of the exercise of local powers, which—thanks to its potential and the freedom it granted to local bodies to strengthen such powers— could lead to perpetuating diversity as we have never so far known it in the context of our unitary State.

NOTES

1. L. Janicot, *Réflexions sur la notion de compétences propres appliquée aux collectivités territoriales en droit français*, AJDA, 2004, p. 1574.
2. According to Article 1 of the Constitution of 4 October 1958: '*La France est une République indivisible, démocratique laïque et sociale. . . . Son organisation est décentralisée*' (France is an indivisible, democratic, secular and social Republic. . . . Its organization is decentralised).

3. DC 25/02/1982, issue no. 82–137 and DC issue no. 82–138, note J. Boulouis, AJDA, 1982, p. 303.
4. Art. l 2121-29 (CGCT—*Code général des collectivités territoriales* or General Code for Local Bodies) for communes, 3211-1 for Departments and L 4221-1 for Regions).
5. JO 8/01.
6. JO 17/08.
7. L. Janicot, prec., p. 1583.
8. J. Caillosse, 'Le savoir juridique à l'épreuve de la décentralisation', local body directory, LITEC, 1988, p. 14, from J.C. Douence, 'La région, collectivité à vocation générale ou spécialisée?', RFDA, 1986, p. 541.
9. R. Carré de Malberg, 'Contribution à la théorie générale de l'Etat', prec., p. 179, cit. by M.C. Rouault, 'L'intérêt communal', thesis, 1991, PUL, p. 240.
10. G. Burdeau, 'Traité de science politique', vol. 2, 'L'Etat', LGDJ, 1980, p. 405.
11. B. Faure, Thesis, 'Le pouvoir réglementaire des collectivités locales', Pau, 1992, p. 277.
12. J.C. Douence, 'La notion de collectivité locale', Ency Collectivités locales, vol. V, Dalloz, 1988.
13. Idem.
14. Ch. Autexier, 'L'ancrage constitutionnel des collectivités de la République', RDP, 1982, p. 615.
15. J. Chapuisat, 'La notion d'affaires locales en droit administratif français', thesis, Paris 2, 1972, p. 12.
16. CE 13/03/1985, Ville de Cayenne et al., AJDA, 1985, p. 376, obs. L. Richer.
17. J.M. Pontier, 'L'Etat et les collectivités locales (la répartition des compétences)', thesis, LGDJ, 1978, p. 573.
18. Respectivement J. Chapuisat, 'Les affaires communales', AJDA, 1976, p. 472, Ch. Autexier, prec., p. 609, G. Burdeau, op. cit., p. 436.
19. B. Faure, Thesis, 'Le pouvoir réglementaire des collectivités locales', Pau, 1992, p. 73.
20. J.B. Auby, 'La loi constitutionnelle relative à la decentralisation', Dt Adm, April 2003, p. 6.
21. J.F. Brisson, 'Les nouvelles clefs de répartition des compétences entre l'Etat et les collectivités locales', AJDA 2003, p. 530.
22. J.F. Brisson, p. 531.
23. B. Mercuzot, 'La subsidiarité à la française', Review Europa Civitas, PU Nancy, 2003, pp. 79–93.

24. Idem.
25. Ibid.
26. Ibid.
27. J. Moreau, 'La loi no. 2004–809 du 13 août 2004 relative aux libertés et responsabilités locales', JCP G, 26/01/2005, p.133; M. Verpeaux, 'La loi du 13 août 2004: le demi-succès de l'acte II de la decentralization', AJDA, 2004, p. 1960.
28. Decision no. 2004-503 DC of 12 August 2004, Official Gazette, issue no. 190 of 17 August 2004, p. 14648, commentary by B. Faure, 'Les relations paradoxales de l'expérimentation et du principe d'égalité', RFDA, 2004, p. 1150.
29. J.M. Pontier, 'La loi organique relative à l'expérimentation par les collectivités territoriales', AJDA, 2003, p. 1715; J.L. Pissaloux, 'Réflexions sur l'expérimentation normative', Dt Adm, November 2003, p. 12.
30. B. Faure, prec, p. 1150.
31. cf. Organic Act of 1 August 2003 that lays down considerable limits.
32. G. Marcou, F. Rangeon and J.L. Thiébault, 'La coopération contractuelle et le gouvernement des villes', l'Harmattan, 1997; L. Richer, 'La contractualisation comme technique de gestion des affaires publiques', AJDA, 2003, p. 972.
33. J.M. Pontier, 'Les nouvelles compétences de la region', AJDA, 2004, p. 1968.
34. Idem.
35. J.M. Pontier, 'Pour une reconnaissance de la notion de collectivité chef de file', RA issue no. 328, p. 402.
36. J.F. Joye, 'La notion de chef de file en droit des collectivités locales', JCl, *Collectivités territoriales-intercommunalités*, July 2003, p. 12.
37. DC issue no. 94-358 of 26 January 1995.
38. B. Mercuzot, 'L'institutionnalisation des chefs de file', in *Les nouvelles responsabilités locales*, a presentation at the Study Session on 5 November 2004, Amiens.
39. Idem.
40. J.M. Pontier, 'Actualité, continuité et difficultés des transferts de compétences entre l'Etat et les collectivités territoriales', RFDA, 2003, p. 35.
41. Communes, 'Intercommunalities', Departments, Regions.

CHAPTER 11

Environment and Local Bodies: What Kind of Decentralization?

FLORENCE JAMAY

The Act II on decentralization neglected environmental issues and with the 13 August 2004 Act on Local Freedoms and Responsibilities[1] very few powers were transferred to the local bodies, raising the issue of the link between decentralization and the environment. A complex and ambiguous issue, it has already been the subject of many research papers, but whether this relationship is compatible or contradictory in nature is yet to be decided. Whereas environmental management is a power that is both feared and coveted by local governments and, in any case, seems to be one of the basic issues at stake, the problem that arises is to what extent decentralization is desirable in this sector. In fact, while decentralization obviously brings about a rapprochement with ground realities, thereby promoting the principle of proximity, it is also fraught with risks.

Until 1983, the State alone was responsible for environmental policies. The 7 January 1983 Act on the division of powers introduced a responsibility-sharing mechanism between the State and local bodies in Article 1, which states:

> the State shall cooperate with Communes, Departments and Regions to protect the environment and improve the quality of life ('*l' État concourt avec les communes, les départements et les régions à la protection de l'environnement et à l'amélioration du cadre de vie.*' (Art. L 1111-2 of the *Code general des collectivités territoriales* or General Code for Local Bodies)

Thus, there is definitely joint responsibility of the State and local governments. However, this power could be exercised either under the exclusive jurisdiction of the State or under joint jurisdiction or through an automatic or optional transfer of power, depending on the sector.[2]

However, the extreme prudence exercised by the legislators as regards the transfer of powers related to environmental issues must be stressed here, as it essentially meant that unlike town planning, which was largely decentralized by the 1982 and 1983 Decentralization Acts, environment still remained basically within the sphere of the State. When the 2 February 1995 Act on strengthening environmental protection was adopted[3] it did not change the basic framework, despite its author's claim of having further devolved environmental policy matters to the department level. This choice was corroborated again by the 13 August 2004 Act.

While the transfer of power mechanism failed to deal with this matter, it has become imperative for local bodies today to take action in the environmental field. A review of their expenditure on this account would suffice to measure their involvement, especially the expenditure incurred by communes, which amounted to € 6.1 billion in 2002,[4] accounting for 11 per cent of these local bodies' total expenditure; most of the money was earmarked for water and waste disposal. On the whole, local bodies bear 58 per cent of the expenditure on environmental protection.

While the Acts were reticent *vis-à-vis* the transfer of powers in the environmental field (I), we should nevertheless bring to light how environmental concerns gained ground amongst local bodies, which have invested extensively in this sector and have been able to devise positive environmental policies (II).

I. A TENTATIVE DEVOLUTION OF POWERS ON ENVIRONMENTAL MATTERS

The result of the reticence shown *vis-à-vis* local bodies was that the State continued to hold most powers in environmental matters. While the State still wished to retain its powers in this sector—and we shall analyse the reasons for it (A)—the local bodies too were striving to develop a local approach to environmental problems (B).

A. Powers that were Retained

The State's reticence in transferring certain powers on environmental matters to local bodies can be attributed to a combination of factors.

First of all, it must be borne in mind that environmental matters are linked to public health (pesticides, genetically modified organisms, dioxins, water quality, air quality, etc.) and public safety issues (industrial risks, natural hazards: floods, risks related to climate change, etc.) and could not be decentralized as a whole because of the resources involved and also because governance in environmental matters fell under the State's competence. Hence, risk prevention activities were primarily the State's responsibility, with the activities of local bodies confined to executing measures taken at the national level.[5] Due to the imperatives of uniform norms, it was considered dangerous to allow local authorities to assess the preventive measures to be adopted, each in their own different way. Further, there were a number of 'special forces' on environmental matters (classified installations, water, genetically modified organisms, etc.) that already existed in this sector, whose presence scaled down the policing powers of mayors.[6] In fact, this explained the revocation of municipal bye-laws adopted by mayors, who banned the cultivation of genetically modified organisms or the installation of mobile telephony antennas, as they wished to implement the precautionary principle in their territory.[7] In fact, to implement such a principle, you need the services of experts, which is beyond the capacity of most local governments. Thus, we may well believe that the implementation of the precautionary principle basically implied that regulations concerning scientific issues that were yet to be resolved could not be decentralized.[8]

The great influence exerted by European Community law over France's national laws (80 per cent of which originate from the Community) would then explain why the State did not wish to abdicate its powers in this sector. For these laws clearly hold the State responsible for ensuring their compliance and implementation. It also needs to be emphasized here that the origin of many pre-litigation procedures instituted against France stemmed from a lack or partial implementation by local bodies of obligations emanating from the European Community laws. There are many examples: the case of water, for instance, insofar as local bodies had a major role to play in the application of the directive on urban effluents. However, the state failed to meet the deadline for building the appropriate facilities for water treatment, in order to achieve the quality levels envisaged in the directive.[9] The case of biodiversity protection is anoter example. There was reticence on the part of the local bodies to implement the Natura 2000[10] directive and also the issue of waste disposal, in which France faced condemnation essentially because of the local bodies' inability to ensure that domestic waste incineration plants complied with the standards established. It must be underlined that as for water and waste disposal, the local bodies' delay in implementing their obligation was due to the heavy investments involved.

Finally, the environment was a high stakes issue and a controversial subject by nature at the national level, and more so at the local level, where there was intense lobbying to abolish protection measures. There was always the risk that local representatives would rather pursue short-term interests, especially those involving economic gain, rather than issues concerning environmental protection.[11] Whereas Article L 2212-2 of the local bodies' general code (*Code général des collectivités territoriales*) stipulates that it is the mayor's responsibility to prevent and manage natural hazards, in practice it was the prefect who drew up risk prevention plans. This practice was the result of the fears expressed in so many words by the legislators with regard to leaving this instrument in the hands of local elected representatives, who might, for example, fail to freeze developments on low-lying flood-prone lands as they could be much sought-after by real estate promoters.[12]

Apart from the State's desire to retain key powers in environmental matters, it also seemed that local bodies found it difficult to come out with a localized environmental approach.

B. Deficiencies in the Local Approach

Local bodies have been struggling to promote a territorial approach to environmental policies. The complex nature of power sharing between them resulted in power dispersal, which made the implementation of localized environmental policies a difficult proposition (1) and, as such, they found it difficult to be acknowledged as a relevant space for dealing with environmental issues (2).

1. *Complex Nature of Power Sharing between Local Bodies*

A glance at these laws would demonstrate the very complex structure of power sharing on environmental matters. There are numerous stakeholders in this field and it is difficult to define each one's responsibility. The complexity was further strengthened by the nature of environmental law itself, composed of legislations adopted in different eras and for different reasons, which piled up on each other with the passage of time to respond to specific issues and were often devoid of coherence.[13] Consequently, environmental norms were not very readable. These two phenomena, combined together, resulted in the lack of consistency and coherence as well as that of transparency in environmental policies.[14]

At first, it seemed that there was a sharing of powers in this field, but none of the local bodies seemed to have played a preeminent role. And secondly, a quick analysis of the various powers exercised shows the lack of expertise of local bodies.

Though Communes seemed to be working in close proximity, with a natural vocation for informing and sensitizing people on environmental issues, it cannot, however, be assumed that they were an appropriate level for managing environmental problems. The smallness of their territory and lack of technical know-how and financial capacity made implementing environmental policies a difficult proposition. Notwithstanding this, certain powers were conferred upon them, whereas it was the impact of other powers—not necessarily directly linked to the environment—that was likely to be significant on this issue.[15]

Their fundamental role lay in establishing and managing local public utilities. Hence, the 15 July 1975 Act assigned waste management to them, entrusting them with the task of waste collection and disposal. Water distribution, and organizing and managing sanitation also fell within their powers. Above all, they had to bear the total expenditure on community sanitation and individual sanitation systems based on the commune's requirements and, in particular, take into account the total population—both inhabitants and seasonal visitors (Art. L 2224-8 of the *Code général des collectivités territoriales*, or the General Code for Local Bodies). The Communes considered these as essential powers on environmental issues. However, they were extremely cumbersome and costly to implement: domestic waste pollutants (waste water and solid waste) management and recycling accounted for up to 89 per cent of the Communes' expenditure on the environment, as they required heavy infrastructure (pipelines, incinerating plants, etc.) whose cost escalated proportionally as national and European norms became stricter.[16] Thus, there arose the issue of funding these Commune environmental policies.

Mayors were empowered to use their local policing powers to enforce environmental policies. In fact, it was the municipal police's duty to ensure order, public safety, security and public health (Art. L 2112-2 of the *Code général des collectivités territoriales*), which implied 'safety and convenience of movement in the streets' and included 'cleanliness, lighting, removal of obstructions, demolitions or repairing of buildings threatening to collapse' (para 1), 'the duty to crack down on the threat to public peace (. . .), noise, including neighbourhood noise' (para 2), 'the duty to prevent, through appropriate measures, and to put an end to calamitous accidents and scourges as well as all types of pollution, such as fires, floods, jetty failures, land or rock slides, avalanches or other natural accidents, epidemics, contagious and epizootic diseases' (para 5). Under the 30 December 1966 Act on air,[17] in his capacity as the person in charge of traffic and parking police, the mayor could intervene and take measures pertaining to environmental protection, and notably, close certain roads to traffic (Art. L 2213-2 of the *Code général des collectivités territoriales*). He could also limit access to or prohibit vehicles plying on certain routes or sectors of the commune where traffic could disturb either the neighbourhood peace or cause air pollution, or in order to protect certain animal or plant species, or in order to protect natural spaces, landscapes or sites for aesthetic, ecological, agricultural, forestry or tourism development (Art. L 2213-4 of the *Code général des collectivités territoriales*). Thus, this kind of policing could have a specifically environmental goal.[18] But we cannot read too much into the powers conferred on the mayor's office insofar as there were several special administrative police forces that came under the Prefect's control (classified installations, water, genetically modified organisms, etc.) and thus limited the mayor's possibilities to intervene.

Apart from their powers in environmental matters, Communes could pursue a veritable environmental protection policy through the powers vested in them for urban development. Indeed, the local urban development documents could be used as tools for environmental protection and management. The 10 July 1976 Act on nature conservation states that 'urban development documents ought to respect environmental concerns' (Article 2). And according to Article 1 of the 12 October 1977 Implementing Order, 'environmental concerns should be taken into account by urban development documents in their procedural framework'. The 13 December 2000 Act on urban renewal and solidarity[19] aimed at further strengthening harmonization between land use policies and environmental policies.[20] And the 3 June 2004 Ordinance[21] lay down that territorial consistency plans and local urban development plans that were likely to have a significant effect on the environment depending on the area to which they applied, had to undergo an environmental evaluation (Art. L 121-10 of the *Code de l'urbanisme* or Urban Planning Code). Reports submitted for environmental evaluation defined and assessed the significant impact that the document could have on the environment and gave a list of measures to be taken to avoid, reduce and compensate negative effects to the extent possible (Art. L 121-11). This integral approach made sure that the rigorous procedures for the preparation of the local urban development plan were strictly complied with, especially the status report,[22] which was henceforth to be submitted along with town planning and sustainable development projects, which defined the general policy for urban development and planning for the commune as a whole (Article L 123-1, al. 2). Local urban development projects could therefore set aside reserved spaces and delineate listed woodlands (Art. L 123-8 al. 8 and Art. L 130-1). They could also delineate natural and forest zones (called N zones) where there would be minimal urban development (Art. R 123-8). Issuing building licenses could enable better environment administration and protection, through compliance with local urban development plans.

The Department, as a local body as well as an administrative district of the State's services, was often considered as the most appropriate level for dealing with environmental issues.[23] Unlike the Commune, it enjoyed both human and financial resources in adequate measure and presented a suitable territorial dimension for a general environmental protection policy while at the same time benefiting from its inhabitants having a sense of belonging, unlike the Region.[24]

The proposals given in the Barnier report on environmental policy clearly favoured the Departments, but they were not followed.[25] No real power transfer took place and the Department was only given simple sectoral or consultative powers. However, it did have the possibility of developing a veritable policy for the conservation of sites, landscapes and natural environments and of protecting natural habitats thanks to the powers concerning sensitive natural areas that were conferred upon it (Art. L 142-1 of the *Code de l'urbanisme* or Urban Planning Code). To do this it was vested with two prerogatives: it could impose a departmental tax to preserve sensitive natural areas and exercise pre-emptive rights over certain zones delineated by the General Council in concurrence with the respective communes. It also had the power to create walking and trekking areas (Art. L 361-1 of the *Code de l'environnement* or Environmental Code derived from Article 56 of the 22 July 1983 Act). Later on it was vested with powers concerning the preparation of domestic waste and common industrial waste disposal plans. But it must be mentioned that since the 2 February 1995 Act, Departments have had the choice to assume these powers, an option that was not very popular since only ten General Councils opted for it. This explains why the 13 August 2004 Act concerning local responsibilities made the transfer of these powers mandatory. Indeed, this measure was not devoid of pragmatism. When shortage of waste water outfall reached threatening proportions,[26] there was evidently a desire to involve local stakeholders in a more active role behind this mandatory power transfer, which was supposed to facilitate people's acceptance of often-undesirable facilities.[27] Finally, Departments also enjoyed a number of consultative and proposal-submitting powers; they were consulted especially while territorial consistency plans were being drawn up, notably by the Prefect, for the definition of the perimeter to be covered (Art. L 122-3 III of the Code de l'urbanisme or the Urban Planning Code) by water development and management plans or marine development plans. The importance of this consultative process should not be disregarded. On their part, Departments could, in fact, be asked to develop orientations and their inclusion could be considered a condition for departmental participation in these projects.[28]

Although by their size, Regions would be the most suitable level for healthy ecosystem management and a meeting point between the urban and the rural, between conservation and development,[29] their powers were, however, limited. They were vested only with initiatory powers for the establishment of regional natural parks, a favourite framework for action by public bodies for preserving landscapes and national and cultural heritage (Art. L 333-1 of the Environmental Code). Since the 27 February 2002 Act[30] on democracy of proximity, they could, on their own initiative or at the request of the concerned owners, classify properties that qualified for natural habitat protection as regional nature reserves. However, they shared these powers with the State (Art. L 332-2 II of the Environment Code). More recently, regions have been granted planning powers. Thus, the 27 February 2002 Act entrusted them with drawing up of regional plans for air quality (Art. L 222-1 of the Environmental Code) as well as plans for special industrial waste disposal, which they could opt out of till the act was proclaimed (Art. L 541-13 of the Environmental Code). It should be emphasized here that this power transfer in no way diminished the State's right over air or waste disposal as it continued to have the possibility of taking over after a formal notice giving an eighteen month deadline, which demonstrated a total lack of faith in decentralization.[31] Although the energy policy is traditionally centralized, Regions could draw up regional wind energy plans[32] for the promotion of harmonious wind energy development, by virtue of the 3 January 2003 Act pertaining to public energy services. Thus, Regions had limited legal powers, but this did not prevent them from framing innovative policies in this field, especially through planning.[33]

Hence, as far as power sharing on environmental issues is concerned, we may say that there is no clear-cut hierarchy between territorial communities. The legislators did not find it fit to discriminate in favour of any one community over the other, which resulted in intervention by a multiplicity of actors, without it being always easy to identify the responsibilities of each of them. Consequently, powers seemed scattered and muddled, which made it difficult to define any clear environmental policy. Indeed, there was a piecemeal allotment of powers concerning water management and supervision. In fact, during discussions on the 1992 water bill, many parliamentarians recommended favouring one particular territorial community over others, but the legislators opted to allot each one of them conservation and development powers, without leaving any scope for the bill under discussion to envisage a reversal of this decision.[34] And yet, the dispersal of powers and the resultant confusion, which adversely affected the understanding and transparency of these laws and brought about a dilution of responsibilities, was often denounced. A clarification thus became necessary and local bodies insisted upon one.[35] It began with a rationalization of power sharing and the definition of each one's responsibilities. It would be interesting to initiate reflection on the identification of a leader for each environmental policy, who would work with other partners. Without excluding the exercise of several layers of powers, this would enable local bodies to coordinate the activities of several others by means of agreements. While the 13 August 2004 Act enshrined this notion, it would be rather difficult to identify a leader—even sector-wise—in this field. And in more general terms, it seems imperative to think about the overall consistency of environmental policies.

Hence, we may say that instead of being the driving force behind the policies, local bodies have emerged, first and foremost, as managers of programmes inspired at the central level.[36] Indeed, power sharing in the field of the environment has reserved supervisory and regulatory powers for the State, while transferring management to local bodies, as is evident in matters pertaining to air, water or waste. While there is a need to clarify relationships among local bodies, there is also a need to rethink the relationship between the State and local bodies, as well as to reflect about the desirable level of decentralization in the environmental field.

2. *Inappropriateness of Local Spaces for Dealing with Environmental Problems*

Given the need to have a global approach to environmental problems, decentralized local institutions could hardly be considered appropriate territorial entities to deal with these issues.[37] Thus, the inadequacy of a local territorial approach can be explained by the fact that local spaces are inappropriate to deal with environmental problems.

Hence, it is rather difficult to define the expertise available at the territorial level in matters relating to environmental protection. This makes it even more difficult to identify the relevant territory for the exercise of a specific power. Especially since environmental law—though made up of patchy regulations of different origins and times—is based on sectoral logic. Thus, while substituting sectoral logic with territorial logic does seem necessary, it is possible only on the condition that the local power-sharing plan creates large homogeneous and consistent 'wholes', which would help provide a certain autonomy to actions undertaken by each local body.[38] Otherwise, sectoral segmentation would couple with territorial fragmentation.[39] And the choice to bestow powers on each local body for every environmental sector leads to an overlapping of local actions and territorial fragmentation that impedes the emergence of autonomous local policies on environmental matters. Thus, we can only regret, along with Michel Prieur, that the organization and regulation of certain sectors such as waste disposal or air pollution have not been transferred to the Regions, pursuant to and in conformity with the framework laws valid throughout the country.[40] Besides, this fragmentation allows the State to regain its stranglehold as a necessary factor for providing coherence and consistency to local actions.[41] Along with the rising costs of environmental policies, there also arises the issue of technical and financial capabilities to manage them.

Further, environmental issues rarely coincide with institutional hierarchies; hence, global regulations become necessary to manage entities that go beyond administrative divisions such as a coastline or mountains.

Faced with such difficulties, a functional territorial approach became the order of the day and new territorial units, more in consonance with physical, ecological and geographical reality were established, such as watershed catchments basins created as early as 1964 in the field of water or national parks, whose main aim was to protect the environmental heritage. Though these entities did indeed make ecological management easier, they also complicated the relationship between the State's decentralized departments and local bodies.[42]

Further, several intercommunity groupings managed important environmental areas such as production and distribution of drinking water (more than 4,000 groupings—especially single-purpose syndicates (SIVU)—covering a population of more than 50 million inhabitants), garbage collection and treatment and waste water purification (more than 2,000 organizations in each of these fields, covering about 59 million people). Although, local bodies' expenditure on environment was about € 21 billion in 2002, more than 90 per cent was financed by communes and their associations. The latter have spent double the amount spent by communes on the environment and the sector accounted for 45 per cent of the total outlay of intercommunity groups.[43] Thus, intercommunality and environmental management seemed to be closely linked, although only commune associations, from among the inter-community structures, enjoy mandatory powers in this sector. Communities of Communes and township committees only enjoyed optional powers in this field—a rather unfortunate situation.[44] The need for a comprehensive approach for dealing with environmental problems and the heavy investments required in sectors such as water (treatment plants), waste (waste disposal plants) or urban public transport systems are the main reasons for the success of such concepts.

While we may conclude the absence of any proper decentralization of powers in the field of environment from this analysis, we should not, however, believe that there is a dearth of local environmental policies formulated by local bodies, based on their initiatory or planning powers.

II. AFFIRMATION OF LOCAL ENVIRONMENTAL POLICIES

Reading the laws alone is not sufficient to understand the role of local bodies in environmental matters. They also undertake appropriation actions and strategies, which implies that environmental problems are handled locally.[45] Proper local environmental policies are thus drawn up by local bodies, as is evident from the amount of their expenditure under this head. Indeed, their expenditure on the environment stood at € 21 billion in 2002, i.e. 1.45 per cent of the GDP or, in other words, € 340 per capita. The major part of this expenditure was earmarked for water management, followed by urban environment and waste disposal. Communes bore the bulk of this expenditure (30 per cent), especially their groupings (61 per cent). Departments (6 per cent) and Regions (3 per cent) spent much less.[46]

Though local bodies are assuming a greater role in this sector (A), their intervention, however, should always go hand-in-hand with counterweights (B).

A. Growing Importance of Local Bodies

Several local bodies have taken initiatives in environmental matters. In fact, Article 35 of the 7 January 1983 Act allows them a wide scope for intervention (Art. L 110 of the Urban Planning Code) by stating that the French territory is the common heritage of the whole nation and every public body is its manager and guarantor within the purview of its powers, thereby making protection an objective in the public interest and, thus, the duty of all bodies. Therefore, local bodies are authorized to intervene in this domain. Further, Article 16 of the 13 August 2004 Act on local responsibilities (new clause 2 in Article L 1111 of the *Code général des collectivités territoriales*) stipulates that Communes, Departments and Regions work together with the State in administering and developing the territories in all their economic, social, health, cultural and scientific dimensions as well as in ensuring sustainable development.

While they might be the source of a host of innovative approaches, rich in a variety of potentials (1), an intensification of decentralization in this sector is not necessarily the best answer for environmental protection (2).

1. *Innovative Approaches*

Some local bodies used contractual mechanisms to develop environmental actions. The implementation of local Agendas 21 should be mentioned here, in particular. These were variations of the Agenda 21 action programme adopted during the Rio Earth Summit, held in 1992. The first steps began to emerge in 1996–7 with Environmental Charters, known today as 'first generation' Agendas 21. Their aim was to implement a new economic approach that promoted sustainable development, while bearing the notion of ecological costs in mind in environmental management. They took shape particularly from 1999 onwards, after the 25 June 1999 Act on Conditions for Sustainable Territorial Land Use and Development led to the formulation of a charter providing for

> joint, sustain-able territory development projects, as per the recommendations laid down in local Agendas 21 of the Agenda 21 programme (. . .) and the basic guidelines on spatial organisation found therein, as well as measures enabling their execution and aimed at strengthening reciprocal solidarity between urban and rural areas (*le projet commun de développement durable du territoire selon les recommandations inscrites dans les agendas 21 locaux du programme Actions 21 (. . .) et les orientations fondamentales de l'organisation spatiale qui en découlent, ainsi que les mesures permettant leur mise en œuvre et visant à renforcer les solidarités réciproques entre la ville et l'espace rural*).[47]

In 2004, one hundred local bodies—for the most part Communes, but also Departments, Regions and Intercommune groups—embarked on the preparation of such a document. Thenceforth, the formulation of Agendas 21 was encouraged by the signing of individual contracts within the framework of State-Region Five-Year Plan contracts. These projects, which generally called for participation and partnership between private and public actors, ought to have promoted cost-effective production and consumption of resources (energy, water, land, air, biodiversity) and been socially responsible towards other countries as well as future generations.[48] Due to the absence of a precise definition of such a document, it is believed to be more of an action programme for sustainable development, bringing together people and other actors. Thus, the Amiens Metropolis Township Committee's Agenda 21 proposes a series of measures 'to institutionalize actions, adopted by the metropolis, pertaining to water, air, natural areas, energy, aesthetic and sound nuisances and waste disposal'.

It was also through the contractual path that the regions' role in environmental matters grew. While its powers were limited, as we have observed, planning made it possible to formulate proper regional environmental policies. State/Region five-year plan contracts—agreements concluded between the State and the Regions with the intention of linking regional level planning to the national level—enabled Regions to eventually establish their priorities in the field of environment.[49] While the initial five-year plan-related contracts incorporated the environment basically through economic development, the last generation five-year plan contracts (2000–6) attached greater importance to it. Thus, in the section on environment in the Styate-Picardie region 2000–6 Plan Contract, the region's share grew from € 1 million in 1994 to € 11 million in 2000. Europe, through its structural funds grant, can reinforce the Regions' initiatory role by contributing to the various operations initiated or coordinated by them. As it gives time to local elected representatives and economic agents to gradually integrate the environment in their strategies, like Michel Prieur, we too may consider that planning allows for a smooth regionalization of environmental issues.[50] The regional plans entrusted by Article 14 of the 29 July 1982 Act to define 'a region's medium-term economic, social and cultural development objectives', which had sometimes turned into specific sections on the environment, were substituted by the 25 June 1999 Act on Conditions for territorial planning and development, which changed the territorial development schemes established by the 4 February 1995 Act.[51] The plan established the basic guidelines for regional medium-term sustainable development, as regards the location of major facilities and services of interest to the region, harmonious development of townships, environmental protection and improvement, natural and urban areas and landscapes, rehabilitation of degraded areas. It had to be compatible with public service plans. It could recommend, in particular, the establishment of environment protection instruments such as regional natural parks, planning directives or a marine development plan.

Thus, it does seem that local bodies seized the opportunities that were offered to formulate environmental policies, knowing fully well that the political pressure exerted by local green politicians, who got themselves elected from 1998 onwards to these bodies, had often provided a decisive impetus for the implementation of these policies. However, some have adopted more offensive strategies today. Urged to play an active role by the people in these sensitive new technology areas, many mayors have taken decisions that were not within their powers to do so in an attempt to deflect national policies likely to threaten the regional environment. Invoking the precautionary principle and making use of their policing powers for this purpose, they have adopted decrees to prohibit the cultivation of genetically modified organisms (GMO) in their communes and the setting up of mobile telephony antennas, and have regulated sludge farming within their communes.[52] However, these decrees were quashed by administrative judges, either on the grounds that they concerned matters beyond mayoral powers because of the existence of special policies that excluded any municipal intercession, or when police support was admissible, on the grounds that there were no special circumstances in the commune or since local authorities refused to apply the precautionary principle to reinforce measures taken at the national level.[53] A section of this doctrine approved of such decisions for the sake of coherence and consistency, which could only be decided at the national level.[54] However, the risk perceived is real, since it is well known that pollination from transgenic plants can contaminate crops in their vicinity, which can then no longer be sold as 'non-GMO' products, which constitutes a prejudice, particularly for the organic farming system.[55] Can we then reproach a mayor's desire to intercede to protect the crops in his Commune, when no regulations exist at present to protect non-GMO crops? Moreover, the Pau administrative tribunal considered the prohibitory order to protect organic farming as valid.[56] The question that needs to be raised here is how the reticence *vis-à-vis* local bodies, especially by Prefects, who systematically refer their decrees to the courts, can go hand in hand with the much vaunted decentralization policy? More so since the drafting of the precautionary principle—an outcome of the charter on the environment—imposed precautionary obligations on all public authorities, including the State as well as local bodies.[57] A certain joint management in this field is perhaps the order of the day if we wish to allow local policies on environment to be formulated.[58] Once again, it is the extent of the decentralization desired that becomes the moot point.

2. *Risks Associated with a More Extensive Decentralization*

Thus, a more extensive decentralization appears to be necessary. Indeed, a certain number of recent legislative changes have opened up new vistas from this point of view, particularly with regard to the role of Regions. Their role in environmental matters could become more extensive and the 22 January 2002 Act on Corsica is doubtless a forerunner for upcoming changes in this respect.[59] In fact, this law has endowed the Corsican local body with full powers to adopt sustainable development and planning plans for Corsica, which would lay down the island's economic, social, cultural and tourism development objectives as well as those of environmental conservation and basic orientations for the island's development. Further, the formulation of different plans for water, air and waste has been decentralized. Thus, in this region, local development has been envisaged in conjunction with sustainable development.[60]

Henceforth, the Regions are empowered to seek a transfer of power on environmental matters, as laid down in the new Article 72-4 of the 4 October 1958 Constitution (5th Republic Constitution).[61] Consequently, the Brittany region sought added powers in the water sector. In a region where water quality has deteriorated due to the presence of large quantities of nitrates of agricultural origin, restoring water purity is reckoned to be of highest priority. Consequently, the region wishes to undertake new responsibilities that would enable it to devise a regional water development plan (SRAGE or *Schéma régional d'aménagement des eaux*) in association with Loire-Bretagne water agency and basin. The region is poised to become a pioneer in matters relating to credit coordination and planning.

But such extensions of power do not come without risks. In fact, local bodies can seize the opportunity for experimentation henceforth available in order to relax regulations found to be too rigid. The risks involved are definitely real, especially since several elected representatives, grouped together in a particularly active association (ANEL),[62] have not ceased to go back to the protection imposed by the 3 January 1986 Coastal Regions' Act, particularly through a number of legislative riders. Besides, it should be pointed out that Article 12 of the 22nd January 2002 Act pertaining to Corsica had already granted the Corsican Assembly powers to amend certain coastal region laws within the framework of Corsica's sustainable development and planning plans.[63] Thus, it could permit new buildings to come up behind the 100-metre strip along the shore, as well as the construction of temporary, light shelters of the grass huts type within the 100-metre strip along the shore, with the exception of housing.[64] The same danger loomed large over the Act governing mountainous regions, which local representatives wish to modify in order promote development (mountain resorts, etc.) to the detriment of ecological protection (ban on constructions along the shores of water bodies).[65] However, the possibilities of exemptions for experimental purposes are excluded 'when the essential conditions of a public freedom or a constitutionally guaranteed right are at issue', which will hereafter be the case of environmental rights in the Charter on the Environment.[66] Furthermore, one may wonder about the risk of increasing territorial inequalities. Given the resource disparities between different regions, rich regions could invest more to protect their environment and lay down stricter laws, thus bringing about a relocation of polluting activities to less well-off regions, which would then sacrifice the environment at the altar of employment.[67] The risk is real, for hasn't it already happened in the case of Metaleurope? There is no surety that decentralization intensifies the difficulties associated with liberal ideas, whose work carries on regardless of institutional choices.

B. Necessary Counterweights

Thus, it becomes apparent that decentralized environmental management must be accompanied by certain number of counterbalancing measures. Although there may be a relaxation of controls in the environmental sphere, the State's role, on the contrary, should be strengthened (1), just as monitoring by citizens should be further deepened.

1. *Preserving and Strengthening the State's Role*

As Jean-Marie Pointier observed, a policy on the transfer of powers to local bodies should go hand-in-hand with a similar transfer of powers to de-concentrated authorities. And the mere declaration of the duties of a State representative—a Prefect—does not suffice. A concrete delegation of specific powers to the directors of de-concentrated departments should also take place.[68] None of these requirements have been met in the environmental field, where the decentralization of powers did not actually go hand-in-hand with a de-concentration of State powers. Thus, the Minister of the Environment does not have de-concentrated departments under him, corresponding to the State administration's different levels. In fact, the only de-concentrated departments that are exclusively and strictly under its authority are those at the regional level: the Regional Environmental Directorates (DIREN or *Direction régionale de l'environnement*), which were set up by the 9 April 1991 decree. Thus, the will to establish complementarity with local bodies is lacking, because only the regional level has a de-concentrated Department under the Ministry of Environment. Moreover, the DIRENs basically assume a consultative and review role and do not actually get involved in the conventional regulatory activities that mark the State's intervention at the local level.[69] Thus, decision-making remains in the hands of the minister or ministers and the prefect, whose role has been drawing a lot of flak, in fact, because his arbitration between the interests under his responsibility often results in decisions that are rarely favourable to the environment.

Further, it has also become indispensable to increase the numerically woefully inadequate workforce of inspecting and monitoring agencies.[70] Thus, although there are 500,000 classified facilities in France, just 27,000 inspections could be carried out in 2003. The monitoring system's inadequacy basically stems from the insufficient number of classified facilities' inspectors, as was emphasized in the inspection commission report in the wake of the Toulouse disaster.

2. *Strengthening Citizens' Monitoring Role*

The expansion of participatory democracy, as is evident form recent laws, is rather sensitive on environmental issues, whether these concern specific laws pertaining to this sector or the fact that the application of general mechanisms in this field is particularly significant. And we may believe that people's participation is particularly vital in this field, although some of the basic powers exercised by local bodies entail decisions that involve ethical choices or deal with risks that directly affect the citizens.

Consequently, different laws have provided for a mechanism to consult the voters: the 6 February 1992 Act on the Republic's territorial administration[71] allows for a consultation of voters on decisions taken by municipal authorities, an option that was extended by the 4 February 1995 Act on Conditions for Public Establishments for Intercommune Cooperation (EPIC—*Etablissements Publics de Coopération Intercommunale*) on territorial planning and development.[72] The same law also introduced the possibility of a public initiative, by allowing a fifth of voters from the electoral list to ask the municipal council or the deliberating body of a Public Establishment for Intercommune Cooperation to hold a consultation on a development operation that falls within its competence. These bodies are beholden to organize such referendums.

The laws that constitute what is known as the Decentralization Act II open up real innovative possibilities for giving a voice to local citizens. Article 72-1 of the Constitution, introduced by a constitutional revision on 28 March 2003 pertaining to the Republic's decentralization organization, thus established two major steps forward. On the one hand, it established the citizens' right to petition, by granting them the right to ask for the inclusion of an issue within their local body's competence in the agenda of its deliberative assembly. Thus, the citizens would have the possibility of submitting a certain number of local environmental questions, which would be beneficial if well-organized local associations used them to demand the local bodies to adopt practices that were respectful of the environment.[73] However, there are limitations to this step forward as it only involves asking the assembly to deliberate on an issue and only when it falls within the scope of its powers.[74] Thus, it would not permit local citizens to question a decision made by the State that would affect their environment (the route of a motorway for example). On the other hand, it provides the representatives of a local body to ask its citizens to decide on issues pertaining to local powers, through a local referendum, whereas the consultations organized previously were purely advisory in nature, which the local authorities were free to follow or not. But the 1 August 2003 organic law, which laid down the modalities of such consultations,[75] limited their scope, first and foremost by only authorizing Communes, Departments and Regions to organize such consultations, thereby excluding inter-commune groupings, which as we have observed, enjoy wide-ranging powers, especially in the environmental field. It went further by imposing the condition that these consultations would have a decisive character only if at least 50 per cent of registered electors participated. If the participation fell below this threshold, the poll would only be considered consultative in nature. Further, the plan submitted for a referendum had to garner the majority of the votes cast. Thus, the validation conditions are very stringent.

The 13 August 2004 Act pertaining to local rights and responsibilities also introduced a certain number of innovations. Albeit this was limited to the commune level only, it extended the possibility of consulting their electors to all the local bodies, but again only on matters that fell within their competence.[76] Moreover, the Public Establishments for Intercommune Cooperation could also take recourse to such consultation for everything falling within their competence and not just planning and development. But above all, it extended the public initiative provided in the 4 February 1995 Act, by allowing one-fifth of the voters registered on the electoral list in Communes and one-tenth of electors in other local bodies to be the direct initiators of a consultation, by means of a petition. Even here, the consultation could be sought only on matters falling within the assembly's competence and the decision to organize a consultation was the sole privilege of the local body's deliberative assembly.[77] Though the exercise of this right remains limited in scope and strictly monitored, the progress of participatory democracy can reap benefits as regards environmental issues. This is because they concern the day-to-day life and future of each one of us, and are likely to arouse interest among the inhabitants.

Thus, as we have seen, the issue of a desirable degree of decentralization on environmental matters is complex. While it is deemed to be potentially beneficial for the environment, there is no assurance that it would lead to better environmental protection. And it is for this reason that the path of experimentation, initiated by the March 2003 decentralization law, opens up interesting vistas. It allows regions to experiment with new practices, which can be truly innovative in the environmental sphere, while at the same time not going outside the legal and regulatory framework. It appears to be a calculated risk and despite everything, it does allow the exercise of 'democracy of proximity' in this sector.

NOTES

1. *Gazette Officielle*, 17 August, p. 15545; R. Romi, La décentralisation et l'environnement : un coup pour rien, *Droit de l'environnement*, March 2005, no. 126, p. 44.
2. M. Prieur, '*Droit de l'environnement*', Paris, Dalloz, 5th edn., 2004, p. 238.
3. *Gazette Officielle*, 3 February, p. 1840.

4. Taking into consideration only the expenditure incurred under the communes' general budget.
5. J.M. Pontier, 'La puissance publique et la prévention des risques', *Actualité juridique du droit administratif,* 33/2003, 6 October 2003, p. 1753.
6. T. Olson, the Government Commissioner, justified the prefects' exclusive powers pertaining to classified facilities for fear of mayors' activism 'which would not necessarily help the cause of safety and technological risk prevention. It requires highly specialised skills and real expertise to take decisions and opt for appropriate measures, and moreover it also presupposes coherence and consistency at the department's level, if not the national level' (State Council conclusions (29 September 2003), at Houillères in the Lorraine basin, *Actualité juridique du droit administratif,* 24 November 2003, p. 2164).
7. Cf. supra.
8. Y. Jegouzo, 'De certaines obligations environnementales : prévention, précaution et responsabilité', *Actualité juridique du droit administratif,* issue no. 21/05, 6 June 2005, p. 1166.
9. Directive 91/271/EEC of the Council held on 21 May 1991 pertaining to urban effluents treatment, *Journal officiel des Communautés européennes,* L 135, 30 May 1991.
10. Directive 92-43/EEC of the Council held on 21 May 1992 pertaining to the conservation of natural habitats and flora and fauna, *Journal officiel des Communautés européennes,* issue no. L 206, 22 July 1992.
11. On this issue, it may be recalled that environmental protection organizations expressed their fears with regard to the draft bill pertaining to national parks and natural marine parks, tabled before the National Assembly in May 2005, which provided for increasing the role of local representatives in creating and maintaining these areas, that it would lead to relaxation of protective measures and a greater priority to economic development to the detriment of conservation.
12. Local representatives obviously did not take kindly to this situation, as is evident by the bill tabled on 23 March 2005 that proposed to modify the conditions for drafting foreseeable flood-related natural hazard prevention plans (no. 2189). The proponents of this bill contended that these plans would help in establishing administrative supervision over urbanistic development by local bodies, thereby appearing as the restoration of lost supervisory powers rather than a risk prevention assistance tool. In particular, they claimed shared powers 'in the spirit of decentralisation laws' in this domain, and that the communities had to be consulted for recommendations and not for information only.

13. P. Albertini, 'Les collectivités locales et l'environnement', *Actualité juridique du droit administratif*, December 1993, p. 838.
14. Local liberty rally, Workshop on 'Environment and Decentralisation', Chartres, October 2002.
15. R. Romi, 'Compétences et actions de la commune pour la protection de l'environnement', *Jurisclasseur environnement*, Fascicule 163, p. 3.
16. Communes and commune groupings earmarked more than € 16.2 billion in their budgets for the environment in 2002. Water and sanitation (waste water treatment and drinking water supply systems) constituted the major expenditure incurred by the communes in this sector, as they accounted for 49 per cent of the total budget allocations of communes and commune groupings for the environment (€ 8 billion), and the second major budgetary head is for domestic waste collection and treatment (44 per cent for operational expenses; € 5.3 billion).
17. *Journal Officiel*, 1 January 1997, p. 11.
18. A. Van Lang, '*Droit de l'environnement*' (Environmental law), Paris, Thémis, PUF, 2002, p. 185.
19. *Journal Officiel*, 14 December, p. 1977.
20. A. Van Lang, '*Droit de l'environnement*', op. cit., p. 183. The new Article 121-1 of the *Code de l'urbanisme* or Urban Planning Code as well as the territorial coherence framework, local urban development plans and commune maps defines the conditions that ensure as following: a balance between urban renewal, controlled urban development, rural area development, on the one hand and preservation of areas earmarked for agricultural and forestry activities and natural areas and landscapes protection, on the other, while adhering to sustainable development goals; Economic and balanced use of urban, peri-urban and rural natural areas, control over travel requirements and vehicular traffic, preservation of quality of air, water, soil, sub-soil, ecosystems, open spaces, natural or urban environment, sites and natural landscapes, reduction of noise pollution, saving noteworthy urban landmarks and architectural heritage, prevention of foreseeable natural hazards, technological risks, pollution and nuisances of any type.
21. 3 June 2004 ordinance on transposition of European Parliaments' directive 2001/42/EC and the Council's 27 June 2001 directive pertaining to certain impacts of environmental projects and programmes, *Journal Officiel*, 5 June 2004, p. 9979.
22. The status report analyses the environment's initial state and evaluates the plan's impact on environment and presents the manner in which the plan takes into account environmental preservation concerns and enhancement (Art. R 123-2 of the *Code de l'urbanisme* or Urban Planning Code).

23. R. Romi, 'Départements et environnement', *Jurisclasseur environnement,* Fascicule 162, pp. 3–4; 'La place du département en matière de protection de l'environnement, vers une revalorisation?', *Petites affiches,* 22 June 1990.
24. G. de Lajudie, 'Les compétences des collectivités locales en matière d'environnement', *Gazette du Palais,* 25 June 1998, p. 766.
25. Report no. 1227 prepared on behalf of the National Assembly's Finance Commission, submitted on 14 April 1990.
26. Due to the lack of suitable treatment capabilities, 26 departments had already been constrained to export their waste to other Departments, and 59 per cent of waste storage facilities would reach their saturation point in seven years; taking into account the time required to implement incinerator or storage projects; 75 Departments were already facing a potential shortage.
27. M.L. Lambert-Habib, 'Décentralisation constitutionnelle et environnement', *Revue juridique de l'environnement,* 1/2004, p. 20.
28. Romi, 'Départements et environnement', *Jurisclasseur environnement,* p. 12.
29. R. Romi, 'Les régions et l'administration de l'environnement: des potentialités à developer', *Actualité juridique du droit administratif,* 1990, p. 457.
30. *Journal Officiel,* dated 28 February 2002, p. 3808.
31. R. Romi, 'La loi sur la démocratie de proximité, un renouveau du droit de l'environnement?', *Revue du droit public,* no. 3/2002, p. 869.
32. Article L 553-4 of the Environmental Code: 'In order to promote the harmonious development of wind energy, Regions may set up a regional wind energy plan, after consulting with the concerned Departments and Public Establishments for Intercommune Cooperation with their own taxation system. This plan would indicate the geographic sectors that appear to be the best suited for setting up facilities for producing electricity by using the wind's mechanical energy.'
33. Cf. supra.
34. Albertini, 'Les collectivités locales et l'environnement', p. 839; bill on water and aquatic environment placed in the Senate on the 10 March 2005 (no. 240).
35. Local liberty rally, Workshop 'Environment and decentralisation', op. cit.
36. A. Rouyère, 'La répartition des pouvoirs locaux. Les approches nationales: la France', in *Les problèmes environnementaux urbains, rôle des collectivités locales, Droit et ville,* issue no. 42, 1996, p. 2.
37. Ibid., p. 19.
38. Ibid., p. 26.
39. J. Chevallier, 'Décentralisation et politiques publiques', *Actualité juridique du droit administratif,* 1992, p. 125.

40. Prieur, '*Droit de l'environnement*', p. 245.
41. Rouyère, 'La répartition des pouvoirs locaux. Les approches nationales : la France', p. 27.
42. Albertini, 'Les collectivités locales et l'environnement', p. 839.
43. *Institut français de l'environnement*, 'Le rôle majeur de l'intercommunalité dans la gestion publique de l'environnement', *Les données de l'environnement*, issue no. 100, February 2005.
44. Prieur, '*Droit de l'environnement*', p. 239.
45. A. Rouyère, 'La répartition des pouvoirs locaux. Les approches nationales: la France' op. cit., pp. 27–8.
46. IFEN, 'Le rôle majeur de l'intercommunalité dans la gestion publique de l'environnement', op. cit.
47. Article 25, *Journal Official*, dated 29 June 1999, p. 9515.
48. Ministry of Ecology and Sustainable Development, '*Les agendas 21 locaux en France*', 2002.
49. Van Lang, '*Droit de l'environnement*', p. 189.
50. Prieur, '*Droit de l'environnement*', p. 249.
51. Article 5.
52. F.G. Trébulle, 'OGM, une illustration de la mise en œuvre du principe de précaution', *Environnement*, JCP, 2004.
53. C. Hermon, 'Police administrative et environnement, Plaidoyer pour une police municipale environnementale', *Droit de l'environnement*, issue no. 121, September 2004, p. 164. Pertaining to GMO: TA Caen, 26 February 2002, Prefect of Basse-Normandie region, Prefect of Calvados c/Vaulx-sur-Seulles Commune, *Environnement*, July 2002, p. 20, issue no. 97; TA, Toulouse, 18 January 2005, Prefect of Haute-Garonne c/Bax Commune, *Actualité juridique du droit administratif*, 21/2005, 6 June 2005, p. 1188. For a different interpretation, see, for GMO matters: TA Limoges, 27 March 2003, Prefect of Indre c/Coings Commune, *Environnement*, July 2003, no. 73 and for mobile telephony: TA Marseille, 9 March 2004, S.A. Orange France c/Port-de-Bouc Commune, conclusions P. Harang, *Droit de l'environnement*, no. 156, March 2005, p. 35.

    It must be noted that the actions taken by communes were later taken up by the regions—around fifteen of them—which adopted bills prohibiting GMO cultivation (both experimental and commercial) in their territory. Brittany also decided to reduce GMO imports and sales, especially in animal feed, which constituted an important milestone in a regional economy largely dependent on poultry and pork production, since it was through animal feed that GMOs entered the food chain insofar as produce from animals fed on GMOs (meat, milk, eggs) were not covered by GMO labelling regulations.

54. Pontier, 'La puissance publique et la prévention des risques', p. 1753.
55. Lambert-Habib, 'Décentralisation constitutionnelle et environnement', p. 26.
56. T.A. Pau, 24 December 2003, Prefect of Gers, *JCP Administrations et collectivités territoriales,* 22 March 2004, 1226, p. 435, note C. Boillot-Burg.
57. Art. 5: When damages, although uncertain in the current state of scientific knowledge, are likely to affect the environment seriously and irreversibly, public authorities can use the precautionary principle to the extent of their powers to see to the implementation of risk assessment procedures and the adoption of provisional and adequate measures in order to deal with the concerned damages.
58. Hermon, 'Police administrative et environnement, Plaidoyer pour une police municipale environnementale', p. 170. For a different opinion see Jegouzo, 'De certaines obligations environnementales: prévention, précaution et responsabilité', p. 1166.
59. Romi, 'La loi sur la démocratie de proximité, un renouveau du droit de l'environnement?', p. 870.
60. R. Romi, 'Les dispositions du nouveau statut de la Corse touchant à l'environnement', *Droit de l'environnement,* issue no. 96, March 2002, p. 61; 'La Corse et l'environnement: de la confirmation à l'expérimentation', *Revue française de droit administratif,* July–August 2002, p. 702.
61. This possibility was provided by the 23 March 2003 Act pertaining to the Republic's decentralized organization (*Official Gazette* dated 29 March 2003), which lays down in Article 5, which in turn modified Article 72 of the Constitution, that 'under the conditions provided for in the organic law, and except when the essential conditions of a public freedom or a constitutionally guaranteed right are at issue, local bodies or their groupings can, when the law or the regulation stipulates thus, depart from the legislative or regulatory provisions that govern the exercise of their powers, on an experimental basis and for a specific purpose and a limited duration, on a case to case basis'.
62. *Association nationale des élus du littoral.*
63. *Journal Officiel,* dated 23 January.
64. Lambert-Habib, 'Décentralisation constitutionnelle et environnement', p. 30.
65. See the plethora of amendments tabled by rural representatives during the discussion on the 23 February 2005 Act pertaining to rural territory development (*Official Gazette,* 24th February) and the consequent changes that took place.
66. Constitutional law of 1 March 2005 pertaining to the Environmental

Charter, *Official Gazette* of 2 March, p. 3697: Article 1: 'Every citizen has the right to live in a balanced and healthy environment'.

67. Lambert-Habib, 'Décentralisation constitutionnelle et environnement', p. 32.
68. 'Les nouvelles compétences de la region', *Actualité juridique du droit administratif*, 36/2004, 25 October 2004, p. 1977.
69. Rouyère, 'La répartition des pouvoirs locaux. Les approches nationales : la France', p. 14.
70. Lambert-Habib, 'Décentralisation constitutionnelle et environnement', p. 17.
71. *Journal officiel*, dated 8 February.
72. Article 86, *Journal Officiel*, dated 5 february 1995, p. 1973.
73. Lambert-Habib, 'Décentralisation constitutionnelle et environnement', p. 28.
74. I. Muller-Quoy, 'Démocratie locale', *Jurisclasseur administratif*, Fascicule 117-10, issue nos. 65–6.
75. This law was itself clarified by the 4 May 2005 decree.
76. Article 122 of the Act; Articles L 112–15 of the *Code général des collectivités territoriales.*
77. Article 122 of the Act; Articles L 1116 of the *Code général des collectivités territoriales.*

CHAPTER 12

Decentralization of Vocational Training: Ambiguities of a National Policy

CATHERINE AGULHON

WHAT KIND OF DECENTRALIZATION?

The decentralization of public action was at the forefront of France's political stage between 2002–5. However, it is a long-term process aimed at rebuilding the powers attributed to different institutions and reorganizing public action regulation—a process that was initiated over twenty years ago. It goes well beyond the national framework as it is being adopted both by centralized and federal States, as much in developed countries as in emerging or developing countries (Mons, 2004). This process is aimed at meeting both political and administrative or financial objectives. It appears to be a tool for good governance, aimed at the territorialization of institutions, budget rationalization, and the equity and quality of services.

Decentralization is of interest to the political scientists, sociologists and economists. It has given birth to research and assessments and has become a subject of investigation. In the field of education and training, supporters of decentralization believe that the regional level is the most effective and relevant in terms of the management of these systems, with the objective of cost reduction and the adaptation of supply to local economic and social needs. However, decentralization that is scheduled by the State and divided into successive phases raises questions, both with regard to the stakes involved and its impact. My participation in the assessments commissioned by the Ministry of Labour in 1998 and 2001 (Coordination Committee, 1998; Méhaut, 1998) has enabled me to throw light on such transfers of power.

In fact, different theories have been advanced to identify the process and build analysis models. While decentralizing government action is a problem in a Jacobin State like France, many justifications are also given for the revitalization of these forms of governance. The term 'governance' itself draws on the shared desire for coordinating a negotiated political action. According to the definition given by Perret (2001), governance—a rather fuzzy notion in the management field—is a society's ability to govern itself through institutions, but also through negotiation, decision-making and control processes. It promotes joint action by several bodies, which has become necessary due to increasingly complex social functions. It takes the form of the contractualization of public action.

This term therefore falls within the framework of a movement questioning State functioning and desirous of redistributing powers and responsibilities—very differently according to the areas concerned. Some assert that State action by the central, bureaucratic government is considered ineffectual and impersonal, unable to adapt to the diversity of local realities. As civil servants do not share the thinking behind the construction of the rules or norms, they lack any sense of responsibility for their application. This criticism of the bureaucracy is nothing new. Decentralization constitutes a reaction to the need to shift the places where rules are drawn up. These new places and spaces enable better identification and better response to local specificities, while enabling the contractualization of actions and the mobilization of political, economic and social actors. However, decentralization forces these actors to reconsider the issue of public interest, questions such as the social construction of equity, the ways of coordinating actions and the issue of efficiency, and above all, the issue of the legitimacy of a less hierarchical and more negotiated and contractualized regulation of public action.

In a collective work, research scholars working with Affichard (1997) proposed different political, economic and sociological approaches in order to understand the revitalization of public action. These approaches once again raise questions about the legitimacy of public action, the rationality of such action, its effectiveness and its fairness. But can one keep a hold on all these parameters, and can decentralization play a key role? The lack of conventions leads to doubts about the rationality of civil servants having to deal with the enormous complexity of situations, looks for the best ways of obtaining the cooperation of interested and calculating representatives. Organizational sociology, for its part, offers its own contributions to the analysis of the local politico-administrative system. It looks at the interplay between the different actors, their interactions and their modalities of cooperation. It highlights the persistence of administrative barriers, the difficulties faced in the territorialization of policies and the low participation of citizens in regional political debate. Finally, the theory of justification drawn up by Boltanski and Thévenot (1991) helps in analysing the logic behind the actions taken. Are we witnessing a change-over from a civic logic to an industrial or even, perhaps, mercantile logic? What is regional action based on? Can its justifications—based on the efficiency and rationality of actions—be associated with the legitimacy and fairness of the said actions? These three theoretical explanations are complementary and focus attention both on the interplay between the actors and on the underlying stakes involved, along with the outcome in terms of organization, rationality, efficiency and legitimacy. The last theory seems particularly heuristic to me and seems to attempt to explain the foundations of the interplay between actors at the regional level.

As can be seen, decentralization once again raises questions on the forms of public action, its rationality and its effectiveness, and the political and social bases of its legitimacy. For some political actors, decentralization does not mean the disengagement of the State which then takes on a more prescriptive and regulatory role. In fact, decentralization promotes a rapprochement between citizens and politics with the aim of ensuring the effectiveness of rules and procedures adapted to locally identified needs. It changes the modes of action and regulation in the public interest and in the interest of the fairness of public action. It is based on a form of governance, widely promoted in recent years, that encourages concerted and negotiated action, contractualization and mutual commitment by the responsible partners. The objective is no longer simply to govern, but to cooperate or facilitate the networking of actors, each with their own prerogatives. In reality, this slow, confrontational decentralization process has not yet established its institutional framework, nor has it reached maturity. It has not reduced tensions between partner institutions, between contradictory thought-processes behind the actions taken (effectiveness and equity), between distinctive identities and concerted action, and between the public interest and competitive actions.

In the education and training fields, decentralization took place in several phases: the State retained control over structural management, i.e. the management of curricula and recruitments, while delegating construction and facilities to the Regional Councils. The most widespread delegation of power took place in the field of vocational training, as the Regional Councils became promoters of a negotiated regional vocational training plan for the youth (*PRDFPJ—Plan Régional de Formation Professionnelle pour les Jeunes*), encompassing school training, apprenticeship and continuous education. This plan's constitution mobilized all economic and social partners involved in training in general. It called for a shared thinking on the institutional and economic bases of regional planning, one that would be rational, effective and fair at the same time. Such delegation of power led to the deployment of assessments commissioned both by ministries as well as Regional Councils themselves (Bel and Dubouchet, 2004). These assessments constituted both an external check on the measures taken and their legitimization, while providing a basis for their reorientation. They did not fail to point out the contradictions troubling the institutions involved, the 'power spaces' taken over by the Regional Councils, and the joint effects of the activities undertaken by institutions on the forms of regulating an incomplete regional vocational training system.

The decentralization process established the legitimacy of regional policies and, at the same time, redefined the powers of the various decentralized departments of different ministries (Education, Labour, health and agriculture)—a process that did not take place without tensions. Each institution wished to retain or expand its prerogatives and each one felt threatened by new modes of functioning and regulation, failing to truly understand their real dimensions or effects. The actors were therefore extremely uncertain, which sometimes led them to turn in on themselves, play a waiting game or, on the contrary, fight against the changes. No immediate consensus was reached in these redeployments. Thus, beyond national acts and prescriptions, decentralization took the path of new inter-institutional negotiations. However, as Thuderoz (2000) observed, negotiation also means conflict and joint settlement of that conflict. Thus, negotiation took on a political guise aimed at regulating the modes of social organization—in this case, essentially the organization of schooling and vocational training.

The effects of decentralization are still being examined, as they are far from conclusive and lend themselves to much polemic. In fact, some believe that the geographical shift in public action calls the republican model of schooling into question (Charlot, 1994; Lelièvre, 1997). Others are of the opinion that it can be justified by the relevance of the issue of local development, which makes it possible to shorten the decision-making chain, involve economic and social actors (professional organizations and trade unions) and give a more operational aspect to public interventions (Casella, 1996). Local development would also help in matching the training offered with the jobs available (which denotes an adequacy-oriented approach to which I cannot subscribe). In fact, the delegation of the powers to various institutions thwarts the logic behind public action, shakes up the institutions concerned, redefines the purposes of training courses and leads to open debates. It changes the organization of vocational training system that is still under construction or reconstruction. Thus, the shift in powers raises questions about the revitalization of a training model 'à la française' (Verdier, 1996; Brucy and Troger, 2000). It calls into question the setting up of professional training schools, against which apprenticeship training or youth integration measures compete. In fact, Regional Councils become the great helmsmen of training content and can promote the development of the courses of study they wish to further, on the basis of the agreements they may have reached, and depending on the specific partner whose support they take (local education authority, labour and vocational training department, professional organizations). They can establish their legitimacy and primacy over the powers concerned or choose to delegate them to other partner institutions. Indeed, it is the diversity of policies adopted that catches one's attention, although no rational justification can be found and although there is no way, so far, of assessing their effects. On the contrary, it is this very diversity that gives a pounding to the democratic foundations of the training policy and calls into question their underlying ideas of justice and appropriateness.

DECENTRALIZATION OF VOCATIONAL TRAINING: A NATIONAL POLICY

Vocational training is a complex, segmented and under-appreciated social sphere and a field of research that is undervalued. But it does have a very long history, both with regard to the education as such as well as labour management and, therefore, the sociology of education and labour.

Over the last twenty years, labour market changes (de-industrialization, the development of the service sector, the introduction of new technologies and the reconstitution of employment), falling job supply and rising unemployment have led to new training policies and brought the issue of initial and continuous vocational education to the forefront. Several reforms have been initiated to implement institutional changes (vocational schools), and improve labour training and skills: professional training, changes in curricula, matching training courses to job vacancies, extension of certain curricula (professional baccalaureate and professional bachelor's degrees). Reforms have also been initiated to improve co-investment in continuous education, provide full staff training (DIF). And of course, validate of work experience, thereby making it an essential factor in establishing certifications and, therefore, qualifications, often taking the place of formal training courses. Each of these reforms and structural changes has led to some pernicious effects that may lead to controversies.

But decentralization is a reform process that changes the management approach for training systems (initial training, apprenticeship and continuous education), that is already segmented. It is expected to lead to the opening-up of fields of training and training courses and draw on the break-up of national rules. It is ambiguous, since it is incomplete, and withdraws the State's power to organize the structure and content of training, to follow the career-graphs of the youth and lead to a certain loss in the system's readability. It puts questions on the legitimacy of regions as political actors, on the forms of inter-institutional interaction it engenders, on the contractualization upon which it is expected to be based, and on the inequalities of treatment to which it leads. Thus, decentralization raises questions about political, democratic or liberal basis, its economic (efficiency, effectiveness and performance) and social (equalization of opportunities) objectives and its institutional and methodological processes.

Two key periods marked the decentralization of vocational training, while two tools ensured its emergence: the planning of supplies and institutional negotiations, to which we shall return further down. The 1983 Act granted Regional Councils authority in matters pertaining to the establishment of a provisional framework for initial training programmes, conducted parallel to education. The Five-Year 20 December 1993 Act No. 93-1313 on labour, employment and vocational training extended the Regional Councils' duties with regard to the drafting of vocational training and education policies. Such delegations of power did not confer total autonomy on them, as they were based on contractualization. In the latter, it is 'partners' responsible for their policy and management that are inducted, endorsed by the assessment of their undertakings. The plan implementation agreement is one of the main tools of this new governance system. It guarantees co-managed and co-steered activities, binding both the State and the Regional Council concerned, while circumscribing the very notion of French-style decentralization.

PLANNING: A REFORM TOOL

One of the powers granted to regional councils is that of planning the provision of vocational training. This implies ensuring consistency between the three vocational training branches, for purposes of rationality. Whence the problem of linkages between initial and continuous training, but also the problem of the interiority or exteriority of vocational training *vis-à-vis* the education system, the interiority or exteriority of education and youth-related measures with regard to the working world. One redefinition inevitably leads to others. The place of vocational training has always been difficult to stabilize and the reforms undertaken are further destabilizing it. Vocational training is becoming an area for the crystallization of political, inter-institutional and socio-economic issues that go well beyond it, taking shape at the regional level.

Since 1983, Regional Councils have had the financial means necessary to implement a housing policy that also gives them a certain visibility that makes citizens recognize them better. While they refuse to conduct themselves as tools of State education policies, they acquire their legitimacy through this visibility, stemming from housing. However, it is schooling-related vocational training and education that offers them the opportunity to prime their weapons and professionalize their interventions. They are trying to mobilize actors with regard to the provisional training programmes and to look for ways for streamlining the training programmes offered. They are bringing together two fields that had existed in total ignorance of each other until now.

These policies once again raise a recurring question: today, in the midst of multiple transformations in the economic, social and educational spheres, what can the presuppositions be for the construction of a relevant training programme system?

Thus, these approaches once again raise the problem of matching training and employment at the regional level, a problem that has more or less been abandoned at the national planning level since the Seventh Plan, as these relations showed a lack of immediacy, publicized in the media due to several demographic, economic and social contingencies (Tanguy, 1986; Vernières, 1993).

THE FIRST PROVISIONAL TRAINING PLANS

Most Regional Councils drew up their first provisional training plan as early as in 1985 and had already revised it in 1989. These plans could either be based on a complete overhaul of the network of training institutions and vocational and technological training establishments or call for a partial rebalancing between the various entities. Regional Councils aimed both at influencing the development of branches that they believed would lead to employment generation and at restructuring training institutes and establishments. They did not wish to limit themselves to playing a merely technical role of building or re-building such establishments.

While preparing the plan, several objectives regarding the measures to be taken had to be reconciled. In fact, there were very few connections between the often very restricted labour demands in the economic sphere, the requirements of the educational sphere that regulate and manage student flows, attempts to raise the training level of the youth, and those of the political sphere with the councils attempting to establish their legitimacy by responding to contradictory social and economic requirements and playing their own role of adjustment and regulation.

Regional Councils have to take into acçount national training policies and prescriptions and the laws and regulations defined by the ministries of education and labour[1] (though without there being any real consensus on the objectives pursued by the two ministries). The council have to organize the different training sectors as ordered by the State laws (creation of vocational baccalaureates in 1985, 1987 Act on the extension of apprenticeship training to all vocational and technical degrees) and reform of courses of study and degrees. And it is within this restricted framework that they attempt to establish a balance—some complementarity finalized between initial training and apprenticeship (and, later, mechanisms to help school-to-work transition). These three channels neither fall under the same institutions, nor the same laws, and nor do they owe their development to the same decision-making processes. Thus, it is up to Regional Councils to find partners and reach agreements with them. On what criteria should such agreements be based?

Regional Councils are attempting to identify the tools and methods they could use to draft the training policy. They are establishing their own technical departments. They are mobilizing regional forums such as the OREF ('Observatoires régionaux emploi-formation', or Regional Employment-Training Observatories),[2] or sometimes centres associated with CEREQ (*Centre d'Études et de Recherches sur les Emplois et les Qualifications*, or Centre for Research and Studies on Employment and Qualifications). They call upon external experts and regional bodies such as INSEE (*Institut National de Statistiques et Etudes Economiques* or French National Institute for Statistics and Economic Studies), ANPE (*Agence Nationale Pour l'Emploi*, or National Employment Agency), CESR (*Conseil Economique et Social de Région* or Regional Economic and Social Council) and DRONISEP (*Délégation Régionale de l'Office National d'Information Sur les Enseignements et les Professions* or Regional Delegation of the National Office of Information on Education and Professions) as well as regional delegations of professional organizations that also try to play a regulatory role in the training offered. The development of expertise capable of determining changes in economic activities, developments in training systems, labour movements and modes of professional integration of the youth, while also being able to place such information in perspective is not an easy task. Expertise at the regional level is being built slowly and variously, depending on the local resources. It will obviously be greater in larger regions, such as the Midi-Pyrenees, the Aquitaine or Provence-Côte d'Azur, while being weaker and stained by different ideological interests in other regions. At this level, the quest for a quantitative fit re-emerges strongly. Various partners are seeking tools for adequately defining the training programmes offered, in an attempt to associate the management of training flows per level, sector and speciality with labour needs, which are extremely difficult to identify. Initially, the process has been progressing as if the Regional Councils have not noticed the criticism of the quantified and mechanical approach to training programme organization at the national level.

In fact, these institutional actors, armed with their prerogatives, want to revitalize the conception of training and break with the national policies, believing that the rise in unemployment proves the latters' inefficiency. They are opting for a more liberal and competitive design, which they claim is more effective, i.e. it can be made profitable immediately. In order to do so, the councils are relying on the demands of the economic sphere and trying to break with the civic and democratic logic that is the State's prerogative. In their concern for immediate returns, they are choosing to develop education and contracts in succession.

Unfortunately, rising demand in the economic sphere is not self-evident. At the national level, professional organizations and chambers of commerce and industry have their own development and training policies. They prepare projected employment contracts (CEP, 'Contrats Prévisionnels d'Emploi') under the aegis of the Ministry of Labour and the Vocational Training Delegation. They still control their own funding and even have their own training institutions, and are therefore also involved in these negotiations. However, these professional organizations do not always have any great representative strength at the regional level and often have a very narrow and partial view of the regulatory processes between supply and demand. So while they may argue in favour of their sector, they do not have an overall view of the changes taking place in it. Furthermore, as most experts have pointed out, even at local level, companies have no control over medium- or long-term labour market changes and do not express real needs. In any case, competition in employment pools between different mobile population groups limits their ability to fine-tune training in accordance with available employment. This method of managing training soon reaches its limits.

In general, the first prospective analyses, which took place between 1983 and 1993, revealed the low innovation capacities of Regional Councils, which generally reproduced the existing supply per branch and per sector, empirically.[3] The management of training as well as that of training needs remains an uncertain and fairly unreliable art, all the more so as job supply trends can vary and level off much faster than any prospective analysis can led us to believe (Paul, 1989; Freyssinet, 1991).

Local boards of education have been and still remain the first ones involved in preparing regional training plans. They had very little expertise in the subject, from 1960 to 1984, the school-zone map that was the key element in managing flows and seats (number of youth to be educated, number of colleges and high schools to be opened, number of teachers to be recruited) was pre-pared at the national level. Decentralization and deconcentration transformed their prerogatives. Instead of implementing plans imposed by the ministry, on the one hand, they have to negotiate their school-zone map with the same ministry and, on the other, with the Regional Council. In fact, a mini-revolution has taken place, which has been analysed by a number of education sociologists (Charlot, 1994; Dutercq, 2001; Van Zanten, 2000). It holds local boards responsible and obliges them to question their objectives, particularly in these fields.

Local boards of education have to reconcile the national policy that they prepare with their negotiations with various Regional Council departments. They are involved in the debates on which technical training plans are developed. They have had to bend before the need for consultation and accept negotiated arrangements.[4]

Finding a synergy between education board policies and regional policies is difficult and these institutions often enjoy rather ambiguous relations. The prospective training plans, then the regional training plan, turn into tools for negotiation, compromise and the contractualization of action. However, local boards of education do not easily accept the Regional Council plans. By playing the game of opening and closing sections[5] and managing teachers' posts, they conduct their own education policies—at least in the public sector. Regional Councils may favour the development of certain fields of activity in the private sector or through education and training, so opposing stakes and conflicts may hinder relations between these bodies. These bodies sometimes play on their complementarity *vis-à-vis* other regional forums, thereby reducing their disagreements due to the needs of their alliance. In reality, their relations swing between consensus and antagonism. I have been able to draw up a typology of the configurations of such institutions since 1994, and can say that there have been very few changes (Agulhon, 1994):

In some regions, Regional Councils build consensual relations: The prospective training plan or the training development plan plays an important role in referencing and projecting changes, both for the Regional Council and the local board of education.

In other regions, regional councils limit themselves to infrequent collaborations: Plans here play a minor role. Inter-institutional debates enable the establishment of joint policies from time to time or alliances *vis-à-vis* other institutions (professional branches, chambers of commerce, etc.).

In other regions there is latent, even open conflict: The Regional Council pursues its own policy and the Board of Education pursues the objectives it has adopted in liaison with those advocated by the ministry, more or less by itself. In such a configuration, competition between the institutions predominates, with the Regional Council favouring the development of other training sectors in its actions (apprenticeship or private sector).

Collaboration between the institutions is still tentative—one trying to either anticipate or overwhelm the other's initiatives and establish its own prerogatives. Local education offices establish their own objectives with regard to the development of various courses of study, while the Regional Council tries to contract alliances with the economic sphere in order to pursue its policies and to do a balancing act between initial training and apprenticeship or continuous training, which may thwart the academic objectives involved.

The analysis of these plans (PRDFPJ) helps us understand the essence of the objectives set by the regions. Three types of plans can be discerned. The first kind resembles the preceding schemes, of which they are simply a renewed version. They divide the recommendations by sector and renew the existing ones. The second type of plan describes the situation prevailing in each of the courses very descriptively and in a very segmented manner. Some are built to accompany the career path taken by the youth: information and orientation, training courses and job access modalities. Finally, the most elaborate describe the various training courses offered per sector or branch, while putting these in perspective with regard to employment in the sector concerned. The plan could be more-or-less based on injunctions, punctuated by vague proposals with no time-frames for implementation, a recapitulative document filled with factual data and statistics or a more forward-looking document, proposing concrete methods to improve the functioning of training systems.

In any case, the Regional Councils are attempting to reorganize the system and control it. They are encroaching on the areas reserved for the local boards of education and the DRTEFP (*Direction régionale du travail, de l'emploi et de la formation professionnelle* or Regional directorate of work, employment and vocational training), their interactions are often contentious. But above all, the task of drafting this plan once again raised the issue of the theoretical foundations of changes in training aimed at employment. Some regions, such as the Rhône-Alpes or Midi-Pyrénées, find themselves at the forefront of this transformation. They have mobilized scholars and centres associated with the CEREQ (Méhaut, 1998). They are trying to change their too often empirical and mechanical approach and also attempting to avoid the pitfalls of appropriateness. However, most regions find it difficult to develop a mid-term operational perspective.

1993: THE BEGINNINGS OF AN INTEGRAL PROFESSIONAL TRAINING SYSTEM

By 1993, it may be said that the Regional Councils had established their legitimacy with regard to their educational policy. While they renovated and improved their establishments, set up a few CFAs (*Centres de Formation d'Apprentis*, or apprenticeship training centres) and implemented a trainers' training policy in the apprenticeship training field, they still found it difficult to base their development of training courses on the projected plan, which was sometimes vague enough to trigger fierce negotiations in the field. However, they had laid the foundations of their legitimacy. The Five Year Act increased their powers. The new training plan's (PRDFPJ) coverage encouraged them to increase the intensity of inter-institutionalism while preparing their objectives and their implementation. However, implicitly, the Regional Councils were expected to successfully implement an institutional 'opening up' at the regional level that had never been implemented at the national level. In order to do so, they had to mobilize all the actors involved in one way or the other, in one field of training or another. And there were several actors involved: decentralized directorates of the ministries of agriculture, health and social action, labour (DRTEFP—*Direction*

Régionale du Travail, de l'Emploi et de la Formation Professionnelle or Regional Directorate of Work, Employment and Vocational Training and DDTEFP (*Direction Départementale du Travail, de l'Emploi et de la Formation Professionnelle*, or Departmental Directorate of Work, Employment and Vocational Training), local boards of education and school inspectorates, AFPAs (*Association Nationale Pour la Formation Professionnelle des Adultes* or National Association for Vocational Training of Adults), ANPEs (*Agence Nationale Pour l'Emploi* or National Employment Agency), all local induction, orientation and information networks, professional organizations, OPCAs and enterprises, as well as all types of training establishments.

The adult continuous training landscape—for youth facing difficulties—was particularly complex. It was built with a series of strata, in emergency conditions, in a precarious training market. Decentralization took place against the background of unemployment, and training was used primarily as a palliative for employment, rather than for improving skills or adaptation to jobs. In fact, this was the way the policy undertaken by Bertrand Schwartz in 1981 was understood. Various directors of professional training pursued it on these grounds between 1982 and 1993, in particular Leignel, who promoted a certain inter-institutionalism and organized training courses for the youth, thanks to the CFI (*Crédit formation individualisé* or Individualized training credit).

In fact, the CFI, which was set up by the DFP in 1989 at Prime Minister Fabius' instigation, was an attempt at streamlining the system. It laid the foundations of a durable operation. Its purpose was to organize and support the long professional transition of the youth to the world of employment, through an intermingling of measures (mobilization, pre-qualification, qualification and work-based training). Its task was to coordinate the activities of the various youth orientation and support services and training organizations, to mobilize enterprises, and connect and adjust training, work-based training and assisted employment activities between them (role of zonal coordinators). The aim was to facilitate the trajectories of the youth by offering them individualized support (role of correspondents) and by creating a synergy between local economic changes and the training programmes being offered. Above all, the aim was to facilitate the organization of a route towards certification through the long-term validation of achievements.[6] The aim was an ambitious one and the actors involved were committed to it, but this objective was only partially achieved.

This ongoing training branch, which was largely funded and organized by the State, included a series of sectoral measures per target group type and led to complex inter-institutionalization. It often tried to meet both social and economic objectives and came up against the complexity of the local development issue (Garraud, 1995). Observers criticized it quite strongly, while training policies and technicians attempted to streamline it. However, always looked upon as relatively temporary, these labile mechanisms created a heterogeneous landscape, whose efficacy was difficult to achieve. The example of youth employment stands testimony to this fact (Agulhon, 2001).

Each region implemented a policy that was more or less related with the mechanisms available and that was more or less parallel to the Ministry of Labour's policies. The policies did not solve the problem of adjusting to youth needs, nor those of companies, and nor did they revolutionize the mechanism or incorporate it properly in a unified training system. They marginally adapted their bidding procedures and attempted to subordinate training providers, located in a restrained market. However, they did manage to understand the difficulty of building a training structure that was rational, efficacious and fair, within the inter-institutionalized framework.

SEGMENTED INSTITUTIONAL REGULATIONS

The Regional Councils came to face institutions that were applying their national directorates' policies. The local boards of education were following the provisions of the 1989 Act, the DRTEFP set up the PAQUE and then TRACE (*Trajet d'Accès à l'Emploi*, or Access Route to Employment) programmes, or youth employment defined by the Ministry of Labour. The ANPE and AFPA had come under a national progress contract. The representatives of professional organizations were also following their national directorates. One of the paradoxes of decentralization was that it accentuated regional disparities, while relying, at the same time, on institutions that reproduced national or operating methods or national directives.

While the issue was that of building a regional training system, it was a slow and difficult process, vitiated by the resistances of the institutions involved, along with several contradictions and constraints. Synergies between the three sectors did not succeed in doing away with the existing segmentations.

For initial training, the changes made by the reforms introduced by the Ministry of Education in the 1980s were maintained: supremacy of the general channel, but the development of a professional channel through professional baccalaureates and of the technological channel through the BTS (Brevet de technicien supérieur or Advanced Vocational Diploma). The opening and closing down of sections by local boards of education was controlled, and the latter's autonomy was therefore restricted.

In the apprenticeship sector, the regions that were traditionally interested in this channel (Alsace, Pays de Loire, Bretagne) continued to further it, while regions that were withdrawing from it tried to compensate for the lack by accentuating quality. The same recommendations were disseminated almost everywhere: training trainers, following up work-based learning and quality contracts signed with the CFA.

The training sector continued, although the youth-related branches were the most disturbed by the Five-Year Act and were the most recently reorganized. The Regional Councils found it difficult to accept the philosophy behind the new mechanism, which was more social than economic, more democratic than efficient. But they also saw it as an area with very few institutions—one in which they could experiment with a truly 'regional' policy linked to the concerned region's specificities and needs (territorialization of the training-employment relationship, adaptation of training to the local economic fabric, investments adjusted to fit the intensity of unemployment and the low skills of the youth).

Thus, the Regional Councils inherited a complex heritage to work with. They wished to play the right role and initiate a new policy. They put the needs of the social and professional integration of the youth into perspective, focusing, instead, on rational and economic objectives that they considered 'efficacious'.

The task of regulating the training offered through regional training plans (PRDFPJ), mediation and negotiation instruments between actors and institutions (Regional Council, DRTEFP, local boards of education and professional branches) still had to search for the logic necessary for its legitimization. The economic logic, territorial logic, social logic and search for rationality came together and excluded each other in a contentious inter-institutional game. Collaborations were still at a trial and error stage. Each institution tried to assert its prerogatives, to establish its legitimacy, and often, to anticipate or go beyond the initiatives of these partners. At the same time, each felt that it had to play a role in mediation or as an interface. These multi-party relations played themselves out in a series of negotiations, interspersed with conflicts and agreements. Contractualization (State-Region Plan Implementation Agreement, Inter-Institutional Conventions) replaced the State's role in regulating by decree, although it did not enjoy the legitimacy to do the same and remained indicative and predictive. It did not have force of law—assessments could only confirm the degree of relevance or relative effectiveness of such laws.

EVALUATION OF REGIONAL POLICIES: A TOOL FOR COHESION?

At the same time, the State (but also the Regional Councils) started assessing the decentralization process and included such assessments in Article 53 of the Five-Year Act. These assessments stemmed from shared inter-institutional steering and *a posteriori* modes of practising democracy. Their role was that of coordinating, controlling and disseminating activities. They questioned researchers both about their methods and their conclusions. They gave birth to prescriptive (Perret, 2001) or critical literature (Tanguy, 1995; Dubet, 1999; Callon, 1999). While the researchers wished to distance themselves from this empirical exercise, alienated from control, some took part in it in the hope of reinvesting it with meaning. Hence, they analysed the relationship between research and assessment, as one frequently relied on the other, and vice versa. A priori, research dominates over assessment, as being based on a theoretical apparatus, the former takes enough time to recompose the social sphere and give it meaning, whereas assessment describes the phenomena in the first instance, in response to an institutional order that circumscribes their scope and the issues involved. In reality, these activities are clearly more interlinked than they seem to be. Just as national planning called upon researchers and favoured research on the training and employment sectors, assessments of the decentralization process brought researchers together to deal with this subject and reveal its various consequences. Various modes of direct (secondment of researchers to institutions) and indirect involvement (translation of assessments into a research problematic) reveal the numerous interactions between spheres that were more complementary than opposed, as M. Callon and F. Dubet (1999) observed.

Above all, assessments drew from the regeneration of forms of control or measurement, although they appeared no less ambiguous for that. They were meant to measure the distances between objectives and achievements and reveal the way organizations functioned. They were based on referentials that constituted both a formalization of the concerned objectives and a measuring tool to assess company activities. They gave birth to the compilation of material and data available and the use of surveys (quantitative and/or qualitative) to establish proof. They therefore used methodologies that had been developed by social science research. They distanced themselves from the research itself, as it was commissioned.[7] Therefore, the research was circumscribed within a framework that was established on the basis of external objectives and, in principle operationalized directly in institutional or organizational restructuring. Thus, both the assessors as well as the assessees interacted within a restricted framework, which influenced the analysis. The content of the assessments depended on the relationship between those commissioning them and the experts involved, the translation and interpretation of the commission by the experts, and then the methods used to restore the assessments to those that had ordered them.

Assessment and evaluation stemmed from the field of expertise that developed since the early 1980s, upstream and downstream of political and social action. Different stakes were involved, to different degrees. They either dealt with limited issues (training activities) or complex institutional functioning. Very often, assessments were undertaken on an emergency basis and in haste, sometimes by experts with very little specialization or others that were so highly specialized that their approach was confined to a rather restricted aspect of the problem addressed. In brief, each of the actors involved (sponsor, partner, expert or consultant) followed their own reasoning, which could influence the interactions required and restrict the scope of the assessment concerned, along with its effects. The choice of experts was no more neutral than that of the subjects of the assessment concerned. In the last resort, the political use to which the assessments were put—whether an assessment of results or processes was concerned—determined the issues involved and the methods adopted.

The assessments in which I took part focused on the institutional reconstruction that established the investigation framework.[8] They had to be conducted on the basis of a pre-established canvas, a referential that structured the contents of the questions and homogenized them for all regions. Furthermore, they were undertaken a very limited period. They made it possible to account for the reconstruction of inter-institutional relations and the political and organizational issues involved in the regions. They did not account for all the impacts of the said reconstruction. These assessments were partial, as they were extremely generic and did a quick review of institutional interactions on the basis of interviews, whose contents were difficult to determine.[9]

Regional institutional actors considered these external assessments as inspections of their activities and verdicts upon their results. They attempted to isolate the assessors, as they were well aware that the assessors came up with their assessment by comparing the discourses heard in each institution (Regional Council Departments, local boards of education, DRTEFP and Infra-Regional Departments, information and orientation centres, educational establishments and training institutes). Thus, assessments took place within the framework of a comparison and negotiation between the assessor and the institutional actors involved in the region. Assessors had to provide guarantees of neutrality and accuracy to obtain the information that would enable them to account for the activities undertaken and the progress made within the given period. Finally, in 2002, the regional council presidents refused to allow the pre-planned official publication of the assessments conducted by the coordination committee appointed by the Minister of Labour. Hence, they refused to make the effects of their policies and the disparities in regional functioning public or visible.

Some questions remain unresolved. Did the assessments sponsored by the ministries (of education and labour) have a monitoring and prescriptive role to play? Could they account for the transformations taking place in the training system? Did they merely register viewpoints and fragmentary data to support a difficult inter-institutional dialogue?

It is clear that knowledge about the processes underway was diluted and that inter-institutional arrangements were diversifying in the light of different regional socio-political contexts. The national information tools *Direction de l'évaluation et de la prospective* (DEP), or Evaluation and Prospective Directorate and *Direction de l'Animation de la Recherche, des Etudes et des Statistiques* (DARES) or Research, Studies and Statistics Coordination Directorate) were losing a certain share of the information they provided, which was taken over very diversely by Regional Councils departments and the OREF. And although the aim was to rebuild a training system, the latter lost its visibility and homogeneity.

CONCLUSION

Decentralization once again raised questions at the regional level that were already being raised at the national level—such as the purpose of the educational system, the construction of a training system and its ideological foundations, the role of institutional and economic actors, the relations between institutions and the harmonization of each one's logic of action. Finally, it raised the issue of the construction of an autonomous, public or private, republican, liberal or hybrid regional training system. It brought into play the issues involved and the forms of democracy.

The Regional Councils gradually established their legitimacy with regard to the implementation of an educational and training policy. And herein lies one of the paradoxes of decentralization 'à la française'. Unlike the forms of autonomy gained by the 'länder' in Germany or Spain's regions, France's regions had to work out a compromise with the State, through the regional prefects who retained enormous prerogatives, through the State's decentralized departments (local boards of education and DRTEFP), and through the plan implementation agreement that specified the duties and prerogatives of the partners involved. Still very young, the Regional Councils had to deal with seasoned institutions, as they did not have the means necessary to conduct their policy on their own. They depended on the alliances that they managed to set up, the disputes they managed to avoid, and the regional economic and social dynamic. They did not always take advantage of national-level thinking about training-employment relations. Rather, they developed their own methodology for building a training system in an empirical but disorderly manner (obviously, variations can be observed, depending on the regions concerned). Moreover, in order to do this, several Regional Councils adopted the logic of immediate economic effectiveness. Thus, since 1983 and more so since 1993, an empirical adequacy of employment training through objectives-based contracts, and adjustment to the policies of narrow branches has prevailed, particularly in the weakest regions. It established itself as a regional training policy, whereas the regulations implemented at the national level no longer acted as effective counterweights. The focus on adequacy was based on a faltering local (infra-regional) regulation, all the more so as it came up against the definition of the local sphere or local 'space'[10] and the reality of a local labour market. In reality, the local sphere is a social construction that is meant to be an area for the coordination of action, beyond the definition of its geographic and administrative boundaries.

These geographic and successive changes in the institutional management of training clearly show that the question of the level and modalities to which training has to be brought up to remain unresolved, while also clearly demonstrating the incapability of the actors to situate these changes. Fifty years of thinking about training policies have led to these changes in the decision-making level. Without resolving the serious issue of building a relationship between training and employment, they have shifted the analysis and idealized the relevance of the local level, as they came up against limitations to their effectiveness at other levels. They underline the slipperiness of training-employment relations, which—far from stemming exclusively from institutional management—depend on a labour market that is both temporary and changing. They accompany and increase regional differences, both in the system's design and in its effects, linked to regional economic and social histories and development.

The place of vocational education is called into question in these multiple redefinitions. Should it stem from the educational system as such and fall under a training system (initial training, apprenticeship, work-based learning and continuous training) that would therefore become autonomous and develop its own internal types of linkages? In reality, this is a problem that has always been faced in the history of vocational training from 1880 to 1960. Since 1919, and again in 1945 (Brucy, 2005; Tanguy, 1987; Troger, 1989), this issue remained highly controversial. The schemes alternatively introduced and withdrawn by the Technical Education Directorate (*Direction de l'Enseignement Technique*) constitute a sign or symbol of this controversy. As we have seen, the Ministry of Education attempted to maintain its hold on certification, although it may have implemented a policy negotiated within the CPC (*Commission Professionnelle Consultative* or Consultative Professional Commission). It controlled and also managed most of the potential initial training systems, although it had to negotiate the creation of establishments and sections with the Regional Council, through the PRDFP (*Plan Régional de Développement des Formations Professionnelles* or Vocational Training Development Regional Plan).

Among the establishments and staff, uncertainties about the legitimacy of Regional Councils and the relevance of their activities were no less strong. Teachers' unions were wary about the effects of reforms, no matter where they came from, revealing the fragility of the position of the training sector. They rejected company internships in 1979 and the setting up of apprenticeship sections in their establishments in 1992. They refused to question the change in the status of LP (*Lycée Professionnelle* or Vocational School) students that would bring them closer to the status of apprentices, unobtrusively objecting to the slippage in the position of LPs in these reforms. However, in reality, the restructuring of the training being provided between initial training and apprenticeship, the networking among trainees in technical schools (creation of apprenticeship sections and development of continuous education in the GRETA (*Groupement d'Etablissements de l'Education Nationale Pour la Formation Professionnelle Continue*, or Groups of National Education Establishments for Continuing Vocational Training) and the blurring of institutional borders between various branches gradually called for a reappraisal of the specificity of the institutionalized system. However, so far, the inertia of the educational system has limited the effects of planned and sometimes confused policies.

Decentralization and its trail of procedures gave concrete expression to the temptation or even the attempts to transform the training system. The competitive, commercial model (which formed the basis of the continuous training system, set up in 1971) that allowed negotiation and adjustment to a considerable extent (training programmes based on economic 'needs', market-based training institutes) replaced an academic and democratic model (that of institutional professional training) steered by the State, not directed by the immediate circumstances, based on equal opportunities and on a more internal rather than an external certifying standard. The actors involved obviously have divided opinions concerning these ideological issues, which, apart from creating inter-institutional tensions, hinders the development of a concerted training policy and leave unresolved the enduring ideal of public service 'à la française'.

NOTES

1. Other ministries involved in training such as the agriculture or the health ministries could also intervene.
2. The OREF were set up in 1989. These observatories are information and coordination tools as well as a tools for the construction of regional data. They rely on data produced by local education boards, the INSEE, the ONISEP (*Office National d'Information Sur les Enseignements et les Professions*, or National office for information on education and professions), the AFPA, the DRTEFP, the ANPE, the CRCI and even the CIA-CEREQ. They produce the analyses requested by regional institutions.
3. This notion of needs is extensively used and abused—it runs through most institutions and remains difficult to comprehend. It is used both to justify comprehensive planning and single, adapted continuing training schemes (cf. J.M. Barbier, 1977), as it is represented as being a present or future expression of a social requirement. Scholars have explored the foundation of this injunction and have demonstrated the liability of labour needs, as well as the fragility of the expression of training needs (Freyssinet, 1991).
4. Schools are also included in these negotiations. In the latter, the issues differ for school principals having to negotiate the training programmes they want and for the teachers and their unions. Indeed, the latter, thanks to their position (external to the institutional debate) can fight more easily at a formal and ideological level and symbolically 'resist the invaders'.
5. C. Agulhon (1989).
6. Permanent skill validation centres were set up. The youth are tested for units that they can capitalize for a diploma (mostly the CAP—*Certificat d'Aptitude Professionnelle* or Professional Aptitude Certificate) that they hold for five years before fully acquiring the Diploma. While this procedure has gained a following, the centres do not operate on a full-time basis. The cost of such a procedure has restricted its general implementation.
7. Assessments, like research, can be commissioned or sponsored by national or local, private or public bodies, on the basis of invitations to tender or proposals. Here, I have examined the assessments or evaluations described in the Five-Year Act and conducted under the aegis of the Coordination Committee of Regional Apprenticeship and Continuing Training Programmes (*Comité de coordination des programmes régionaux de l'apprentissage et de la formation continue*)—an inter-institutional steering body.
8. The Five-Year Act, in its Article 53, provided for assessments of processes and their effects every three years and an inter-institutional monitoring committee organized the procedure. It delegated the organization of the 1995 and 1998

assessments to the CEREQ and was directly responsible for the 2001 assessment, calling upon consultants and researchers through invitations to tender. In 2001, it selected three consulting firms and three research laboratories, which shows both the Committee's indifference to the expertise-label or research-label and the competition today between these bodies in bidding for government tenders. Researchers often reinvested these works in scientific publications, whereas experts did not do so as often.

9. A number of institutional actors prepared these meetings and used an extremely selective discourse, which was politically correct and which ironed out tensions, difficulties and failures. They resisted providing any elements of proof (precise data, reports and reviews of activities). Thus, they were co-authors of the assessment process.
10. There too, each institution developed its own definition and its own borders for what it defined as a local area. District and the national education plans' priority educational zones, employment zones and the DRTEFP's employment pools, Regional Council '*pays*' or villages overlapped and were superimposed alongside the State administration's departments and cantons, not to speak of towns and built-up areas, town and country planning zones, etc.

REFERENCES

Affichard, J., *Décentralisation des organisations et problèmes de coordination: Les principaux cadres d'analyse*, Paris, L'Harmattan, 1997.

Agulhon, C., 'Evolutions des formations industrielles en lycée professionnel: de la politique scolaire nationale à la concurrence entre les établissements', *Education et Formations*, 21,1989.

———, *L'enseignement professionnel. Quel avenir pour les jeunes?* Paris, Les éditions de l'Atelier, 1994.

———, 'Les relations formation-emploi. Une quête sans fin', in F. Cardi and A. Chambon, *Les métamorphoses de la formation*, L'Harmattan, Logiques sociales, 1997.

———, 'Autour des mots "formation, professionnalisation des Emplois-Jeunes"', *Recherche et formation*, INRP, issue no. 37, 2001.

———, 'Les politiques régionales de formation professionnelle, du référentiel commun à la politique locale', *Education et Sociétés*, issue no. 16, 2005.

Barbier, J.M. and M. Lesne, *L'analyse des besoins en formation*, Editions Robert Jauze, 1997.

Bel, M. and L. Dubouchet, *Décentralisation de la formation professionnelle: Un processus en voie d'achèvement?*, Editions de L'Aube, Essai, 2004.

Boltanski, L. and L. Thevenot, *De la justification. Les économies de la grandeur*, Paris: Gallimard, NRF Essais, 1991.

Brucy, G., 'L'enseignement technique et professionnel français. Histoires et politiques', *Les cahiers de la recherche sur l'éducation et les savoirs*, issue no. 4, 2005.

Brucy, G. and V. Troger, 'Un siècle de formation professionnelle en France: la parenthèse scolaire?' *Revue française de pédagogie*, issue no. 131, 2000.

Callon, M., 'Ni intellectuel engagé, ni intellectuel dégagé: la double stratégie de l'attachement et du détachement', *Sociologie du travail*, 1, 1999.

Casella, P. and A. Jobert, 'Régionalisation de la formation professionnelle: les enjeux du Plan régional de développement des formations professionnelles des jeunes', Rapport CNRS, Travail et Mobilités, Nanterre, 1996.

Charlot, B. and M. Figeat, *L'école aux enchères*. Paris: Editions Payot, 1979.

Charlot, B., *L'école et le territoire: nouveaux espaces, nouveaux enjeux*. Paris: Armand Colin, 1994.

Coordination Committee, '*Evaluation des politiques régionales de formation professionnelle*', 1993–6 Activity Report, La Documentation française, 1998.

Dubet, F., 'Du côté de l'action'. *Sociologie du travail*, 1, 1999.

Dutercq, Y. and A. Van Zanten, 'L'évolution des modes de régulation de l'action publique en éducation', *Education et Sociétés*, 2, 1998.

Freyssinet, J., *Pour une prospective des métiers et des qualifications*. Paris, La Documentation française, Report for the Tenth Plan, 1989–92, La Documentation française, 1991.

Garraud, P., 'La mise en œuvre des politiques de lutte contre le chômage par la formation: les contraintes du service public de l'emploi en France', *Sociologie du travail*, no. 4, 1995.

Lelièvre, C., *L'école à la française en danger?*, Paris, Nathan, 1996.

Méhaut, P., A. Richard and C. Romani, 'Décentralisation de la formation professionnelle et coordination de l'action publique' *Travail et Emploi*, no. 73, 1998.

Mons, N., 'Politiques de décentralisation en éducation : diversité internationale, légitimations théoriques et justifications empiriques', *Revue française de pédagogie*, no. 146, 2004.

Paul, J.J., *Les relations formation-emploi*, Paris: Economica, 1989.

Perret B., *L'évaluation des politiques publiques*, Paris, Repères, La Découverte, 2001.

Tanguy, L., *L'introuvable relation formation-emploi*, Paris: La Documentation française, 1986.

———, 'Le sociologue et l'expert : une analyse de cas', *Sociologie du travail*, 3, 1995.

Tanguy, L., C. Agulhon and A. Poloni, 'Les institutions d'enseignement technique court : genèse et évolutions', *Revue Française de Pédagogie*, no. 78, 1987.

Troger, V., 'Les centres d'apprentissage de 1940 à 1960: Le temps des initiatives', *Formation-emploi*, nos. 27–8, 1989.

Thuderoz, C., *Négociations*, Paris, PUF, 2000.

Van Zanten, A., 'Massification et régulation du système d'enseignement. Adaptations et ajustements en milieu urbain défavorisé', *L'Année sociologique*, vol. 50, no. 2, 2000.

Verdier, E., 'L'insertion des jeunes 'à la française' : vers un ajustement structurel' *travail et emploi*, no. 69, 1996.

Vernieres, M., Cujas (ed.) Formation emploi, enjeu économique et social. Paris: 1993.

Contributors

CATHERINE AGULHON is Senior Lecturer in Sciences of Education, University Paris Descartes, CERLIS. Her research is focused on vocational training and relations between training and employment and on the problems of transition of young people. She is now involved in studying the university reforms from a comparative and European point of view.

LUCY BAUGNET is Full Professor in Social Psychology at University of Picardy Jules Verne. She was the head of Doctoral Studies College in Human and Social Sciences and previously Associate Professor at Free University of Brussels. Her politications mainly focus on geopolitical identities and societal approach of political issues. This is developing with the research team: CURAPP UMR-CNRS no. 6084.

NATHALIE DEVEZE-SANSON is Junior Lecturer in Public Law, University of Picardy Jules Verne, Amiens, Research Team CURAPP UMR-CNRS no. 6054, Member of a Municipal Council.

BUDDHADEB GHOSH is Senior Fellow at the regional branch of Institute of Social Sciences, Kolkata. Prior to his retirement from West Bengal state civil services, he was Director, State Institute of Panchayats, Kalyani.

OLIVIER GIRAUD is a research fellow in political science at the Centre Marc Bloch in Berlin. He works on comparative public policy analysis. His research areas are industrial relations, vocational training systems as well as social policy (care). He is very much interested in the comparative study of federal systems (Germany, Switzerland, India, etc.) and in the analysis of policy discourse.

ANAND INBANATHAN is Associate Professor of Sociology, Institute of Social and Economic Change, Bangalore.

FLORENCE JAMAY is Senior Lecturer in Public Law, University of Picardy Jules Verne Amiens, CURAPP-CNRS no. 6054. Her doctoral thesis was on the right to information in the sphere of environmental law. The focus of her work is on the evolution of the right to information and the right to participation of citizens in environmental law and the development and the stakes of the participatory democracy.

GIRISH KUMAR is Senior Fellow, Indian Institute of Public Administration, New Delhi. Earlier he was Senior Fellow & Head, Politics & Society Division of Centre de Sciences Humaines.

ISABELLE MULLER-QUOY is Senior lecturer, Faculty of Administrative and Political Sciences, University of Picardy Jules Verne and member of the research team CURAPP UMR-CNRS no. 6054.

M.A. OOMEN is former Director, Institute of Management in Government, Thiruvananthapuram, and Senior Fellow, Institute of Social Sciences, New Delhi.

MAHI PAL is from the Indian Economic Service. Presently, he is attached with the Union Ministry of Panchayati Raj, Government of India, New Delhi.

FRANÇOIS RANGEON is Professor of Administrative Sciences at the Faculty of Administrative and Political Sciences University of Picardy Jules Verne. He directed the Research Team: CURAPP, UMR-CNRS no 6054 for five years and was member of the scientific council of the research group on local administration in Europe (GRALE). As a researcher, he had the responsibility of research programmes in the regional pole in social and human sciences and is the author of important publications on local democracy, public policy, general interest and local development.

Index